Common Core Dilemma

Common Core Dilemma

Who Owns Our Schools?

Mercedes K. Schneider

Foreword by Carol Corbett Burris

TEACHERS COLLEGE PRESS

TEACHERS COLLEGE | COLUMBIA UNIVERSITY

NEW YORK AND LONDON

Published by Teachers College Press, 1234 Amsterdam Avenue, New York, NY 10027

Library of Congress Cataloging-in-Publication Data

Schneider, Mercedes K. (Mercedes Katherine)
    Common core dilemma— : who owns our schools? / Mercedes K. Schneider; foreword by Carol Corbett Burris.
      pages cm
    Includes bibliographical references and index.
    ISBN 978-0-8077-5649-2 (pbk. : alk. paper)—ISBN 978-0-8077-5650-8 (hardcover : alk. paper)—ISBN 978-0-8077-7376-5 (ebook)
    1. Common Core State Standards (Education) 2. Education—Standards—United States. 3. Education and state—United States. 4. Business and education—United States. I. Title.
    LB3060.83.S357 2015
    371.010973—dc23

                                                                    2015003323

ISBN 978-0-8077-5649-2 (paper)
ISBN 978-0-8077-5650-8 (hardcover)
ISBN 978-0-8077-7376-5 (ebook)

Printed on acid-free paper

Manufactured in the United States of America

22 21 20 19 18 17 16 15   8 7 6 5 4 3 2 1

To Diane Ravitch,
who was proud of me
before I had an Amazon ranking

A wrong sum can be put right: but only by going back till you find the error and working it afresh from that point, never by simply *going on*.

—C. S. Lewis, The Great Divorce

Contents

Foreword

Common Core. These are probably the most controversial words in education reform today. The Common Core standards have critics who are conservative and critics who are liberal. Libertarians view the Common Core standards as an overreach of federal power and an intrusion by the national government into the curricula at both the state and local levels. The involvement of both President Obama and Secretary of Education Arne Duncan through the Race to the Top Program fans the flames of their suspicions.

Progressives who criticize the Common Core view it as an affront to the democratic governance of public schools and school districts. They are suspicious of the involvement of venture philanthropists, such as Bill Gates, who spend millions promoting the standards. They worry that the standards are too attuned to the interests of business, rather than the interests of children.

Which side is right? Interestingly, both the critiques of the left and the right can, at the same time, be correct. We are living at a time when the role of special interests in our government is greater than ever before. If our democracy is morphing into an oligarchy, as many have claimed, then both libertarians and progressives share the same concern because government and financial and business interests share the same agenda.

Worries about the Common Core, however, extend far beyond political consternation. The standards have been criticized for being developmentally inappropriate, too bound to the reading of informational text, filled with "fuzzy" and confusing math, and far too closely tied to big, standardized national tests. Indeed, the Common Core was conceived at the same time as the PARCC and Smarter Balance testing consortia. Those who created the Common Core did so with the intent that American students would take common exams based on common standards.

And those tests, and their consequences for children, have not been warmly received. Early Common Core tests caused proficiency rates to drop like a stone. Young students in New York State, for example, come home frustrated by long exams with questions that are far more difficult and complicated than those they have seen in the past. At the same time, reformers and politicians aligned with the contemporary reform agenda use Common Core test results to make their case against teacher tenure and public schools. Throughout it all, teacher and parent support for the Common Core has also dropped like a stone.

Many now ask, what are these standards and where did they come from? From the very beginning of the Common Core's development to the present, Mercedes Schneider has told the story. She has written about the Common Core not only through the lens of a teacher, but with the care of an investigative reporter. Even those who disagree with her point of view do not question her knowledge, her accuracy, or her facts.

In *Common Core Dilemma: Who Owns Our Schools?*, Schneider puts all she has learned about the Common Core in one volume. She writes to inform. She helps her readers understand why the Common Core was created and how it came to be. She introduces the key players and organizations that are most responsible for the standards' creation. She explains the mindset of those who promote the Common Core, and explains the funds they receive for their advocacy.

Mercedes Schneider bursts the myth that the Common Core State Standards were authentically developed by teachers and challenges the notion that they were even developed by states.

She explains how the Common Core was "pitched" to Bill Gates and outlines the role he has played in its promotion. And she shows how the international publishing and standardized testing giant, Pearson Corporation, has its interests tied to the Common Core as well.

Throughout the volume, Schneider makes the case for why the standards were doomed from the start, and why it is important that we recognize not only the flaws in their creation, but the flaws in the standards themselves.

Schneider makes the case that it is time to "turn the page" on this ill-begotten educational experiment. As readers turn the pages of the fascinating and meticulously prepared account, they will be compelled to agree.

—Carol Corbett Burris
Rockville Centre, New York

Acknowledgments

I have such respect and gratitude for Diane Ravitch, who saw the threads of a book in my blog posts on the Common Core and encouraged me to weave those threads into what has become this book. Many thanks also go to Jean Ward, who was enthusiastic about the possibility of this book before I wrote the first word and who has carefully and expertly guided this project. I am also grateful to a number of friends and colleagues who encouraged my work on this book, some even unknowingly. Among them are fellow blogger and education activist Anthony Cody; my friends Seth and Katie Stiles, Patsy Schramm, Noel McNany, Ken Kimberly, and Lori Hobren; and colleagues Sandy Marshall, Jeff Burgoyne, and Billy Percy. I would also like to thank my mother, Mary Louise Schneider, for valuing me and respecting my love for solitude, a quality that is unusual among her five children and that lends itself to writing books.

A special mention to Janna Robertson for her efforts to raise the funds necessary for fees associated with this book and for her own financial contribution to my work. Thank you, Janna. I am grateful also to those who contributed financially: Badass Teachers Association, Nancy Bailey, Lee Barrios, Jillian Caci, Laura Campbell, Marguerite Coffinet, Elaine Cooper, Kim Cosmas, Wendy Duke, Peter Greene, Terry Kalb, Elise Kampfer, Christine Langhoff, Dominique Magee, Gus Morales, Susan Muchmore, Ray Nichols, Rosemary Pearce, Dorothy Petrie, Mary Porter, Diane Ravitch, Gloria Roman, Elaine Romero, Denise Scallan, Jo Ann Scott, Buffy Sexton, David Siegel, Adam Silver, John St. Julien, Laurie Taylor, Charlotte Vrooman, Lesa Wilbert, and the numerous anonymous donors.

To all who have sent me a kind and encouraging word regarding this book, whether in person or via email or social networking, I thank you as well.

And as always, I thank the Lord Jesus Christ, who has given me the ability to research and write and who has graciously provided the people necessary to make this Common Core book a reality.

Introduction

The Quandary of Who Owns America's Schools

Who owns our schools? Who is in charge? Certainly neither the local school board nor the classroom teacher. They haven't the money and influence. Instead, it is those who hail from outside of the classroom, nonprofits, joined by those in business whose minds are preoccupied with the incredible profit potential of CCSS, and even by those at the federal level who, like spider to fly, lure states into the constrictive CCSS web. In the end, America will pay for this power grab unless teachers and parents, students and administrators, legislators and boards of education resist misguided and selfish efforts to promote the unwholesome idea of test-centered standardized education.

Attempting to empower those who would resist prompted me to write this book.

Educators and the American public must understand what CCSS is—its history, development, and intention—in order to combat this fiscally and otherwise costly, gross blunder of an educational product.

When I first heard of CCSS, in early 2010, I was in a department meeting at the high school where I teach sophomore English. I learned from one of our assistant principals that Louisiana would be replacing its state standards with a new set, to be called the Common Core. I learned that CCSS was not yet finished, but that when it was, it would be better than our current standards if for no other reason than there would be fewer standards. I also learned that CCSS was to be phased in over a three-year period, at the end of which our students would be expected to complete new, CCSS-aligned English and math assessments that were going to be more difficult for students to pass—even though said assessments had yet to be created.

Thus, in early 2010, like many teachers across the nation, I was encouraged to embrace the new standards even though they were not yet finished, and I was told that the tests associated with these unfinished standards were going to be difficult ("rigorous"), even though the tests could not possibly exist yet if the standards themselves were not even complete.

Talk about flawed.

These unfinished standards were being imposed on our district in top-down fashion. I did not find out until March 2014 that back in May 2009, our governor and state superintendent had signed our entire state-wide education system on for what was undeniably a state-by-state, na-tionwide education experiment.

When I first heard about CCSS on that winter 2010 morning, I held no negative opinion of the situation. I trusted my assistant principal, and if she were enthusiastic about this up-and-coming revolution in standards, I was fine with it. Plus, I liked the idea of fewer standards. In truth, at that point the entire CCSS-and-assessments concept was purely theoretical. In addition—and this is noteworthy—this upcoming CCSS announcement preceded Louisiana's shift to grading teachers using student test scores and to using letter grades to evaluate (and punish) schools and school districts.

I was in my fifteenth year of full-time teaching, and I had never had my professional performance tied to the standardized test scores of my students. Another component of CCSS—one inherently designed to break public education—is its creators' intention *since inception* to wed common standards to high-stakes assessments. I have heard individuals time and again argue for CCSS without the assessments. But CCSS was never intended to be without high-stakes assessments. My colleague Pe-ter Greene captured this idea well when he noted that saying one wants CCSS without its assessments is like saying one prefers the front end of a horse but not the rear: It's all one horse.

My purpose in writing *Common Core Dilemma—Who Owns Our Schools?* is to offer readers a foundation regarding the origin, develop-ment, and promotion of the CCSS. Though carefully publicized as the product of a seemingly democratic, state-level process, CCSS is a tool of control in the hands of a privileged, well-connected, and amply financed few. In these pages I examine the educational environment in America in the decades leading up to CCSS, and I consider key organizations and individuals involved in creating, financing, promoting, and other-wise fostering and profiting from CCSS as part of a spectrum of so-called "test-driven reform." Thus, this book is not an analysis of the standards themselves, nor is it a chronology of CCSS backlash. That noted, what is written in these pages will enrich readers' understanding of both the stan-dards themselves and the much-publicized, teacher, parent, and student rejection of CCSS.

As it stands, CCSS is a hurriedly produced product intended to impose high-stakes outcomes onto those without power over it. In general, CCSS is not owned and valued by those required to institute it—current American public school teachers and administrators nationwide. This alone makes CCSS destined to fail.

Each of the eleven chapters that comprise the body of this book highlights the CCSS-induced, American education power grab, and the debilitating issues that make CCSS both unhealthy for American public education and unsustainable as an education framework. The first chapter concerns the history of education legislation contributing to the creation of CCSS, particularly former president George W. Bush's No Child Left Behind, with its dependence on high-stakes testing outcomes to "prove" that education was occurring—or else. NCLB was a misguided, punitive reauthorization of the Elementary and Secondary Education Act (ESEA) of 1965. NCLB was itself a doomed effort to control American public education, and CCSS is yet another effort to supposedly improve American education by hijacking local control.

The second and third chapters concern the governor- and business-supported nonprofit Achieve, Inc., with its wholehearted endorsement of standardized test scores as proof positive of education attainment. Not only this, but Achieve quickly strayed from its intended purpose as a standards and assessments "clearinghouse" to a standards and assessments *evaluator*. Achieve brought the profit-driven business mindset into education and opened the door for viewing teachers and students as assets or liabilities via its American Diploma Project (ADP), which focused on developing a common set of standards for American high schools.

Chapter 4 concerns two key organizations that joined forces in first promoting ADP and then CCSS: Education Trust and the Fordham Foundation/Institute. Ed Trust operates on the assumption that education standardization promotes educational equity and that top-down change is best because it is fastest. Flawed, flawed. Fordham Foundation/Institute is willing to sell to the public at all costs a CCSS that it claims to be a universally superior set of standards, when in fact a state-by-state comparison to already existing state standards show this to be false. Tragic.

Then there is the CCSS "contract," the Memorandum of Understanding (MOU) that the CCSS "owners"—the National Governors Association (NGA) and Council of Chief State School Officers (CCSSO)—composed as a means of securing a commitment from top state officials to supposedly lead their states in developing CCSS, as well as advancing the plan for common assessments. The resulting CCSS legally belongs to

NGA and CCSSO. Thus, "state-led" means nothing more than two high-ranking state officials in each state committing their unsuspecting state education systems to what would become a set of inflexible standards tied to punitive assessments. This part of the CCSS-induced, public school ownership battle is detailed in Chapters 5 and 8.

Since CCSS did not emerge from teacher practitioners and other education stakeholders, the CCSS concept required a well-orchestrated, intentional public relations effort. CCSS "lead architect" and edupreneur David Coleman and his nonprofit, Student Achievement Partners (SAP), was available not only to guide CCSS writing but also to publicly promote the completed CCSS product. The public relations component of CCSS was also written into the CCSS MOU and included enlisting national-level organizations to assist with promoting CCSS to the public. A key component of the CCSS promotion involved promoting teacher and administrator "approval" of CCSS via publicized survey outcomes. However, for a number of these CCSS-promoting surveys, both survey construction and reporting are flawed. The CCSS sale noted above is detailed in Chapters 6 and 7.

Chapter 10 concerns what former President Clinton believed would sink a national standards effort—federal involvement. Despite Clinton's advice, NGA and CCSSO dared to include a section on "the federal role" in CCSS. In short, the federal government was to "offer incentives" to states for CCSS implementation, teacher development, and common assessment development. In his role in promoting the CCSS that he obviously wants, U.S. Secretary of Education Arne Duncan comes as close as is possible to overstepping the federal role in state education affairs without *technically* crossing the line. Nevertheless, his hovering right on the edge of what is allowable by federal law has hardly endeared him to a suspicious public, a flaw contributing to impending CCSS failure.

CCSS financing is not only tied to the federal government. As Chapter 9 details, in 2008, two CCSS "insiders" asked Bill Gates to bankroll CCSS. It would cost millions to create and nurture CCSS. Gates was offered no guarantees that states would follow through with implementing CCSS—so he made sure to finance as much of a guarantee of CCSS "implementation" success as possible. Gates envisioned the need for "mass education" to be brought "to scale" in a manner that would benefit mega-corporations—like Pearson. Indeed, as noted in Chapter 11, Pearson was clear about its plans to "embed" itself in American education by way of CCSS. Therefore, to Gates and Pearson, CCSS is best viewed as a promising vehicle for marketing education. In the name of educating children, profitability assumed center stage—an exploitation that is indeed tragic for its corporate-serving end.

So there we have it in brief: the prominent players in the CCSS game—the ones who would snatch local control away from the locals in the name of standards that they publicize as higher than previous state standards, though even that is open to dispute.

Those who love and respect the locally controlled American classroom—and resist its takeover by profiteers or by right-minded but misguided nonprofits who, for funds received, must produce studies, plans, influence, and results—need not despair.

We *can* correct this misdirection.

The course down the CCSS path is not irreversible.

CHAPTER 1

Gradually Leaving Education Behind
No Child Left Behind and Its Predecessors

When I was in college in Colorado working on my doctorate, I used to take driving trips to St. Louis, Missouri, to visit friends. The drive would take me across the entire state of Kansas—over 440 miles. Many times during those trips, I had to monitor the position of dual storm systems, from both the north and west, meeting to form one terrific storm right in the middle of the state. Individually, the storms were problematic, often because of strong winds that could easily push 18-wheelers off of I-70. However, when two systems came together, it was something to witness, reminding me of scenes of impending destruction from science fiction films. On one occasion, I was driving between two systems after evacuating the interstate—black sky to my right and to my left, with only a sliver of sunshine straight ahead. Another time, I missed the storm system itself but drove through the aftermath: scores of vehicles apparently blown into the median and left by their owners over a stretch of more than 100 miles.

When I think of the creation of the Common Core State Standards (CCSS), I am reminded of the Kansas storms, for CCSS is the nexus of other education "brewings" that united in the birth of CCSS. One such major contributor was the No Child Left Behind (NCLB) Act of 2001,[1] signed into law on January 8, 2002.[2] Before I delve into the wonder that was NCLB, allow me to offer a brief history of the legislation that brought America to that point, beginning with the original Elementary and Secondary Education Act (ESEA) and highlighting specific components of ESEA and its pre-NCLB revisions and selected, related documents that have left their mark in the form of CCSS and its fraternal twin, "common" assessments. Then I promise to land this chapter in the "accountability" frying pan of a failed NCLB.

Allow me to also caution readers that this history of events leading up to the creation of a "common core" is a history captured primarily in legislation and government reports. As a result, readers might be tempted to dismiss the content of this and a few subsequent chapters as "dry" and therefore unimportant. After all, delving through legislation and research reports hardly sparks images of adventure and intrigue. Nevertheless, I ask my readers to bear with me in this excavation of a history that produced not only the "common standards" idea, but also the "common assessments" designed to inseparably accompany those "common standards."

And now, let us go back to 1965 and President Lyndon B. Johnson's ESEA.

ESEA IN 1965; COLEMAN REPORT IN 1966

Made into law on April 9, 1965,[3] ESEA was considered "the most expansive federal education bill ever passed."[4] (You see, you're already unexplainably drawn in.) ESEA introduced Title I funding to assist schools with educating children in poverty, along with funding for libraries, state departments of education, research, and other education-impacting services.[5] In 1968, ESEA was amended to include Title VII funding for bilingual education.[6] The idea behind ESEA was that more government funding of education for the poor would help combat poverty—namely, more children would graduate from high school. Thus, ESEA was a move toward the federal government's involvement in offering earmarked money to states (as opposed to offering general, federal financial aid). In the case of ESEA of 1965, administration of federal funding was left to the states in order to counter the appearance of too much federal control over state education decisions—a decision that ESEA-reauthorization NCLB attempted to emulate with less success. (More to come on this front.)

Not everyone was keen on ESEA. The Coleman Report of 1966 challenged[7] the efficacy of ESEA by reporting that children of color did not make marked gains "as measured by their performance on standardized achievement tests." The report was conducted only 1 year following the passage of ESEA, and both the insufficient passage of time between ESEA enactment and the conducting of the Coleman study, and the study's clearly documented inequalities of racial segregation, confound any reported result of the outcomes of ESEA on fighting poverty. However, one notable issue of the Coleman Report is its reliance on standardized tests to measure educational "success" of schools:

> The schools bear many responsibilities. Among the most important is the teaching of certain intellectual skills such as reading, writing, calculating, and problem solving. One way of assessing the educational opportunity offered by the schools is to measure how well they perform this task. Standard achievement tests are

available to measure these skills, and several such tests were administered in this survey to pupils at grades 1, 3, 6, 9, and 12.[8]

Though not directly used to "grade" schools, the Coleman Report's mistaken assumption that student standardized test scores would be useful in assessing the "effectiveness" of individuals/entities beyond the student would find expression as a key component of NCLB and ultimately CCSS.

Another notable issue with the Coleman Report's usage of standardized testing concerns the authors ignoring the greater, life-quality ramifications of the utter saturation of racial injustice and inequality on the greater culture, especially in the South. The researchers believed that "culture bound" testing was justified because, in their view, particular attributes were necessary for students of color to have success in a world that the report had just indicated was clearly biased against them:

> These tests do not measure intelligence, nor attitudes, nor quality of character. Furthermore, they are not, nor are they intended to be, "culture free." Quite the reverse: They are culture bound. What they measure are the skills which are among the most important in our society for getting a good job and moving up to a better one, and for full participation in an increasingly technical world. Consequently, a pupil's test results at the end of public school provide a good measure of the range of opportunities open to him as he finishes school—a wide range of choice of jobs or colleges if these skills are very high; a very narrow range that includes only the most menial jobs if these skills are very low.[9]

The above words from the Coleman Report illustrate how complex it is to determine for others what exactly contributes to "success" in our world. Moreover, these words show how blind test administrators can be to the manner in which their own perceptions of the world interfere with both test selection and the utility of test results. The "skills most important" for Whites to be successful in a predominately White society that is often openly hostile to the "success" of its members of color differ from those that may be deemed "most important" by the oppressed members. In short, it was naïve to believe that people of color in 1960s America would "get a good job and move up to a better one" and that being bound to "only the most menial jobs" was absolutely connected to "low" academic skills.

I have spoken with some of my students of color about their academic performance and have learned that among certain subgroups in our society, even today, academic achievement is frowned on as an attempt to "be White" or is viewed as an affront to subgroup acceptance. I have also learned from individuals who were young adults of color in the 1960s that the "skills" deemed "most important for success" included avoiding situations in which one had to deal directly with White people, and if those could not be avoided, to not look Whites in the eye and to not speak unless spoken to.

And I continue to teach students of color who are learning such "White society survival" lessons from elders in their homes and communities.

None of these social complexities can be captured via the outcomes of standardized tests.

The Coleman Report did publicize the importance of a child's formative years at home on later success at school.[10] Furthermore, Coleman Report commissioner, former U.S. Education commissioner Harold Howe, was a key influence in desegregating schools in the South via stipulations associated with Title I funding.[11] Nevertheless, in its use of standardized tests to "measure" U.S. education "success" on the heels of ESEA authorization, the Coleman Report established the beginnings of an expectation that student standardized test scores might be utilized (never mind invalidly so) to measure schools and even teachers.

ESEA IN 1994: THE IMPROVING AMERICA'S SCHOOLS ACT

Prior to NCLB in 2002, ESEA was reauthorized five times (1972, 1978, 1983, 1989, and 1994).[12] Fortunately for my readers, I will not examine every reauthorization prior to NCLB. On the contrary, for our purposes, it will suffice to focus on only the 1994 reauthorization preceding NCLB. I will only note that for all reauthorizations, Title I funding remained ESEA's centerpiece. The 1994 reauthorization, the Improving America's Schools Act (IASA) of 1995, introduced the idea of "a core of challenging state standards" for all students and included the expectation of curricular "alignment"—and associated, state-determined assessments:

> The IASA replaces the piecemeal structure of the old ESEA. ESEA programs will now be integrated into a state's overall school improvement efforts, *focused around a core of challenging state standards*. ESEA programs now promote the alignment of all education components—curriculum and instruction, professional development, school leadership, accountability, and school improvement—so that every aspect of the education system works together to ensure that all children can attain challenging standards. . . .

These goals seem at first look intrinsically worthwhile. However, there is a hitch.

> Title I will *ensure greater accountability through the use of state assessments that measure students' progress toward new state standards.* The same standards and assessments developed by a state for all children will apply to children participating in Title I. These two fundamental changes in Title I—the role of high academic standards and the use of state assessments—will help ensure that Title I is an integral part of state reform efforts, rather than another add-on federal program.[13] [Emphasis added]

Standards and assessments were new to ESEA via IASA; however, they were left to the discretion of states to create and to measure. The IASA state-honoring flexibility (an overused word in our current climate of education reform) also introduced into ESEA the idea of the "waiver," which states were "encouraged to request . . . if they [found] that statutory or regulatory requirements inhibit[ed] the effective implementation of effective programs or reform efforts."[14] Leaving standards and assessments up to the states would be a concept partially retained in NCLB.

A refreshing decision that former President Clinton made in regard to the writing of the 1994 ESEA reauthorization was to appoint school superintendent and former high school teacher Thomas Payzant to the position of Assistant Secretary for Elementary and Secondary Education. Regarding his active role in IASA, Payzant recalls:

> People appreciated having a practitioner take a leading role in the development of legislation. I used my experience to explain the impact particular legislation would have on schools and districts.[15]

I commend Clinton for exercising common sense in appointing a former teaching practitioner to a federal education post and for allowing the man to draw on his practical experience in informing education legislation. Nevertheless, such input guarantees neither successful policy creation nor suitable implementation.

GOALS 2000

Before the 1994 reauthorization of ESEA in the form of IASA, the Clinton administration enacted HR 1804, otherwise known as Goals 2000, in January 1994.[16] Based on the groundwork of a 1989 "Education

Summit" including then-President George H. W. Bush and the nation's governors and briefly called America 2000,[17] Goals 2000 purported to "provide a framework" for the 1994 ESEA reauthorization and included lofty yet not easily obtainable or measurable national education goals, such as "all students will start school ready to learn" and "every parent . . . will devote time each day to helping [his or her children] learn."[18] Goals 2000 did attempt to offer wraparound services, including those to help "train and support" parents and to address children's nutritional and physical developmental needs. Nevertheless, the goal that "every parent devote time each day to helping children learn" is noble yet unrealistic. Some parents simply do not have the time given their work schedules and other life responsibilities; others might be academically challenged themselves.

What Goals 2000 did acknowledge was that the primary responsibility for a child's well-being rests with home life, not school life. Such responsibility cannot be addressed via state or national education standards for schools, and certainly cannot be measured using standardized assessments. Neither Clinton (nor G.H.W. Bush before him) pretended that it could. However, Goals 2000 does include language that puts the United States in competition with other nations, such as the astounding "goal" that "by the year 2000, United States students will be first in the world in mathematics and science achievement."[19] Goals 2000 also set the "goal" that "by the year 2000, the high school graduation rate will increase to at least 90 percent."[20]

A word is needed here regarding the problematic nature of graduation rate terminology divorced from clear, universally accepted definitions.

Declaring "graduation rate" is a tricky prospect because the term *graduation rate* can be defined in any number of ways. For example, in measuring "cohort graduation rate," the U.S. Department of Education defines a "graduate" as one who completes high school in 4 years, with other adjustments:

> The final regulations define the "four-year adjusted cohort graduation rate" as the number of students who graduate in four years with a regular high school diploma divided by the number of students who entered high school four years earlier. . . .[21]

The definition of graduation rate restricted in the manner above will certainly yield a lower percentage of graduates than one that takes into account graduation in 5 years' time, or graduation from an alternative program that yields, for example, an equivalency diploma.

If one considers "graduation" as involving a student's completing either traditional or nontraditional high school programs in four years or more but who persist in such programs until completion results in a traditional high school diploma or its equivalent, then the United States has met this 90 percent goal, as noted by education historian Diane Ravitch in her book *Reign of Error*:

> The US Department of Education uses the four-year completion rate as a gold standard; this method produces the lowest possible graduation rate. It does not account for students who take more time to graduate or who earn a GED.
>
> The four-year graduation rate is one way to measure graduation rates, but it is not the only way. Many young people take longer than four years to earn a high school diploma. Some graduate in August, not May or June. Some take five or six years. Others earn a GED. When their numbers are added to the four-year graduates, the high school graduation rate is 90 percent. . . .
>
> . . . it is also accurate to say that 90 percent of those between the ages of eighteen and twenty-four have a high school diploma.[22]

The important lesson from the shifting manner of defining graduation rate is that numbers suit the definitions to which human beings restrict them. There is nothing absolute in reporting a statistic called "graduation rate." One should take care to consider the definition associated with a number before forming judgments about those to whom the number might be applied as a label.

If one considers the expanded definition that Ravitch offers of graduation rate, then the American education system is not evidencing the "crisis" that modern corporate-minded education "reformers" are pushing as the very foundation for promoting CCSS and its assessments.

That noted, the hidden (and restrictive) commonly used federal definition of "graduation rate" is not the most troublesome aspect of Goals 2000 as viewed in retrospect from today's CCSS standpoint.

Of all the doors opened for statistical obsession via Goals 2000 and culminating in CCSS and its "common" assessments, perhaps the most influential was the Goals 2000 desire for national standards. Note that Goals 2000 holds national standards separate from state standards and not as an automatic (nor coerced, nor mandated) replacement for state standards.[23] In fact, the Clinton administration was overly careful in stating that the national standards were "voluntary" and were to be certified by a panel to be appointed by Clinton (the National Education Standards and Improvement Council, or NESIC), and reviewed by a separate goals panel.[24] Nevertheless, some viewed the inclusion of the call for national standards as "hurting" the Goals 2000 effort. Among these was *Baltimore Sun* contributing writer Kerry diGrazia:

> Support for Goals 2000 erodes with the looming prospect of national curriculum standards—standards designed to provide a way to meet the goal that "all students will leave grades 4, 8 and 12 having demonstrated competency over challenging subject matter."
>
> Development of the standards was initially pushed by the Bush administration—which provided federal funds for the development panels—and embraced by the Clinton administration.
>
> But the release of proposed standards, paired with the GOP sweep last fall, turned what had seemed like a consensus into a heated debate, within the education community and among politicians in Washington.[25]

As it turns out, appointments to Clinton's national standards council, NESIC, were never made.[26] A contributing factor likely to have quelled any further open discussion of national standards was National Endowment for the Humanities chair Lynne Cheney's public rejection of the national history standards, which she helped finance—and later criticized as follows:

> The things that we have done that are successes, the triumphs, the progress that we have made are not given sufficient emphasis, so that students . . . would have a very warped view of our past.[27]

Cheney's disapproval of national history standards content was fueled by the public perception that such standards were created in secret. As UCLA Professor Gary Nash recounts:

> [Conservative American radio talk show host] Rush Limbaugh told his television followers that the National History Standards were created by "a secret group" at UCLA, and many other hostile critics of the standards, such as Lynne Cheney's employee John Fonte, repeatedly called me the "principal author" of the guidebooks. This was a clever way of persuading the public that these were standards from hell. After all, it was much easier to convince people who had not read the books that the guidelines were deeply biased and unbalanced if they could be pictured as the product of one person's mind or the minds of a small group rather than the laborious collaborative product of a large number of educators, classroom teachers being foremost among them.[28]

The American public is distrustful of a federal role in promoting national standards. In the case of the national history standards, the federal government initiated the effort but did not hide the writing via secretive committee. Moreover, the Goals 2000 national standards effort was not tied to federal funding, and there was no push for states to surrender their standards via two signatures on some memorandum of understanding and later a requirement to receive federal ESEA funding, as was later the case with CCSS.

There was also no call to tie national standards to national tests. However, even in the pre–Goals 2000 days of America 2000, the New York State Department of Education observed:

> Liberals were wary of the [state] testing provision, stating that more tests alone would only demonstrate the widely known fact that poor and minority students perform at lower levels. . . . An assortment of experts, advocates, and academics expressed concern about the increasing potential for national testing.[29]

Goals 2000 does not read like a federal takeover of education; moreover, the document includes no language related to national testing. And yet the public was still skittish. Apparently, legislators were as well. Prior to Clinton's Goals 2000, when the effort belonged to Republican President G.H.W. Bush, even fellow conservatives were already concerned about the growing federal role in education.[30] It seems that Cheney's 1994 rejection of the national history standards was enough to tap into such concerns. In January 1995, the Senate decisively rejected the national history standards in a 99–1 vote.[31]

The idea of a set of national academic standards had become tainted.

Though Goals 2000 did not successfully produce a set of national academic standards, it was successful in producing the first-ever national standards for arts education.[32] It seems that no Cheney and Limbaugh counterparts objected to federal association with standards in dance, theater, music, and visual arts.

Overall, Clinton's Goals 2000 stalled. It did not translate into the profound education overhaul that G.H.W. Bush and Bill Clinton planned for it to be. It did, however, provide a platform for an increased federal role in state education in the form of the 2001 reauthorization of ESEA: NCLB.

NO CHILD LEFT BEHIND (NCLB)

I don't know of any dedicated teacher who does not wish he or she had the time and other resources to guarantee that no child would fall behind academically. Rather than coming alongside teachers in order to help them accomplish this goal to the best degree possible, in NCLB, former President Bush points a finger at "failed" American public education and applies punitive, so-called "accountability" measures to aim for his own completely unrealistic goal of "100 percent proficiency in math and reading by 2014"—which Sue Whitney, special education advocate and research editor of Wrightslaw, argues really meant only 95%.[33] Interestingly, Whitney casually observes circa 2004, "It will be a decade before we need to worry about whether the 95% factor is appropriate."[34] In her comment, Whitney dismisses the general, punitive attitude of a federal mandate that included costly sanctions to the education systems in states that did not meet NCLB terms.

The 2001 U.S. Department of Education–archived executive summary of NCLB is the first time I read the term *failing school*:

> [In December 2001] President Bush secured passage of the landmark No Child Left Behind Act of 2001 (NCLB Act). The new law reflects a remarkable consensus—first articulated in the President's No Child Left Behind framework—on how to improve the performance of America's elementary and secondary schools *while at the same time ensuring that no child is trapped in a failing school.*
>
> The NCLB Act, which reauthorizes the ESEA, incorporates the principles and strategies proposed by President Bush. These include increased accountability for States, school districts, and schools; greater choice for parents and students, particularly those attending low-performing schools; more flexibility for States and local educational agencies (LEAs) in the use of Federal education dollars; and a stronger emphasis on reading, especially for our youngest children.[35] [Emphasis added]

Based on this executive summary, NCLB appears similar to its ESEA-reauthorization predecessor, IASA. However, an important distinction is the use of standardized tests to measure state-determined "adequate yearly progress" (AYP)—and the consequences for districts' not meeting AYP. The "failing" school is the school that "performs low" on standardized tests. As education historian Diane Ravitch observes, "The passage of No Child Left Behind made testing and accountability our national education strategy."[36] Indeed, the NCLB executive summary notes as much:

> The NCLB Act will strengthen Title I accountability by requiring States to implement statewide accountability systems covering all public schools and students. These systems must be based on challenging State standards in reading and

mathematics, annual testing for all students in grades 3–8, and annual statewide progress objectives ensuring that all groups of students reach proficiency within 12 years. Assessment results and State progress objectives must be broken out by poverty, race, ethnicity, disability, and limited English proficiency to ensure that no group is left behind. *School districts and schools that fail to make adequate yearly progress (AYP) toward statewide proficiency goals will, over time, be subject to improvement, corrective action, and restructuring measures* aimed at getting them back on course to meet State standards. Schools that meet or exceed AYP objectives or close achievement gaps will be eligible for State Academic Achievement Awards.[37] [Emphasis added]

There it is: The fate of state education rests on the results of state standardized tests. Though NCLB purports to be testing "challenging state standards," the truth of the matter is that when tests are linked to high-stakes consequences ("corrective measures"? "restructuring"?), high test scores become an end unto themselves. Nothing attached really matters—only the numeric outcome. In the case of NCLB high-stakes testing, states had to demonstrate based on state test scores that general achievement was high, as well as subgroup achievement.

Under NCLB, if standardized test scores determined that given schools "needed improvement," districts suffered the added burden of shuttling students to other schools "of choice" in order to remove children from "failing schools." The NCLB executive summary entitles this section "More Choices for Parents and Students"; however, the information is undeniably punitive to schools, school districts, and states:

The NCLB Act significantly increases the choices available to the parents of students attending Title I schools that fail to meet State standards, including immediate relief—beginning with the 2002–03 school year—for students in schools that were previously identified for improvement or corrective action under the 1994 ESEA reauthorization.

LEAs (local education agencies) must give students attending schools identified for improvement, corrective action, or restructuring the opportunity to attend a better public school, which may include a public charter school, within the school district. The district must provide transportation to the new school, and must use at least 5 percent of its Title I funds for this purpose, if needed.

For students attending persistently failing schools (those that have failed to meet State standards for at least 3 of the 4 preceding years), LEAs must permit low-income students to use Title I funds to obtain supplemental educational services from the public- or private-sector provider selected by the students and their parents. Providers must meet State standards and offer services tailored to help participating students meet challenging State academic standards.

To help ensure that LEAs offer meaningful choices, the new law requires school districts to spend up to 20 percent of their Title I allocations to provide school choice and supplemental educational services to eligible students.

In addition to helping ensure that no child loses the opportunity for a quality education because he or she is trapped in a failing school, the choice and supplemental service requirements provide a substantial incentive for low-performing schools to improve. Schools that want to avoid losing students—along with the portion of their annual budgets typically associated with those students—will have to improve or, if they fail to make AYP for 5 years, run the risk of reconstitution under a restructuring plan.[38]

This NCLB executive summary excerpt makes a few issues clear. First, school districts that serve the neediest populations, arguably the ones that need additional funds most, run the greatest risk of losing their Title I funding for not meeting test score–based goals. Sadly, the Bush administration completely ignores the established correlation[39] between socioeconomic status and standardized test scores. In his article *Why Standardized Tests Don't Measure Educational Quality*, UCLA Emeritus Professor James Popham explains,

> One of the chief reasons that children's socioeconomic status is so highly correlated with standardized test scores is that many items on standardized achievement tests really focus on assessing knowledge and/or skills learned outside of school—knowledge and/or skills *more likely to be learned in some socioeconomic settings than in others.*[40] [Emphasis added]

That his entire NCLB law actually tested factors external to the school environment more than internal factors was apparently lost on Bush, an irony that had him "leaving American public education behind" as he put his NCLB mission first. To be fair, NCLB was a rare instance of legislation with bipartisan support, but this speaks to the importance we all place on education, not the soundness of NCLB provisions.

A second issue revealed in the NCLB executive summary involves the pressure for all schools to prove that they could produce AYP-satisfying test results—or risk having their schools taken over for "restructuring"—including the firing of administration and teaching faculty.[41] Moreover, the fiscal pressures on schools were not only related to Title I funding; they also included the additional unfunded costs of fulfilling NCLB's AYP requirements. As New Jersey Representative Scott Garrett notes,

NCLB changed the focus from the education of our kids to bureaucracy and accountability issues. Because of that, money had to be spent elsewhere. According to the GAO (Government Accounting Office), 41 percent of the financial support and staffing at state education agencies was needed to satisfy federal regulation. *In other words, the federal government was the cause of 41 percent of the administrative burden at the state level, despite, on average, providing just 7 percent of the funding. . . . NCLB will cost states about $1.9 billion between 2002 and 2008.*[42] [Emphasis added]

This NCLB-induced fiscal pressure leads into a third issue: States controlled the determination of AYP as well as their selected standardized tests (and associated cutoff scores). That is, in order to escape NCLB punishment of lost freedom via such issues as "restructuring," states could set easily attainable goals. As Representative Garrett observed in 2007:

The goal of No Child Left Behind was to raise achievement by setting standards. Instead, what we've accomplished is a proverbial race to the bottom. The states understand all too well how to game the system . . . and they realize that if they simply lower their standards, then they could say, "Hey, we met our goal and we get our funding, and we don't have any of the additional restrictions." So NCLB provided an incentive for states who once had a good standard to lower that down much lower.[43]

And state AYP goals varied widely in quality.[44] Indeed, the variance among state AYP goals (and the resulting determinations of proficiency), particularly when considering the inconsistency of state test results when compared to those of the National Assessment of Educational Progress (NAEP), is a criticism[45] that would feed into the need for common standards.[46] And never forget: CCSS common standards are intended to have common assessments[47] in order to address the problem of state education autonomy in education assessment.

For 5 years, NCLB had its chance to "save" American public education. It was due to be reauthorized in 2007. The year 2007 came and went; the bipartisan support that had reauthorized ESEA in the form of NCLB in 2001 was no more. Neither the Senate nor House produced viable legislation leading to reauthorization, and reauthorization appeared less likely as 2007 turned into 2008—a presidential election year.[48] One election year led to another (2012), and still there was no NCLB reauthorization. In 2012, in its report entitled *NCLB's Lost Decade for Educational Progress*, FairTest offers the following severe judgment of NCLB and its failure to close achievement gaps via heavy reliance upon standardized testing:

Ten years have passed since President George W. Bush signed No Child Left Behind (NCLB), making it the educational law of the land. A review of a decade of evidence demonstrates that NCLB has failed badly both in terms of its own goals and more broadly. It has neither significantly increased academic performance nor significantly reduced achievement gaps, even as measured by standardized exams.

In fact, because of its misguided reliance on one-size-fits-all testing, labeling and sanctioning schools, it has undermined many education reform efforts. Many schools, particularly those serving low-income students, have become little more than test-preparation programs.[49]

All of the NCLB emphasis on test-related punishment did not put American education on the utopian road to 100% proficiency in reading and math by 2014. In 2007, this was obvious. In fact, to individuals with common sense, the disconnection with reality that led to the original assertion of proficiency perfection was obvious from the outset.

After 5 years of NCLB—with its test-driven consequences—NAEP scores remained flat.[50] If the evidence of NCLB success was supposed to be astounding improvements in standardized test scores, then even by such a shallow standard (pardon the pun), NCLB failed. The federal government was not willing to openly admit as much. When it came to facing the 2007 reality of a failing NCLB, both Bush and Congress floundered. However, behind the scenes and in other arenas, the push to improve upon NCLB-in-limbo was already in the works.

CHAPTER 2

Achieve and Its "Common Core of Standards" Master Plan—Part One

A key factor contributing to the creation of the Common Core State Standards (CCSS) was the known-yet-unacknowledged failure of No Child Left Behind (NCLB) by the time of its supposed 2007 reauthorization. With its focus on standardized test scores as the ultimate measure of educational success, NCLB was not going to propel the United States into the superstar limelight as the nation with 100% student proficiency in reading and math. Among NCLB complications was a lack of consistency among states regarding what constituted adequate yearly progress (AYP), which was supposedly tied to state standards and evident on state assessments (and also on the National Assessment of Educational Progress [NAEP]).

One lesson taken by test-driven-reform proponents from NCLB failure: Consistent standards would be necessary to make American education work. In its November 2007 annual meeting, the Council of Chief State School Officers (CCSSO) had begun promoting the idea of volunteering to compose national standards in apparent anticipation that the federal government would push states in such a direction, presumably because NCLB was floundering. (More to come on this CCSSO decision in Chapters 3 and 5.) However, as noted in Chapter 1, the idea of national standards received a very public blow when first National Endowment for the Humanities chair Lynne Cheney and then the U.S. Senate openly and decisively rejected the national history standards in 1994. The idea of national standards was met with a general distrust of federal government interference in state education affairs.[1] In fact, in addressing the 1996 education summit organized by the National Governors Association (NGA) and chiefly comprised of governors and business executives, President Clinton "tacitly acknowledged that any federal involvement in school reform would kill it."[2] Thus, in this national education summit in 1996, much of the discussion concerned improving state standards as opposed to creating national ones.

As education historian Diane Ravitch observed in 1996:

> This past spring [March 1996], when IBM and the National Governors' Association convened a national education summit to renew support for higher standards, the conventional wisdom among participants was that the pursuit of national standards had self-destructed. Both Republican and Democratic governors made clear that they wanted no part of national standards. The future of standards, they insisted, would be determined by the states.[3]

In her 1996 writing as a member of the Brookings Institution, Ravitch was for national standards, not federally created standards, but it is clear that she did not foresee the possibility that common standards (and associated assessments) could be promoted by the federal government and could comfortably feed into the profit motives of education businesses.

At both G.H.W. Bush's 1989 educational summit and the 1996 NGA educational summit, business interests were seated at the table with governors. (The 1996 summit also included "education experts" whereas the 1989 summit did not.[4, 5]) However, although some summit attendees wished for more of a focus on "choice options,"[6] it is important to note that the possibility of privatizing public education in order to convert public tax money into substantial "education profit" was not an idea that was overtly promoted. Thus, the business presence at the 1989 and 1996 education summits was not pushing for the privatization of public schools.

One critical idea that came out of the 1996 NGA education summit was that of a "national nonprofit organization allied with states and business interests that could serve as a clearing house for information and research on standards and assessment tests."[7] Note that this new "clearinghouse" was accorded nonprofit status. The creation was not just a committee or a consortium. In other words, and importantly, the newly created entity was designed to operate with cash flow. Thus, this late-1990s standards-and-assessments–focused creation held tax-exempt status and thus could accept tax-deductible donations from businesses and philanthropies with interests in influencing the development (and subsequent implementation and related products) of standards and assessments. As previously noted, I do not believe that the goal of the 1989 and 1996 education summits was to turn attention to privatizing public education. However, in retrospect, the formation of education nonprofits provided an entrance for funding education privatization and doing so under the radar, in the guise of seeming benevolence. Surely, a nonprofit would not advance for-profit motives . . . right?

As the 2014 influence of business and philanthropy upon the direction of American education continues to speed out of democracy-fostering control, it is important to recognize that the organization responsible for creating the proposed "standards and assessments clearinghouse" nonprofit—the National Governors Association (NGA)—had already established its own nonprofit in August 1974—the NGA Center for Best Practices.[8] So, what we had in the late 1990s was the NGA—already possessing a nonprofit and therefore vulnerable to sway via the wishes of individuals and groups providing the tax-exempt donations it accepts—creating another would-be vulnerable nonprofit—this time focused on collecting and distributing information on educational standards and assessments.

That newly NGA-created nonprofit—a supposed standards and assessments "clearinghouse"—would come to be known as Achieve, Inc.[9] The organization formally received its nonprofit status in May 1997.[10] As it gained power in the standards-setting arena, Achieve would perform a key role in the creation and promotion of CCSS.

For now, let us focus on those early days of Achieve—the Relatively New Nonprofit on the Standards and Assessment Block.

ACHIEVE, WHO'S YOUR DADDY?
WHY, IT'S IBM CEO LOUIS GERSTNER, JR.

Created in 1996, Achieve, Inc. has a board comprised of governors and business CEOs.[11] Thus, in Achieve, Inc., business interests have fashioned for themselves a seat at the NGA table of American education issues.

Notice who still is not seated among this intended decisionmaking group: the teacher practitioner. (Sigh.) Nevertheless, the guys there, they think they know how the American public school classroom should work.

"But from whence cometh this 'Achieve'?" you ask.

If one individual could be credited as Achieve's creator, that person would be IBM CEO Louis Gerstner, Jr. The products of a politico-corporate marriage that should never have happened, both the 1996 national education summit and the resulting "entity," Achieve, Inc., are the unfortunate education consequences of the corporate mind.

In a keynote address at the 1995 NGA annual meeting, Gerstner apparently felt qualified to forcefully promote his views about American education because, as he said to the governors, he has "spent a lot of time on education." In regard to his noneducator audience, he added, "So have many of you. We all have scars to prove it." Not actual, practical, classroom-teaching "scars." Just those top-down, shape-the-system-from-the-outside "scars."[12]

In his 1995 speech, Gerstner was quick to add that he is a businessman, and his words betrayed his perception that running America's schools is like running a company: "But I've also spent a lot of time helping troubled companies get back on their feet. It's hard work. Lots of hard work, and invariably it involves lots of structural change."[13]

Based upon his rally-the-troops speech, it was obvious in 1995 that Gerstner planned to "structurally change" American education. He strongly campaigned for "a fundamental, bone-jarring, full-fledged 100 percent revolution that discards the old and replaces it with a totally new performance-driven system." And according to Gerstner, that *must* involve national standards *now*:

> I want to suggest three, and only three, priorities for public education for the next year (1996): The first is setting absolutely the highest academic standards and holding all of us accountable for the results. Now. Immediately. This school year. Now if we won't do that, we won't need any more goals, because we are going nowhere. Without standards and accountability, we have nothing. . . .
>
> If we don't face up to the fact that we are the only major country in the world without an articulated set of education standards—and without a means of measuring how successfully we are reaching them, we're lost before we get started. . . .
>
> We cannot be sidetracked by academicians who say it will take five years just to set the standards.[14]

Interestingly—and despite the 1994 Cheney incident tarnishing the national standards idea for fear of a federal takeover—then–Secretary of Education Richard Riley applauded Gerstner for his speech.[15] However, it seems that any thinking individual realizes that it is nonsense to demand national standards "now" and to not realize that standards development of such magnitude should require care in organizing teacher practitioner involvement for planning, drafting, review, testing, modification, and voluntary adoption—and that making any set of standards inextricably bound to high-stakes assessments kills the effect of the standards by placing undue focus on the outcomes of the tests and not the learning to be acquired via the standards.

But Gerstner was a businessman, and a successful one, which means his forcefulness had paid off for him in the past—and apparently it did so with the governors in 1995 as well. He focused on the 1983 report *A Nation at Risk* as the reason for his "immediate" urgency. Even though

12 years had passed and America still somehow managed to retain its position as a world power—and even though America did not become a world power by trying to "keep up" with other countries—the governors in attendance bought the education reform "urgency" that Gerstner was selling. Also, it is clear from his speech that Gerstner perceived teachers not as professionals but as part of a problem that required corporate-generated solutions—and the governors swallowed this teacher-as-scapegoat perspective, too. Indeed, near the end of his speech, wealthy businessman Gerstner announced his intent to hold an education summit the next year—in 1996—one that would be composed of governors and business interests—with a smattering of "education experts"[16] to serve as "resource people."[17]

It is from that 1996 summit—the one alluded to previously in this chapter by Diane Ravitch and the first one initiated by business and hosted at Gerstner's IBM conference facility[18]—that the entity that would become Achieve, Inc. was born. As noted in the 1996 NGA education summit report:

> A series of actions that will establish K–12 academic standards, assessments, and accountability for student performance, and to improve the use of school technology to reach high standards are under way as a result of the 1996 National Education Summit. Commitments to action came from 40 governors and 49 corporate executives who attended the meeting on March 26 and 27 at the IBM Corporation's Executive Conference Center in Palisades, New York.
>
> *Within weeks of that meeting, the National Governors Association adopted a proposal to create a non-governmental organization* to serve as a clearinghouse for standards information and benchmarks and public reporting.[19] [Emphasis added]

How humorous to consider that governors were trying to create a "nongovernmental agency." As previously mentioned, they did succeed in creating a nonprofit, and nonprofits tend to belong to those who make the donations—if not the federal government, then philanthropists, or businessmen like Gerstner—who know what American education needs by observing it from the outside

ACHIEVE: FORGET "CLEARINGHOUSE"; LET'S EVALUATE

Through Achieve, the business mindset of competition and profits would find a fixed foothold in the area of traditionally collaborative and non-profit-focused public education. Such is clear in Achieve's drawing on the business practice of benchmarking standards—comparing standards to those of competitors—in this case, to the standards of other states and countries—and to the bottom line of assessment results.

Achieve quickly became more than a standards and assessments clearinghouse; it became a standards and assessments *evaluator* and *advisor.*

Big jump.

In his 1995 NGA speech, Gerstner wanted a set of national standards "now"—for the 1996–1997 school year. Even Achieve, Inc. could not achieve that degree of urgency. But the new clearinghouse *could* exert itself by proclaiming itself a standards authority.

In 1998, Achieve conducted its *Academic Standards and Assessments Benchmarking Pilot Project.*[20] For this trial Achieve tested the educational standards and assessments of two states, Michigan and North Carolina. In justifying its purpose, a number of truths are made clear. First of all, Achieve had been put in a position to judge state standards and assessments, and such a position inherently holds power. In its 1998 report on Michigan's results, Achieve noted the following regarding its seemingly benign position and purpose:

> Achieve is involved in benchmarking for another important reason: states have traditionally had limited access to quality, trustworthy information about education standards and assessments. . . . States are increasingly looking for an independent, credible place to turn to for advice on these issues.[21]

Achieve views itself as independent and credible. The organization does not appear to acknowledge its own susceptibility to enforcing the competition-centered, profit-driven mindset of its business CEO board members in determining what constitutes education success, including which components of such success are not readily apparent and therefore unable to be measured.

The influence of business on education was in seed form in the late 1990s—a seed that would sprout and flourish under the pressure of a "failing schools" message that was yet to come.

As part of its astounding shift from standards collector to standards evaluator/advisor, Achieve does attempt to establish the credibility of its standards-grading process by noting that it has enlisted the assistance of established organizations that were well versed in identifying "exemplary standards":

> We have designed a comprehensive and rigorous process for benchmarking a state's standards and assessments against exemplary models in each of the core

academic subjects. The process we have developed analyzes standards and assessments as a package, rather than simply standards alone. In addition to analyzing the rigor and quality of the standards and tests, we have measured the degree of alignment between the two. During the pilot, the Council for Basic Education (CBE) conducted the standards benchmarking, while the Learning Research and Development Center (LRDC) at the University of Pittsburgh led the assessments analysis. Both organizations have extensive experience working with states and districts to design and review standards and assessments. We also took advantage of the considerable knowledge and expertise of the U.S. National Research Center for the Trends in International Mathematics and Science Study (TIMSS), located at Michigan State University (MSU). . . .

   The Council for Basic Education (CBE) designed a process for benchmarking standards to uncover the strengths and weaknesses of state standards by comparing the standards to state, national, and international "benchmark" standards that are recognized for their quality and/or for producing high student achievement.[22]

It does appear that Achieve tried to ensure a high-quality process for evaluating state standards and offering recommendations for improvement. Nevertheless, although the goal of this standards-examining effort might not have been to arrive at a single set of national standards, it is easy enough to travel in that direction when comparing the standards of any number of states with a limited collection of standards that are considered ideal—the benchmark. What Achieve appears not to have considered is whether benchmarked standards are effective when they are divorced from their contexts. For example, in this 1998 pilot study report, Achieve notes that its international example was Japan. However, one must consider Japanese education standards in the context of Japanese culture (including the values of the group over the individual); the Japanese pressure on high school graduates to be accepted into prestigious colleges; and the degree to which college acceptance determines potential career advancement in Japan.

   Is it fair (or useful, or even necessary) to use Japanese education standards as an American model if American society and Japanese society differ to such a degree that the uninformed observer could not possibly mistake one for the other?

   Doing so seems like quite the stretch in "comparability."

   In benchmarking standards, there is also the question of whether promoting a narrow education ideal is even possible or desirable in a nation with such cultural variety within and among its 50 states. In its 1998 report, Achieve notes that it tried to offer multiple examples of "good" standards. However, despite its statement about recognizing standards for their quality and/or for producing higher test scores, its judgment of "good" hinged upon NAEP and TIMSS scores—a narrowed, test score–based ideal.

Next, regarding Achieve's declared "independent" and "credible" position, those leading the standards quality determination should consider the degree to which a group of predominately middle-aged, almost exclusively White male leaders (one governor on Achieve's 1998 board was of Asian descent)[23] is able to provide informed leadership regarding systems dynamics (such as those that affect minority members of society) that might complicate a seemingly clear connection between standards and assessments. (In 2014, the Achieve board of directors continued to be all male and all White except for one Black member.[24])

No women.

Only a single (token?) male of color.

I find this glaring lack of gender and ethnic/racial balance highly problematic. These predominately White men form a board of directors that is attempting to alter the heart of American education via standards and assessments.

On to other notable issues.

In its 1998 report, Achieve notes that one of its consultant groups, CBE, "worked with content experts and seasoned classroom teachers to develop new tools and systematically analyze the state standards."[25] And those involved with Achieve attempted to offer "various perspectives and characteristics of good standards."[26] Still, the determination of "good standards" was ultimately "guided" by NAEP and TIMSS results. In short, in selecting benchmarking models, NAEP and TIMSS scores influenced the determination of "good" standards because, well, those test scores mean a lot to "policymakers and the public":

> Because of the increasing importance to policymakers and the public of the state-level National Assessment of Educational Progress (NAEP) assessments and the Trends in International Mathematics and Science Study (TIMSS) results, evidence from NAEP and TIMSS guided our [benchmarked standards] selections (promoted as "exemplar" standards). We used the assessment frameworks that form the basis for the NAEP assessments in reading, writing, math, science, US history, civics, and geography. While these documents provide various levels of detail about the content and skills that students need to do well on the NAEP assessments, and some are more useful than others, they are nonetheless the principal standards that communicate to the public the expectations for student achievement on these important assessments.[27]

In 1995, IBM CEO and (one year later) Achieve board member Gerstner *did* emphasize his expectation that the national standards he demanded America needs "now" should be connected to standardized tests.

In that same 1995 NGA speech, as Gerstner hammered home America's need for national standards, he alluded to America's greatness in landing a man on the moon[28]—which happened in the absence of a standards movement.

A Gerstner blind spot in his message for standards urgency.

Back to Achieve's 1998 benchmarking report.

The report continues by noting that international standards models (i.e., like those in Japan) were selected based upon TIMSS results. (Only Japanese standards were available for international benchmarking in the 1998 pilot.)

So, let us absorb what we have here: Achieve purports to offer multiple models of state standards identified as exemplary in order to offer states choice and variety regarding what Achieve holds as exemplary. However, in the end, all exemplary standards models are identified as such based not only on a state's NAEP results (or, in the case of Japan, TIMSS results) but also on how well those exemplary models *conform to the NAEP assessment frameworks.*

As far as any American standards are concerned, exemplary equals "NAEP assessment framework conformity."

Let's set American public education up to teach to the NAEP test and call it exemplary.

Let's throw in some international exemplary standards judged by completely isolating those exemplary international standards from any greater cultural perspective and instead narrowly focus on TIMSS results.

Why?

Because NAEP and TIMSS are "important assessments."

In this 1998 report, Achieve also makes a comment that would change as the business mindset of measured outcomes came to seize American public education: "Achieve's benchmarking efforts are *not designed to grade or rank states.*"[29] [Emphasis added]

Achieve maintains that its goal is not to grade or rank. And yet, Achieve acknowledges that it relies on the outcomes of standards grading as performed by the American Federation of Teachers (AFT) and Fordham Foundation (known better as the Fordham Institute, by 2007)[30] to inform its review of Michigan's standards in this pilot.

Achieve notes that it wants to break with the standards-grading idea, yet it relies upon two organizations known for grading state standards to advise it in evaluating state standards.

Really?

Particularly through the Fordham Institute, the publicized grading and ranking of state standards (and the declaration of state standards deficiency) would indeed travel on a 1990s-established trajectory made possible by the punitive nature of NCLB and its common standards-requiring offshoot, Race to the Top (RTTT).

And here Fordham is in 1998, having found for itself a home in the sparkling-new, "independent" standards and assessment "clearinghouse"—which is not just the initially purposed *storage* for state standards but the quickly morphed *evaluator* of state standards—Achieve.

It seems that Achieve might have been deluding itself that it was not promoting standards grading given subsequent wording regarding education accountability and the arguably inflated role of standardized testing as an accountability end-all:

> In order to understand the full extent of what states expect of their students, we feel it is important not only to look at academic standards, but also at the tests states use to measure those standards. *Tests are the critical link between setting standards and holding education systems accountable for achievement.*[31] [Emphasis added]

The pairing of ideas—saying "we don't mean to grade" while emphasizing test scores—is like fashioning an arrow and painting a target, all while declaring to have no intention that the two should interact.

The inclusion of a business philosophy on benchmarking provided a bow.

As its 1998 pilot report indicates, Achieve *intended* to meld education and business practice—a concept that was gaining popularity among education administrators in the 1990s. I recall attending a workshop with my Louisiana school principal in 1992 to help with quality control in our school. I also remember hearing my Georgia school principal make references in numerous faculty meetings in 1994 to teaching as being a "business" and my students as "customers."

Achieve assumes that because benchmarking is an accepted business practice, it should also be an accepted education practice—without considering the striking differences between business operations and school operations—not the least of which is that the American education "product" is a human being:

> Benchmarking is a highly respected practice in the business world. It is an activity that looks outward to find the highest goals for performance and then measures actual business operations against those goals. *Benchmarking in education is a logical extension of this business philosophy.* . . . [32] [Emphasis added]

Benchmarking in business is *money-centered*. It is about profits versus costs, and assets, and net worth: that is, assets minus liabilities.[33] This leads to yet another truth inherent in Achieve's 1998 report: the danger of viewing human beings—in this case, teachers and students—as either assets or liabilities—to the school's profit venture. Given that student test scores were becoming the revered and preferred outcome measure of academic success, it is easy to see how the business model of education could easily promote the valuing of good test-takers over poor ones and high-scoring schools over low-scoring ones.

Finally, based on the findings of its pilot, Achieve offers Michigan the following unusual advice regarding what Achieve determined was a lack of fit between Michigan's "broad or vague" standards and its "high expectations" assessment system. Let us first consider this nugget:

> As we see it, there are two strategies Michigan could pursue to communicate more clearly its academic standards to educators and the public. The state could revise the existing standards to better reflect the expectations on the assessments, or it could develop and distribute supplementary materials that clarify and extend the existing standards and forge a better connection with the assessments. *Revising the existing standards would likely be more complicated and could send the false signal that the state is changing the direction of its reforms. On the other hand, creating new documents that would serve as a bridge between the existing standards and the assessments would continue and deepen the state's present course in education reform.*[34] [Emphasis added]

Even though Achieve has determined that Michigan's standards could use improvement, *Achieve advises against it because of public perception.* Achieve's advice: Forget our advice to improve standards. Instead, just rig the standards by adding another layer to the process. Call it a "bridge." This way, the public will not be upset by—what? The truth that standards are being altered?

Achieve was willing to advise states to do less than what it deemed best in order to manipulate public perception. In the end, Achieve was willing to sacrifice what it deemed quality standards for political expediency.

Choosing political expediency over educational quality would reveal itself in Achieve's promoting the idea that 48 states and two territories contracted to use "common" standards in 2009—before such standards even existed.[35]

Back to 1998 and that Achieve pilot report.

Achieve continues with its advice for Michigan not to touch deficient standards and instead to add a "cover yourself" layer that would be made available to the public:

> The states that have had the most success with this strategy—creating a clarifying set of materials—have made those documents the centerpiece of their public engagement campaign. In Oregon, for example, a broad set of standards similar to Michigan's Curriculum Frameworks have been superseded by a clearer, more explicit set of expectations that directly speak to the content and rigor of the assessments. Massachusetts has also produced a clarifying set of documents that bridge the standards and assessments. These new documents contain standards that better define what will be assessed on the state tests and also contain examples of test questions. Most importantly, the new sets of materials in both states are sent to schools and parents in preparation for the state tests.[36]

It is interesting that the terminology used to promote CCSS ("clear, understandable, and consistent"[37]) is similar to the language Achieve used in 1998 to promote state usage of a patch to connect standards and assessments—especially for preparation for the state tests.

All of the work Achieve invested in its pilot study, all of the care it took in establishing a process for reputable organizations to evaluate and advise about standards, all of the justifying benchmarking, all of the detail in writing advisory results for the pilot state, Michigan, and in the end, it's the assessments that are accorded supreme importance.

Lesson learned here from Achieve: Standards serve assessments. And by 1998, Achieve was only getting started in its attempts to shape state standards into what would later become those voluntary standards intended to be empowered via high-stakes assessments, and that governors and state superintendents just happened to sign on for 11 years later, in 2009.

In the next chapter, the Achieve journey continues as this standards-clearinghouse-turned-standards-evaluator hosts its own education summit and creates its own project to create and promote its ideal high school standards.

CHAPTER 3

Achieve and Its "Common Core of Standards" Master Plan—Part Two

In 1995, IBM CEO Louis Gerstner, Jr. addressed the NGA national meeting, telling governors that a then-12-year-old "urgency" was placing national security squarely onto the American public school classroom, and that the solution was a set of national standards, which must be created and instituted now. Although Gerstner's demand for "national standards now" was amazingly unrealistic, NGA did decide to create a nonprofit that was supposed to serve as a standards clearinghouse—but quickly became a standards "authority" instead—Achieve, Inc. The almost exclusively White male board of Achieve, Inc. was divided between governors and business executives.

Supposedly concerned with "closing the achievement gap," Achieve, Inc. exited the starting gates by reinforcing the "us versus them" mindset between well-positioned, influential individuals outside of the classroom and teacher practitioners. No need to meaningfully involve teachers in changes that Achieve, Inc. had already decided needed to be instituted.

It is only a matter of telling teachers what they are expected to do.

That would require more high-profile meetings, of course.

1999: THE YEAR OF ACHIEVE-PROMOTED, NATIONAL ACCOUNTABILITY

In 1999, Achieve sponsored a national education summit. Co-sponsors included the Business Roundtable, Council of the Great City Schools, Learning First Alliance, National Alliance of Business, National Education Goals Panel, and the National Governors Association. Rather than conduct a detailed examination of each organization, I will simply highlight the focus of what this summit deemed important in a message signed by the summit's co-chairs Governor Tommy Thompson of Wisconsin,

Governor James Hunt of North Carolina, CEO Louis Gerstner of IBM, and CEO John Pepper of Procter and Gamble:

> The nation's governors, business leaders and educators have been hard at work in recent years pushing America's public schools toward world-class performance. Virtually every state now has academic standards in the core subjects that students are expected to meet, up from about a dozen states three years ago. *The majority of states now test student achievement against these standards in English and mathematics, and most report those results publicly. This represents significant progress from the mid-1990s, when many questioned the need to set rigorous targets for schools and hold them accountable.*[1] [Emphasis added]

Yep. The focus is on "testing student achievement against standards."

Governor Thompson stated, "Today, it's about the three A's, not the three R's . . . accountability, achievement, and alignment." He noted, "The consequences for those students that don't measure up are severe."[2]

Wow. "Love of learning" just took a kick in its rear.

In an oddity, the summit's action statement notes that "rich curriculum in every school" is a "priority." However, the language about accountability and consequences sets the tone of this summit not as one seeking to enrich learning and support teachers in this effort but as one emphasizing rewards and consequences that motivate performance—the ultimate "performance" being higher test scores.

According to this summit, teachers are expected to perform as well.

I know: Let's pay teachers based on student "achievement." We'll call it "pay for performance."

I find myself envisioning poodles performing for treats tossed to them by governors and business CEOs who "mean business."

Demeaning for teachers and students alike.

A reading of the summit overview document unmistakably shows that the goal of this summit was to "face the tough challenge posed by raising standards and measuring results"; to "refus[e] to back down"; to "redouble efforts" to make "higher" standards and "measur[ed] results" "happen together."[3]

President Clinton—who created a Goals 2000 national standards committee that failed to materialize (see Chapter 1)—"praised governors and CEOs for keeping the standards movement going" and urged summit attendees "to hold firm against any backlash that comes when real accountability is first put in place."[4]

These very words could have been used to describe the 2009

Governors Symposium—the one at which it was announced that "46 states and three territories already signed on to the Council of Chief State School Officers and the National Governors Association–led initiative to develop a set of common core standards that are fewer, clearer, and higher. . . ."[5]

Here is some more 1999 Achieve summit language that is familiar when one considers the push for CCSS:

> When stakes are high, states must ensure that their standards are worthy targets and that their assessments are accurate measuring sticks. In the Action Statement, governors pledged to benchmark their states' standards, assessments, and accountability systems against those of other states and nations and report the results publicly.[6]

In the case of CCSS, the common standards were simply declared worthy. They were never tested on a smaller scale prior to full implementation. As noted previously, most states (as it happens, the governors and state superintendents) signed on for CCSS with no idea about what the outcome might be. They agreed to tie their state education systems to an as-yet-uncreated set of standards. As for making certain that assessments tied to standards are "accurate measuring sticks": The standards must first exist before this can be done. Furthermore, in both 1999 and in 2009, those who are enthusiastic about the education summits do not appear to consider whether standardized tests can actually capture the information that is useful in determining whether students have actually mastered knowledge and can translate it into real-world situations.

Regarding assessments, the phrase "accurate measuring sticks" really bothers me.

I'm again envisioning those trained poodles.

Then there's the question of the usefulness of benchmarking, which I have already discussed. In its 1998 test of only a couple of states' standards, Achieve performed the benchmarking ritual and then advised Michigan to keep its standards anyway. Moreover, Achieve advised Michigan follow a politically expedient route that had been taken by Oregon and Massachusetts. Interestingly, the question of the quality of Oregon's and Massachusetts' standards was not the issue; "building the information bridge" between standards (no matter the quality, apparently) and assessments was. Where would this mighty 1999 education summit's call for accountability and admiration for rigorous tests end up?

Why, with a 2001 summit, of course.

2001: NAEP LOOKS NICE, SO WE DONE GOOD

The focus in 2001 was on 2000 NAEP scores and how they had risen. Not sure how that was proof of the efficacy of the standards- and assessment-based reforms declared in 1999; however, summit attendees were able to celebrate the NAEP gains made from 1996 to 2000.

It seems to have escaped those celebrating that NAEP only tests students in two subjects (reading and math) in two NCLB-mandated grade levels (grades 4 and 8; NAEP is also given to grade 12 but is not mandated by NCLB). Whereas it might be a less biased measure of math and reading achievement than state standardized tests, NAEP is narrowly defined to progress (for all practical purposes) in just two subjects for only two grade levels.

The connection between reform "success" and NAEP scores is a loose one, at best.

The 2001 summit briefing guide does offer two notable comments. First, it includes a word about upcoming education legislation:

> The president and Congress are poised to enact legislation that will accelerate the pace of these reforms. States will be challenged to expand testing and accountability systems, intervene in chronically low-performing schools, and close the achievement gap that continues to separate the advantaged and disadvantaged.[7]

And just what "reform-accelerating legislation" would that be?

The No Child Left Behind Act of 2001.

Second, in its acknowledgments, Achieve mentions Chester Finn, president of the Fordham Foundation, and Kati Haycock, president of Education Trust.[8] This threesome—Achieve, Fordham Institute, and Education Trust—would become indispensable in establishing and promoting CCSS. Prior to CCSS, however, the Education Trust, Fordham Foundation/Institute, and the National Alliance of Business would ally and produce "a common core of English and mathematics academic knowledge and skills, or 'benchmarks,' that American high school graduates need for success in college and the workforce": The American Diploma Project (ADP).[9]

AMERICAN DIPLOMA PROJECT

The grand flaw in ADP is its overarching goal of directing education into the narrow, business-serving direction of "knowledge and skills most demanded by higher education and employers."[10] In other words, learning for the sheer joy of learning—learning for learning's sake—was scrapped in favor of a market-serving perspective. While it is true that high school students and their parents want to feel confident that school is preparing students for a successful life, narrowing this goal and tying it to business interests creates a twisted, corporate-feeding distortion. In this view, education is ultimately valuable only if it receives the nod of approval from business.

Creativity, innovation, invention, risk, self-expression—these are life-enriching qualities that prove difficult to benchmark—and much more difficult to measure on standardized tests. Nevertheless, this is the direction that Achieve chose to pursue with ADP—a project that was *the* undeniable precursor to CCSS.

ADP was officially launched the same year as NCLB: 2001. By 2004, ADP released a report called *Ready or Not: Creating a High School Diploma That Counts*. The question is, a high school diploma that counts for what? In the report, ADP opens by stating that the American high school diploma should designate "adequate preparation for the intellectual demands of adult life." It then states that universities and employers currently "all but ignore the diploma, knowing that it often serves as little more than a certificate of attendance."[11]

Wow.

In its negative view of the value of the high school diploma, it seems that ADP has emulated Achieve "father" Louis Gerstner, who told governors in 1995, "We have given high school diplomas in this country to a whole generation of Americans who cannot basically read those diplomas—they are functionally illiterate."[12]

Such a severe indictment on the diploma is not justified. I know of no university that admits students who have no high school diploma or recognized equivalent. Furthermore, in advertising jobs, employers note the level of entry education required—and often, they list 'high school diploma or equivalent." Yet ADP's (and Gerstner's) sensational declaration of the utter lack of value of the American high school diploma would serve useful to their purpose in manufacturing a problem: of defining American education as failing.

Now, keep in mind that only 2 years before ADP was founded—in 1999—Achieve declared its push for accountability for state standards and associated assessments a success based on 2000 NAEP scores. So, with ADP, the story seems to be that American education is a success *until high school* (recall that high school is not measured by the NCLB-mandated

NAEP), and that the call for "higher" standards and measurable outcomes on standardized tests only worked for lower and middle grades that could be showcased using the NCLB-mandated NAEP.

In its 2004 report, ADP assumes that the high school diploma should readily connect to "high performance, high growth jobs."[13] As a result, ADP declared that the American high school was failing because it did not set "clear academic expectations that have currency beyond 12th grade."[14]

Yet reading, comprehension, critical thinking, writing and speaking, the ability to communicate and work with groups, and the ability to apply math and computer skills are all skills honed in high school that transfer to life, the workplace, and higher education. As for the American high school diploma's ensuring college entrance readiness, ADP complains about the variety of grades that "cannot be compared from school to school" and of "a confusing array" of college entrance exams that are "unrelated to any of the tests students have taken already."[15] Such is certainly an argument for "sameness"—for creating a single high school exit assessment that is snap-locked in its alignment with a single, U.S. college entrance exam.

The failure of the American high school (and postsecondary system), they say, rests in its *variety*.

Interestingly, CCSS architect David Coleman—who became president of the College Board following his CCSS stint—admits in 2014 that the best predictor of college success is high school grades.[16] This is the president of a testing company publicly admitting that his standardized tests cannot effectively compete with teacher-assigned high school grades—which vary from school to school and teacher to teacher—in accurately predicting a student's postsecondary success.

I think ADP just experienced a profound blow to its logic that variety is bad and sameness is superior.

During the course of my high school career, I took six classes a year with six different teachers. I completed high school in 4 years. For some courses, I had the same teacher, but for most, I changed teachers. So, throughout high school, I had perhaps 18 different teachers, who all agreed via their grading that I was an A–B high school student. Moreover, all agreed that I would do well in college. The single—voluntary—standardized test that I took in high school, the ACT, confirmed their agreement.

When I was admitted to Louisiana State University in January 1985, the university based its admissions decision on my high school grades, my class ranking, my teacher recommendations, an entrance essay that I wrote as part of my application, and my ACT score.

My ACT score complemented my high school teachers' determination of my abilities via their grades of my performance as part of my high school transcript as well as their written recommendations.

Viewing my ACT score alone says nothing about my work ethic, my ability to persevere, my ability to work with others, or my creativity—all qualities that contribute to a fulfilling, productive, satisfying life not only for me alone but also for those with whom I interact.

Back to that 2004 ADP *Ready or Not* report.

ADP cites a 28% remediation rate for the 70% of graduates enrolling in postsecondary institutions. It assumes that this remediation rate means that the high school diploma is worthless, that a credible high school diploma would guarantee that the bearer is ready for on-level college coursework. Not necessarily so. A contributing factor related to the potential need for postsecondary institutions to offer remedial courses is that colleges and universities are allowed to admit students conditionally. Sadly, another motivating factor for colleges is the additional revenue stream created by heavy enrollment of students in multiple remediation courses. Thus, some students whom the postsecondary institutions deem to be academically marginal are offered an opportunity to prove themselves. Moreover, American high school students are allowed the choice to complete a high school course of study that does not lead to college. However, students might later decide to pursue college. (ADP even admits that the specifics of high school coursework selection affect college student attrition.[17] In other words, some students select courses that do not foster subsequent college success.) Also, students need not produce honor-roll-worthy grades in order to complete high school. ADP should ask the question of whether or not a straight-C student should be expected to require some remediation upon college entrance. Then there are students who do well overall but who might struggle in a single subject, such as math or English. Such students might even be on the honor roll for overall B averages, for example. (An A in English might compensate for a hard-fought C in math.)

Indeed, the reasons for a notable percentage of college applicants' requiring remedial coursework are numerous. One should not speedily conclude that a student's need for remedial coursework automatically and directly reflects on the quality of coursework behind the high school diploma.

As Philip Schlechty notes in the first chapter of his book *Shaking Up the Schoolhouse:*

America's schools are far better than many critics say and many American citizens are terribly ignorant about the public schools. Not only do they underestimate present performance, they overestimate the performance of schools in the past.

In the not-too-distant past a significant number of Americans were literally illiterate in that they could not decode words on the written page. Today, 99 percent of all adult Americans can read in the sense that they can decode words. The illiteracy rate that concerns us today is the functional illiteracy rate. Nearly half of adult Americans are functionally illiterate; they cannot read well enough to manage daily living and employment tasks that require reading skills beyond a basic level. Literal illiteracy has been eradicated. What remains to be eradicated is functional illiteracy, which represents a newer, higher standard.

Taking a romantic view of the past in relation to the present often translates into misguided policies and acerbic commentary, summed up in the battle cry "back to the basics." But how, it should be asked, can we go back to where we have never been?[18]

In general, America has made progress in terms of literacy. Yet literacy is not the only issue that has changed over the years. The expectations that business owners have of America's schools have also changed. There has been a shift that in itself shows the progress of American society in general. Once focused on the role of the American education system in preparing American youth for vocational employment, business leaders are now more concerned with academic preparation.[19] In their concern, business leaders are dissatisfied with high school graduates who are functionally literate. They apparently want more. Nevertheless, it is possible in this country for one to become a company executive and still depend on the grammar and spell-check features now common to word-processing software programs.

Food for thought.

Here is the reality of American public education in our time: It is possible for American students to graduate with a high school diploma and be functionally literate—not skilled in the use of the rules of grammar, not proficient at spelling, not voracious readers. Nevertheless, according to a study published in 2010 by William Wood of James Madison University, functionally literate individuals (Woods calls these individuals "less literate") also tend not to have achieved a high school diploma, with only 27 percent holding a high school diploma or equivalent.[20] Thus, if one thinks of literacy as a continuum, then those achieving a high school diploma tend to operate at a more advanced level of functional literacy.

Does this increasing rate of functional literacy mean that there is no room for improvement in the American high school? Not at all. As a high school English teacher, I am always seeking ways to make my classroom operations more efficient. By doing so, I might devote more one-on-one consultation time to students to coach them on their writing and help them increase their knowledge of the world, thereby improving reading comprehension and fostering critical thinking. However, the ADP goal of producing a single set of English and math standards—and tying such standards to common, standardized assessments—is misguided and is based upon the premise that sameness equals quality and that sameness tested will somehow translate into a level of academic functioning unprecedented in the history of American public education.

Even former president George W. Bush—the man who introduced and strongly promoted NCLB and its "100 percent proficiency in math and reading"—admitted in a 2001 Yale University commencement address to being a C student in college.[21] Moreover, being a C student in college does not usually begin in college. In a 2013 meta-analysis of variables predicting college GPA by cognitive psychologist Daniel Willingham, high school GPA was in the mix, as were SAT and ACT scores, the grades students set as their ideal targets, and the ability to persist academically.[22] Thus, it is likely that Bush was not a stellar student academically in high school, either. Indeed, his high school academics are described by Michael Kinsley of CNN as being "ordinary."[23]

For ADP, the high school standardized test results were all that mattered in the end. And because testing outcomes have been tagged as the ultimate mark of success, the standards associated with such tests have become rigid. The standards must be immovable in order to connect to the tests. And in situations in which standards and assessment become rigid, curriculum also runs a major risk of being hijacked by administrators mesmerized by the thought of ever-higher test scores.

It was clear that ADP wanted a single, unified, national high school diploma. It did not declare this overtly; to do so would be to sound dangerously federal. However, the message is implied in this ADP promotion:

> Although high school graduation requirements are established state by state, a high school diploma should represent a common currency nationwide. Families move across state lines, students apply to colleges outside their own state and employers hire people from across the country. States owe it to their students to set high school expectations for high school graduates that are portable to other states.[24]

In its 2006 report, *Closing the Expectations Gap*, Achieve reported that five states—California, Indiana, Nebraska, Wyoming, and New

York—had completed the ADP alignment process, meaning that the business community has indicated that the high school standards "reflect their skill demands."[25] However, Achieve was able to verify that ADP standards had actually been incorporated in only two states: California and Indiana. Moreover, by the time Achieve had published its 2011 *Closing the Achievement Gap* update, ADP was no longer the focus. CCSS had taken the Achieve–Ed Trust–Fordham center stage.[26] But let us not get ahead of ourselves. Let us consider Achieve's ADP status in 2008.

2008: ADP EXPANDS INTO CCSS

It should come as no surprise that Achieve would seek to extend its ADP to all grade levels. After all, national standards and associated assessments were IBM CEO Gerstner's intention 13 years earlier in his 1995 "urgency" speech to governors.[27] All grades "need" common standards and assessments. According to Achieve, previous state standards did not consider the expectations of colleges and businesses in setting such standards:

> Before the ADP benchmarks identified what students need to know to succeed post-high school graduation, state standards reflected a consensus among subject matter experts about what would be desirable or important for young people to learn. They did not take into account what postsecondary institutions, training programs and employers expected of high school graduates.[28]

Achieve then commended 22 states for aligning their high school standards with ADP standards. However, Achieve added that not only would not enough states be aligning with ADP, ADP standards would not be enough. More alignment was supposedly needed, and Achieve was balanced right on the edge of a "state-led" idea for a *single set* of K–12 standards. Notice this careful sales job, which started as a supposed review of ADP yet quickly turned to "Say, this 'common core' of standards in English and math happened to emerge from states involved in ADP":

> What have we learned from the work of these leading (12 in English, 16 in math) states? Whether students are headed directly to work or to postsecondary education, employers and faculty agree that high school graduates need increasingly similar levels of rigor. When states take the lead, and use college- and career-readiness as their goal, they will develop rigorous standards that prepare all students for success. *A critical mass of states has arrived at a common core of standards in English and mathematics as a byproduct of their deliberate, voluntary*

efforts to align their high school standards with the demands of college and careers.[29]
[Emphasis added]

There it is: the seed idea for CCSS in a published report. Notice the emphasis on the "states" "arriving at a common core." Also notice the inclusion of the term *voluntary*. Never mind the ADP push to enlist states in the common high school standards effort. When it comes to a full-on, K–12 "common core," the "states" took the lead.

In some respects, it seems that Achieve continued to be cautious with where it was headed with this "common core" promotional. Two ideas in Achieve's 2008 *Out of Many, One* report lead to this conclusion. First, Achieve is careful to state that "common" does not imply a single set of standards. Under the heading, "Common Does Not Mean Identical State Standards," Achieve writes:

> *While state standards from these states share a common core, they are not identical.* The ADP Core forms a foundation of college- and career-ready expectations, *but does not necessarily constitute four full years of content in English and mathematics.* How states choose to construct a rich classroom experience for all four years of high school varies from state to state. *A number of states include content in their standards that are outside the scope of, or more rigorous than, the ADP benchmarks. For example, a number of states include in their mathematics standards rigorous content that is particularly important for students interested in pursuing further education and careers in Science, Technology, Engineering or Mathematics (STEM) fields.*
>
> States also differ with respect to the organization of their standards, their level of specificity and the amount of detail provided. [30] [Emphasis added]

That, right there, is not the current CCSS. However, as one will see in reading the subsequent chapter on the CCSS MOU (memorandum of understanding), the National Governors Association (NGA) and Council of Chief State School Officers (CCSSO) included language to guarantee an inflexible, rigid "core" that would make the above statement by Achieve little more than window dressing.

The second statement that sets the 2008 *Out of Many, One* report teetering on the edge of what we know as CCSS (but not being exactly CCSS) is the statement that standards should not be rigid. Under the heading, "Real World Standards Must Be Dynamic, Not Static," Achieve states:

> The knowledge and skills required for postsecondary success will continue to evolve as the global economy changes, technology advances and new societal

challenges and opportunities emerge. . . . Standards help translate our under-standing of those evolving requirements into the curriculum and so must be updated periodically.

States therefore must establish regular schedules for reviewing and updating their standards. . . .

States do not revise their standards at the same time and so can—and should—learn from those who precede them. The result will be not only an evo-lution of standards in individual states, but also a common core of college- and career-ready standards among the states.[31]

In noting that states do not revise standards at the same time, Achieve is showing that it is right on the CCSS precipice—not quite there, but ex-tremely close. Again, the CCSS MOU would attempt to incorporate this standards-revision "flexibility" by including language that betrays just the opposite: top-down "permitted" revisions on a schedule to be deter-mined by CCSS owners, the National Governors Association (NGA) and Council of Chief State School Officers (CCSSO).

The 2008 Achieve report includes language that has become euphe-mistic for everything the CCSS wants to appear to be without offering supporting evidence. For example, the Achieve report includes the phrase "college and career ready." CCSS proponents parrot this phrase ad nause-am in order to fix the idea in the minds of the American public that CCSS can guarantee these outcomes as indisputable truth. Notice also that the "demand for college and careers" is actually an expression for postsec-ondary education and (especially) the business world. In this regard, it is important to keep in mind that Achieve is comprised of governors and business CEOs—not university presidents. Thus, the "demands" regard-ing "college and career" arguably belong to business CEOs and politi-cians (i.e., governors).

Now, a word about Achieve's statement about the "critical mass" of states arriving at a "common core of standards." Achieve does not com-ment regarding how many states it takes to form a "critical mass." Two? Three? Four? Achieve had already had a challenging and only modestly successful battle in trying to prod 50 states to "voluntarily" institute its ADP standards and align those standards with assessments.

Notice also that the Achieve sales pitch for CCSS reads as if CCSS has already been developed. The "critical mass" has already "arrived at a common core of standards." However, this Achieve report was written in 2008—2 years before writing on the CCSS was finished.

More than likely, a few governors, state superintendents, and busi-ness leaders hatched the *idea* of CCSS and were using this report to first float the idea in order to begin to shape the thinking of state leadership in general. Indeed, there was a November 2007 CCSSO meeting in which the idea of states' producing "voluntary" national standards before the federal government forced the states to do so [32] and ADP was indirectly represented.[33] (More on this "idea hatching" issue in Chapter 6 on the organization Student Achievement Partners.) And let us not forget Gerstner's forceful 1995 message regarding the need for national standards "now." However, in 2008, Achieve was not promoting "common" standards and assessments with Gerstner force. On the contrary, 2008 Achieve was gingerly promoting the "common standards" idea. The formalized CCSS commitment—signing on the dotted line, literally—would come in 2009. But for then, in 2008, a key was to sell the concept of "common." Details were to come soon—including how to fund an unprecedented effort at converting American education to sameness in two core subjects.

Continuing with Achieve's "common core" sales pitch: It is important to steer opinion away from federally instituted national standards. To this end, Achieve attempts to reassure states that they are really still in control. Sure, Achieve wants states to relinquish control and go with the "common core" standards crowd, but to say so directly is to forfeit the potential sale:

> Each state is responsible for setting their own academic standards, *consistent with their constitutional responsibilities. Federal efforts to influence—let alone direct or determine—state standards have met with stiff and effective political resistance.* This report demonstrates that state education policymakers—focusing on their own goals, working with their own constituents and on their own timetables— will put in place rigorous, competitive standards that prepare all students for college and careers.[34] [Emphasis added]

Come now. If the standards are to be "common," in reality, much of this "your own state standards" will have to go. Groupthink, not individuality, will be center stage. Continuing:

> Voluntary, state led alignment efforts that have resulted in a common core should not be confused with calls for the federal government to set national standards. *The common core discussed in this report came about organically, through action by individual states, working in their states to identify what their high school graduates need to know. The common core reflects the reality of the world*—that there is fundamental knowledge in English and mathematics that all graduates must know to

succeed and that is not bound by state lines—*but the common core also respects the traditional role of state decision making in education.*[35] [Emphasis added]

Achieve declares that CCSS "reflects the reality of the world." Forget all that "state autonomy" talk—sameness is the name of the game. Since variety is not necessary, autonomy is not, either.

CCSS is the hub of reform. Achieve must sell the "common" idea so that test-driven reforms are anchored:

> With the necessary and intentional leadership from states, there is every reason to think that a common core of college- and career-ready expectations can—and should—be reflected in virtually every state. Getting standards right is not just an academic exercise. Rigorous state standards anchored in real world demands can and should drive the rest of the states' education reform agenda—including graduation requirements, assessments, accountability and data systems. Only then can the gap between students being proficient and being truly prepared be closed.[36]

CCSS was never meant to stand alone. It was meant to unite the test-driven reform package. In the above excerpt from the 2008 report entitled *Out of Many, One*, Achieve makes this "common standards as the center of a test-driven-reform package" idea undeniably clear.

With the 2008 *Out of Many, One* report, Achieve placed the nation on the edge of CCSS—a single set of K–12 standards. In some respects, the content of the report belies the expectation that "common" would not result in the rigid CCSS that would require a Memorandum of Understanding. However, in many more respects, Achieve's vision for "standards unity" across the United States is unmistakable.

By 2007, NCLB was declared a failure. In 2008, Achieve publicized its "common standards" plan. This is no coincidence. With test score–centered NCLB, state autonomy over standards and assessments was a proven flop. The key was to convince governors and state education superintendents to "voluntarily" relinquish individual state education functioning in the name of "necessary and intentional state leadership," and a seed for this had already been planted in the 2007 CCSSO annual meeting. Achieve knew it could not publicly demand the relinquishing of state rights over education; however, it offered the carefully balanced report that only needed the slightest nudge to fully morph into CCSS.

CHAPTER 4

Playing in the Achieve Sandbox
Education Trust and Fordham Institute

In 2001, Achieve launched the American Diploma Project (ADP) (precursor to the Common Core State Standards [CCSS]) with the assistance of three other nonprofit organizations: the National Alliance of Business (NAB), the Education Trust, and the Thomas B. Fordham Foundation/Institute.[1] One year later, in 2002, NAB folded,[2] so that left the Education Trust and Fordham Foundation/Institute as Achieve's two primary buddies in promoting the idea of a K–12 "common core of standards" that "a critical mass" of states just happened to decide was necessary in order to "drive the rest of states' education agenda" in "closing" the "achievement gap."[3]

But what are this "Education Trust" and this "Fordham Institute," you ask?

The goal of this chapter is to answer that question and more, for both Education Trust and Fordham Institute are providing a public face to the CCSS push.

KATI HAYCOCK AND HER EDUCATION TRUST

Pinning down the exact year that the Education Trust was created has proved difficult. It could be that Education Trust was formed "in 1990 by the American Association for Higher Education (AAHE)," according to both *Education Week*[4] and the Jesuit Catholic university Canisius.[5] However, the U.S. Department of Education lists Education Trust's founding year as 1992,[6] and the National Assessment Governing Board says it was founded in 1996.[7]

According to Education Trust president Kati Haycock's biography on the George Mason University (GMU) website, Haycock founded the Education Trust in 1992 as a unit within AAHE, consistent with her professional history in "closing the achievement gap":

In 1973, Kati Haycock was asked by the President of the University of California to ensure, pursuant with recent legislation, that undergraduate enrollment in the University of California ("UC") system reflected the state population as a whole. Haycock became the first director of student affirmative action for the UC system. She decided to return to school to pursue her Master's in Education, and soon after her graduation founded and served as President of The Achievement Council, an independent statewide organization *focused on closing the achievement gap* in California's low-performing, predominantly minority schools. In 1989, she became the Executive Vice-President of the Children's Defense Fund in Washington D.C., the nation's largest child advocacy organization. Haycock's achievements led her to establish the Education Trust in 1992, a unit within the American Association for Higher Education that helps schools launch reform efforts aimed at improving outcomes for minority and low-income students. Haycock is currently Director of the Education Trust, which has grown to become its own entity. Haycock serves as the principal spokesperson for the Education Trust. . . .[8] [Emphasis added]

What is clear is that in April 1997, the Education Trust was granted non-profit status.[9] This nonprofit status allows the Education Trust to collect a whole heap of cash from those whose wills are bent on implementing "reforms" of their pleasing, not the least of which is CCSS. (More to come in Chapter 9 on such "benevolent," democratic-process-overriding "philanthropy" that has been dumped into the Education Trust and other test-driven, reform-minded nonprofits' bank accounts.)

Haycock's bio as it is listed on the GMU website is the most comprehensive information publicly available on her professional experience, yet it mysteriously begins in 1973 with a request from a university president for her assistance with affirmative action admissions. No hint of what might lead a university president to solicit Haycock's leadership for affirmative action, including no specifics on Haycock's undergraduate degree and no mention of Haycock's having any classroom teaching experience.

Haycock guards the knowledge of her own education background. On June 5, 2014, I emailed Haycock with the following: "I am seeking specifics on college degrees earned by Kati Haycock—degree type, year of graduation, and field."

This information on a high-profile individual who purports to be an education expert should be readily available to the public.

Haycock briefly responded to ask why I wanted to know. I informed her about this book and my references to her involvements with No Child Left Behind (NCLB) and the American Diploma Project (ADP) and indicated that I had not been able to locate information on her degrees.

She responded that she holds a bachelor's in political science from the University of California at Santa Barbara and a master's in education policy from UC–Berkeley.

Haycock is not a teacher. She is, however, a highly influential individual who is promoting her vision of a test score–centered American classroom.

It's like writing cookbooks without ever having prepared a meal.

Back to Haycock's Ed Trust machine:

The purpose of the Education Trust, according to the Canisius website, is "to encourage colleges and universities to support K–12 reform efforts."[10] Such a statement complements the Education Trust's mission, as noted on its website:

> The Education Trust promotes high academic achievement for all students at all levels—pre-kindergarten through college. Our goal is to close the gaps in opportunity and achievement that consign far too many young people—especially those from low-income families or who are black, Latino, or American Indian—to lives on the margins of the American mainstream.[11]

Efforts to assist society's disenfranchised should happen. However, the corporate reform push of narrowly defining "high academic achievement" as improved standardized test scores is problematic. Focus on test scores does not help empower the powerless. Instead, it promotes a competition among schools to secure students who are easier to educate—and those students tend not to be the ones requiring additional assistance to "close" a test score–measured "gap." Haycock fails to realize as much in her 2013 argument cautioning approval of NCLB waivers before the Senate Health, Education, Labor, and Pensions Committee.[12] In that testimony, Haycock approved of NCLB for its requirement that schools be "held accountable" to report test score results on "groups of children who lagged behind."[13] She applauded the idea of schools "teach[ing] *all* their students to the same state standards"[14] without regard to the pressure this would put not only on schools and teachers, but also on subpopulations of students who entered the NCLB "competition" at a disadvantage.

Of course states were going to seek "waivers" from such pressures—pressures that Haycock has never known firsthand. Like most corporate reformers, Kati Haycock is no classroom teacher and certainly no classroom teacher facing the test score–producing pressures of NCLB.

Haycock's perspective on what best produces school "reform" betrays a pervasive ignorance of those pushing so-called education reform from a perch external to the American schoolhouse.

In a 2011 *Phi Delta Kappan* interview, Haycock discusses her view of fast change, an idea that has become a hallmark of corporate, "top-down" reform:

> Experience has convinced me that change will occur faster if it's driven from the top, from college or high school. When colleges demand, high schools change; when high schools demand, elementary and middle schools change.[15]

Keep in mind that in its 2008 *Out of Many, One* report, Haycock's Education Trust (and Achieve, and Fordham Foundation/Institute) tried to convince states that CCSS "emerged" from the states—that it was not "top-down."

So, the idea behind CCSS, and the idea behind the failed NCLB, was to "demand change" from the "top," which in the case of NCLB, was the federal government. However, "demanding change" implies that those demanding have the ability to leverage serious consequences if the mandated change does not occur. In the case of NCLB, schools that did not meet their "adequate yearly progress" (AYP) goals[16] could lose funding or even be taken over for "restructuring"—a euphemism for firing faculty and administration. And what was the measure of desired change? Two-dimensional, standardized test scores. According to the U.S. Department of Education (USDOE) in 2002, "A State's definition of AYP is based primarily on the State's academic assessments."[17]

As was the case with NCLB, states buying into CCSS would need to be convinced by those promoting it (including USDOE) to participate in the "demanded" change. For NCLB, federal money was the lure. The same would be true for CCSS, with U.S. Secretary of Education Arne Duncan's 2009 announcement of an education competition in which states could vie for millions in American Recovery and Reinvestment Act (ARRA) funding, with commitment to CCSS being a virtual prerequisite for federal dollars.[18] Haycock is not only for federal involvement; she is for federal *law* demanding and restricting state autonomy in educational matters. According to Haycock, federal law is necessary to force states to "move policy" in a way that "benefits" low-income and minority students:

> *Federal law is essentially a shortcut to changing practice.* It's not a perfect shortcut. You certainly can't neglect what's going on at the state and local level, and we have to invest more in helping professionals improve. *But federal policy is the most powerful single lever that we have.* . . .
>
> If you asked me which level—federal, state, or local—is most likely to be

concerned with low-income and minority students and most likely to move education policy in a way that will benefit them, it's the federal level. . . .

Does that mean that I'm confident that the federal government will always
play a positive role? No. *But I have more confidence that the federal government will
remain focused on producing more equitable outcomes for poor and minority kids than
I do that the 50 states or the 15,000 local school districts will.*[19] [Emphasis added]

Again, the incredible flaw in Haycock's position is the federal narrowing of achievement to equal high scores on high-stakes tests. However,
federal law overturning the "separate but equal" inequity and requiring
integration of schools had a major *positive* impact. Indeed, this was an area
where federal enforcement was needed to address injustice and produce
change. In contrast, requiring student learning to be equated with a narrow, annual standardized test score is not. One of the well-publicized in-
sistences on the CCSS website is that CCSS is "not a curriculum."[20] One
could certainly debate that point (and I do so in Chapter 11 of my book
A Chronicle of Echoes).[21] Nevertheless, the tight connection between standards and curriculum is indisputable. Notice how Haycock talks about
her perspective that "standards-based reform" entails "assisting" teachers
with curriculum, well, because they just need "our" (top-down?) help
figuring out how to translate standards into practice:

I certainly have changed my mind around issues of curriculum. In the very early
days of standards-based reform, we thought it was enough for states to make the
goal clear and that teachers should be free to figure out how to teach to it. I think
I was dimly aware that most teachers probably couldn't do that very well, but
I got swept up in the thinking that, with enough support, teachers could bring
their practice into line with standards. It would take some time, but it wouldn't
take forever.

It's the countless conversations I've had with teachers themselves that have
convinced me that, especially for low-income kids, educators want and need far
more guidance, support, lessons, units, assignments for teachers. We shouldn't
be leaving things like the orderly development of vocabulary and background
knowledge to individual teachers to figure out. Even if they're really good, they
can miss something that's hugely important. . . . [22]

Haycock keeps referring to some "we" who is apparently not the classroom teacher.

Does Haycock believe that those outside of the classroom are better
equipped to determine curriculum than those inside? Such thinking promotes the idea that a fear of high-stakes (punitive) outcomes can make

the most seasoned teachers doubt themselves and lean on those "top-downers" with zero classroom experience for direction.

In the end, all the talk about the freedom to choose curriculum really is no freedom at all. If the standards are rigid and fixed and the high-stakes assessments are tied to the rigid, fixed standards, then for those controlling and promoting the rigid, fixed standards and associated assessments to also "help" with curriculum decisions should be no surprise—and that was part of the plan, even in 2008, as noted in this press release by the National Governors Association:

> Content standards specify the knowledge and skills that students need at each grade level. These standards must be supported by an aligned and clearly articulated system of curriculum, assessments, teacher preparation and professional development, textbook selection and appropriate supports for students.[23]

In 2008, the plan for CCSS included aligning the entire top-down "reform" process: standards, curriculum, and assessments (and professional development, and data collection). No sense in Haycock's getting swept up in believing that teachers should be expected to exercise professional judgment over their teaching by being expected to know how to select curricular materials.

The problem for teachers lay in having standardized tests as the high-stakes outcome. Being expected to teach to the test is inevitable in situations in which standardized tests are the end-all, be-all. Teachers do not want to be declared failures. They do not want their students to be declared failures. They do not want their schools to be underfunded, or placed on probation, or "restructured." When trapped in a twisted, test-driven "reform" situation, teachers will try to make it work—even if it means relying upon "professional assistance" from the very ones who imposed the test-driven reforms.

Like Patty Hearst with her kidnappers, many teachers will see their standardized-assessment-forcing destructors as necessary friends. And Haycock has positioned herself to be one of those top-down, test-driven, necessary people—all in the name of being an advocate for disadvantaged students.

She's been doing so since 1973, when a California university president sought her assistance for their affirmative action program. No one impugns Haycock's caring for children of color. What is problematic is the wrong-headed insistence that these children will be helped by a complex bureaucracy of policies, practices, curriculum, materials, and tests forced on schools in punitive, high-stakes fashion.

As for top-down involvement from the federal government in state education affairs, Haycock is in favor. Now, that 2008 *Out of Many, One* report on the American Diploma Project—a report involving the work of Haycock's Education Trust—certainly does not state an overt desire for federal involvement in common standards development; to do so would have killed the CCSS prod of governors' "discovering" common standards. (Recall President Clinton's hint to avoid mentioning federal involvement in reforms, that such a mention would "kill" the reforms.)[24] However, in 2012 reflections on the perceived problems of NCLB implementation, one-time Education Trust research and policy director Kevin Carey (with Ed Trust from November 2002 to August 2005),[25] observes that the NCLB "high water mark" of federal government control over state education was not enough to ensure airtight state compliance:

> When we dug into the details of NCLB implementation, there were already troubling signs. *While the law marked a high water mark of federal control over K–12 education*, it was still, relatively speaking, not far from the ocean floor. NCLB gave states vast discretion to set standards, choose tests, and decide what test scores would yield a passing grade. The technicalities of the law's accountability regime created openings for ruthlessly inventive state bureaucrats to excuse their low-performing schools from scrutiny and sanction. Teachers unions that had been excluded from the negotiating table began waging an increasingly public fight against the law. States-rights Republicans did the same.[26] [Emphasis added]

One can take two notable points from Carey's summation of the NCLB creation and enforcement processes: First, the implication of Carey's belief that even the "high water mark" of federal control was not enough for NCLB feeds the idea that the federal government must assume a stronger role in future standards and assessment reform efforts. Second, even if they are not at the center of the development process, teachers' unions must somehow be pacified regarding their role at "the negotiating table."

In its position of planting and fostering the 2008 common standards idea leading to CCSS, the Education Trust, along with CCSS-promoting partners Achieve and Fordham Foundation/Institute, appears to have learned lessons from NCLB's failure, lessons that have translated into action for CCSS. The federal government would be involved by dangling ARRA money in front of states in order to entice involvement in CCSS,[27] and pre-CCSS state agreement[28] would be tied to governor and state superintendent signatures on a detailed CCSS "Memorandum of Understanding" (MOU). Furthermore, the CCSS MOU would not only outline the "state-led" standards creation process; it would also specifically identify teachers' unions as contributors (albeit on the fringes) of the CCSS development process.[29] (More to come on the details of the CCSS MOU in Chapter 5.)

Since its earning nonprofit status in 1997, Haycock's Education Trust has been busy in its attempts to advance the spectrum of test-based reform associated with CCSS, including CCSS-linked assessments and data collection. According to IRS Form 990, the Education Trust is the controlling entity for three other nonprofits: the U.S. Education Delivery Institute,[30] Edinnovations,[31] and the Data Quality Campaign.[32]

According to its 2013 tax form (filed in March 2014), Edinnovations is a shell organization that has no money but does have three "directors" working 20 hours each per week on who knows what.[33] The U.S. Education Delivery Institute is functional; it includes the following mission on its 2011 tax form:

> The US Education Delivery Institute (EDI) is an innovative non-profit organiza-
> tion that focuses on implementing large-scale system change in public education.
> Our mission is to partner with K–12 and higher education systems with ambi-
> tious reform agendas and invest in their leaders' capacity to deliver results.[34]

Notice how official the name "U.S. Education Delivery Institute" sounds—like the name of a government agency. However, the U.S. Education Delivery Institute's mission statement conveys the organization's intent to "invest" in what it determines to be "ambitious reform agendas" that "deliver results."

One guess as to what "delivering results" could possibly mean.

Certainly CCSS, associated curriculum, professional development, assessments, and data collection qualify as "large-scale system change." And the Education Trust, via its U.S. Education Delivery Institute, is up for the top-down challenge.

The third Ed Trust–controlled nonprofit, the Data Quality Campaign (DQC), is its most active. Created in 2005 by former National Governors Association "policy monitor" Aimee Guidera,[35] DQC is described as follows:

> The Data Quality Campaign (DQC) is a national, collaborative effort to en-
> courage and support state policymakers to improve the availability and use of
> high-quality education data to improve student achievement. The campaign will
> provide tools and resources that will help states implement and use longitudinal
> data systems, while providing a national forum for reducing duplication of effort
> and promoting greater coordination and consensus among the organizations fo-
> cused on improving data quality, access and use.[36]

DQC "encourages and supports states" in data collection. DQC is a data collection hub, and Haycock's Ed Trust is the parent organization of DQC. Haycock is also a member of the DQC board of directors.[37]

DQC offers what it considers the "Ten Essential Elements" of "state-level" data collection.[38] I will highlight a few such elements here as I examined them in a November 2013 post on my blog.[39]

The first on the list is a "unique student identifier," or a means of identifying students by number "to get a complete picture [of student educational progress] as students move through their education careers."

The disclosure of this unique identifier appears to be the one issue that parents and students 18 or older can still opt out of as per U.S. Secretary of Education Arne Duncan's 2012 modified Family Educational Rights and Privacy Act (FERPA).[40] That is, states can still collect data on these students and link the data to this unique identifier. However, the identifier can be "kept secret from those accessing data at parental request." Yet how many parents know about this or have ever been directly informed?

Make no mistake: The identifier does not go away. It is still there whether parents want it to be or not.

The second "essential element" is the need to collect demographic data on students. Though it offers free lunch and special education status as examples (information that would be a violation of privacy for teachers to disclose but would be open to agencies and hackers), DQC does not close the door on exactly how much demographic data could be collected.

The fifth "essential element" introduces teachers into the mix, the goal being to connect specific teachers to students. DQC declares this is necessary in order to assess the effectiveness of teacher training programs. Given what I know about the privatizing push to annihilate traditional public education, I can readily see such data being used to punish teachers. DQC insists that data will not be used "to blame and shame."[41] On the contrary. DQC endorses the Teacher-Student Data Link Project (TSDL), "a cross-state, collaborative effort focused on developing a common, best practice definition of 'Teacher of Record' and business processes for collecting and validating linked teacher and student data."[42] Common sense would dictate that if it takes over $3 million[43] to establish a clear connection between student and teacher, then basing teacher and school and state "performance" on student test scores is too risky a venture for achieving so-called "accountability."

In the eighth "essential element," DQC argues that collecting student dropout and graduation data "provides the clearest picture of whether students graduate, drop out, or move." However, as noted previously, there are any number of ways to define "graduate" and, by extension, "dropout." Indeed, the lack of any consistent definition of "graduate" or "dropout" allows for constant manipulation of graduation and dropout data. Is a "graduate" one who completes high school in 4 years? Five years? Via GED? Via night classes? What if a student leaves high school without a diploma and decides to return the following year? Is this student a "drop-in"?

Shifting definitions of "graduate" and "dropout" make this eighth "essential element" a potential field day for pro-market reformers to declare victory or judgment according to whichever suits their purposes at a given moment.

The ninth "essential element" is also a corporate reformer field day: "Rigorous exams like ACT, SAT, AP, and IB." Here we go again with the standardized testing emphasis. There is no mention of the potential use of student test scores to fire teachers and close schools—as has already been done under NCLB. The DQC explanation is benign—the use of test scores simply to inform.

Don't you believe it.

The tenth "essential element" notes the need for "a robust data audit system." Here's a question: To whom will this audit system be accountable? Therein lies a primary problem with test-driven reform: The consequences are high for those being "held accountable," but in the top-down world of corporate-modeled education reform, those at the top—like Haycock, her Ed Trust, and her associated nonprofit DQC—are accountable to no one, unless it is to corporate, government, and association funders.

And yet, running a nonprofit associated with supposedly reforming American public education proves quite profitable for those not held accountable themselves. Even though I will postpone any major discussion of CCSS funding for subsequent chapters, allow me to note that on its 2012 tax form, the Education Trust reported $9.7 million in contributions and grants as part of its total revenue of $11 million. Total assets amounted to $15 million. Haycock reported working 38 hours per week for just over $300,000 (compensation from Ed Trust plus estimated "other" compensation).[44] On its 2012 tax form, U.S. EDI reported $3.8 million in expenses—all payable to the Education Trust.[45] Haycock sits on the U.S. EDI board (unsalaried) and contributes a reported 1 hour per week. It's a similar story for DQC: On its 2012 tax form, DQC reported $2.8 million in expenses—again, all payable to the Education Trust.

Haycock sits on the DQC board (unsalaried) and contributes a reported 2 hours per week. All three of these interconnected organizations—Ed Trust, U.S. EDI, and DQC—benefit from the test-driven spectrum of reforms centered around CCSS.

FORDHAM FOUNDATION/INSTITUTE

In promoting "common standards," Achieve relied upon the Fordham Foundation/Institute. The prominent "faces" of the Fordham Foundation/Institute are its president, Chester Finn, and its executive vice president, Michael Petrilli (who has since become president upon Finn's retirement).

Finn has been in the classroom—for a single year, as part of an internship for his master's program at Harvard. As Finn notes in his book *Troublemaker*:

> The summer I graduated from college (1965) [Harvard University, with a bachelor's degree in U.S. history], I began the Master of Arts in Teaching program at the Harvard Ed School, specializing in social studies, in which field Massachusetts certified me as a secondary teacher. After a hasty summer of practice teaching, I was placed at Newton High School as a full-time intern teacher for the 1965–6 school year. Despite my previous tutoring, camp counseling, and summer classroom gigs, this was my first big solo teaching job. And I wasn't much good at it.[46]

There you have it: the extent of Fordham Institute president Chester Finn's classroom teaching career. By 1968, Finn followed former Harvard professor Daniel Patrick Moynihan to the White House to assist re-elected president Richard Nixon "with urban affairs."[47] Finn's very brief teaching intern year is absent from his contemporary biographical information, including his bio for the Fordham Institute,[48] the U.S. Department of State,[49] and the Hoover Institution.[50] It seems that the only biographical sketch that mentions Finn as a "high school teacher" is the sketch promoting *Troublemaker*.[51]

Below is a sampling of what Finn chooses to highlight about his career (taken from his Fordham Institute bio):

> Chester E. Finn, Jr., scholar, educator and public servant, has devoted his career to improving education in the United States. As Senior Fellow at Stanford's Hoover Institution, chairman of Hoover's Koret Task Force on K–12 Education,

and President of the Thomas B. Fordham Institute, his primary focus is the reform of primary and secondary schooling.

Finn has led Fordham since 1997, after many earlier roles in education, academe and government. From 1999 until 2002, he was John M. Olin Fellow at the Manhattan Institute. In 1992–1994, he served as founding partner and senior scholar with the Edison Project. He was Professor of Education and Public Policy at Vanderbilt University from 1981 until 2002. From 1985 to 1988, he served as Assistant Secretary for Research and Improvement & Counselor to the Secretary at the U.S. Department of Education. Earlier positions include Staff Assistant to the President of the United States; Special Assistant to the Governor of Massachusetts; Counsel to the U.S. Ambassador to India; Research Associate at the Brookings Institution; and Legislative Director for Senator Daniel Patrick Moynihan.[52]

For some reason, Finn believes himself qualified to lead the charge in evaluating and grading state education standards. Though his bio appears impressive, it is "top-heavy": Like Haycock, Finn was quickly launched into the world of influencing education policy without any substantive practical experience to warrant such a prerogative. Lofty titles and positions aside, neither is qualified to spearhead a national standards effort.

I wrote about the Fordham Foundation/Institute under the direction of Finn in my book *A Chronicle of Echoes.* Here is an excerpt on the Fordham Foundation/Institute's history:

> The Thomas B. Fordham Institute was created in 1959 in Finn's childhood hometown of Dayton, Ohio. Thelma Fordham Pruett, Fordham's widow, funded the Institute, which was not education-specific until Mrs. Pruett's death in 1997. In 2007, the Institute was combined with the Fordham Foundation. The Fordham Institute website describes the Institute as the "public face of nearly all that Fordham does." . . .
>
> Fordham is a "think tank" that promotes a corporate reform agenda in education. It operates via donations from some highly influential funders who endorse (and often, actively promote) the same push for privatization as does the Finn-directed Fordham. Finn and others promote their views via publications and endorsements. Fordham also presents awards in recognition of individuals it believes best exemplify the privatization agenda. . . .
>
> Under the direction of Chester Finn, the Fordham Institute is a well-financed privatization force. On its website, Fordham lists as its "policy priorities" three issues: "standards-based reforms," "quality choices," and a "reform-based system." First, concerning Fordham Institute's (and Finn's) priority of standards-based reforms:[53]

"... We press for the full suite of standards-based reforms ... including (but not limited to) careful implementation of the Common Core standards (CCSS) for English language arts (ELA) and mathematics ... rigorous, aligned state assessments *and* forceful accountability mechanisms. ..."[54]

The Fordham Foundation/Institute's intention to promote CCSS is certain. And despite Achieve's declaration that its benchmarking "was not designed to grade or rank states" (see Chapter 2), Achieve chose to involve Chester Finn and the Fordham Institute—known for grading standards since 1997[55]—the same year that Chester Finn became Fordham Foundation president.[56]

Finn is not alone in his self-appointed state standards evaluation and grading. At the helm with him is Michael Petrilli, who is now president. Petrilli holds a bachelor's degree in political science from the University of Michigan (1995).[57] On that slim foundation, he has inflated his importance and built a major career in educational policy, as noted on his Fordham Foundation bio:

> Mike Petrilli is an award-winning writer and one of the nation's most trusted education analysts. As executive vice president of the Thomas B. Fordham Institute, Petrilli helps to lead the country's most influential education-policy think tank and contributes to its Flypaper blog and weekly Education Gadfly newsletter. He is the author of *The Diverse Schools Dilemma: A Parent's Guide to Socioeconomically Mixed Public Schools*, published in 2012. Petrilli is also a research fellow at Stanford University's Hoover Institution and executive editor of Education Next. Petrilli has published opinion pieces in the *New York Times, Washington Post, Bloomberg View*, and *Wall Street Journal* and has been a guest on NBC Nightly News, ABC World News Tonight, CNN, and Fox, as well as several National Public Radio programs, including All Things Considered, On Point, and the Diane Rehm Show. He is author, with Frederick M. Hess, of *No Child Left Behind: A Primer*. Petrilli helped to create the U.S. Department of Education's Office of Innovation and Improvement, the Policy Innovators in Education Network, and Young Education Professionals. He holds an honors-level bachelor's degree in political science from the University of Michigan.[58]

Petrilli joined the Fordham Foundation/Institute as program director and chief of staff in 1997, the year that Finn became Fordham's president. Petrilli served in the capacity of chief of staff until 2000, at which time he left in order to become "vice president of community partnerships" for the virtual charter school company K12. That lasted only 1 year, at which time Petrilli began working for the U.S. Department of Education in the newly created Office of Innovation and Improvement.[59]

What credentials do the members of Fordham Foundation/Institute's leadership have that qualify them to evaluate and grade state standards? Only the desire to do so—and the glory that comes from media recognition. As former Fordham Foundation/Institute board member Diane Ravitch notes:

> Back in the 1990s, when I was on the board of the Thomas B. Fordham Foundation (now the Thomas B. Fordham Institute), we began rating state standards and assigning letter grades to the states. Much to our surprise and delight, the media ate up the ratings. Whenever we released our grades for the states, there would be big stories in the newspapers in almost every state, and it helped to put TBF (Thomas B. Fordham) on the map.
>
> Now, TBF—a conservative advocacy group for accountability, high-stakes testing, and choice—has become a major promoter of the Common Core.[60]

In an attempt to clarify Fordham Foundation/Institute leaders' view of their qualifications for leading a state-standards-grading effort, I emailed Ravitch the following question on June 6, 2014:

> Diane, would you mind giving me a statement about how it was that Fordham Institute believed itself qualified to grade state standards in the first place?
>
> I'd like to include it in my book.

She thought it was a good question. Here is her response, dated June 7, 2014:

> Fordham has no particular expertise.
>
> The decision to grade state standards was motivated by the belief that it would encourage states to make their standards more rigorous if TBF developed criteria for comparison, engaged experts in the field to read and compare the standards, then released a report card to the media. *This process had the auxiliary but real benefit of making TBF the arbiter of state standards. . . .*
>
> *No one questioned whether there was a connection between standards and achievement. No one questioned the grading.* [Emphasis added; ellipsis as per Ravitch's request]

Assigning grades to state standards put pressure on states to consider the image that the Fordham Foundation/Institute would promote of the states before the public; it put the Fordham Foundation/Institute in the news, and it afforded Fordham clout before the media and in the public eye.

Being regarded as nonprofit, self-styled expert standards-grading arbiters has paid off nicely. On its 2012 tax form, the Fordham Foundation reported total assets exceeding $48 million.[61] The foundation's related organization, the Fordham Institute, reported $9 million in total assets,[62] with $1.3 million of that amount coming from the foundation.[63] (Recall that as of 2007, the Fordham Foundation supports the operational arm, the Fordham Institute.)

Since grading state standards put the Fordham Foundation/Institute "on the map," so to speak, it should come as no surprise that in July 2010—only one month following the official completion of CCSS [64]—Fordham Institute released a report of its (1) grading of the standards of all 50 states and the District of Columbia; (2) grading of CCSS; and (3) comparing state standards to CCSS. The report was entitled *The State of State Standards—and the Common Core—in 2010.*[65]

CCSS did not outshine all state-level ELA and math standards even by the Fordham Institute's own admission. California, Indiana, and the District of Columbia earned equal or superior grades from Fordham for both ELA and math; 11 additional states were declared "too close to call" compared to CCSS in ELA; and nine states were "too close to call" in math. Still, the language of the Fordham Institute report clearly declares CCSS "the winner." In December 2013, I examined the Fordham Institute *State of State Standards* report in a post I entitled "The Fordham Strong Arm of Letter Grades for State Standards"[66] and found it a slanted effort to promote CCSS. Below is an abbreviated version of my post, including Fordham Institute's standards-grading criteria and letter-grade descriptors, and inconsistencies between Fordham's state standards grades and state NAEP scores—the ultimate measure in American education success for decades by would-be reformers.

Fordham Institute's grading of state standards is a remarkably biased effort to sell the public a new product named CCSS.

Read on:

The 2010 Fordham Institute Letter Grades

In 2010, in an effort to promote the CCSS as "clearly superior to standards in most states," Fordham assigned letter grades to CCSS and to all state standards.

They gave CCSS an A-minus in math and a B-plus in English Language Arts (ELA). Fordham notes, "Neither is perfect. Both are very, very strong." Who, exactly, decided that CCSS should have an A-minus in math and a B-plus in ELA?

Well, 10 names are listed as associated with the 2010 Fordham report: four authors (Sheila Byrd Carmichael, Gabrielle Martino, Kathleen Porter-Magee, and W. Stephen Wilson); four additional contributors (Daniela Fairchild, Elizabeth Haydel, Diana Senechal, and Amber M. Winkler), and two (Finn and Petrilli) offering the foreword.

Thus, 10 individuals either used or otherwise promoted a highly subjective rubric reproduced in Appendix A of the report to arrive at their overly influential judgments.

Here are some examples from the rubric:

Seven points: Standards meet all of the following criteria: Standards are top-notch in terms of the content chosen. The coverage of the subject is suitable, good decisions have been made about what topics to include, and nothing of importance has been overlooked. . . .

Four points: Standards fall short in one or more of the following ways: At least 35 and up to 50 percent of crucial content is missing.

Three points: Standards fall short in one or more of the following ways: There are serious problems, shortcomings, or errors in the standards, although the standards have some redeeming qualities and there is some evidence of rigor.

Then, there's the ELA and math-specific criteria, which still are amazingly broad. For example, in high school (grades 9–12), one must judge that standards include "grade-appropriate works of outstanding American literature and that writing" reflects the defining characteristics of various grade-appropriate writing genres.

And in math, Fordham's "content-specific criteria" include no grade-level designations—and also no mention of calculus.

Fordham is able to fit all of the criteria used to brand a state's entire set of K–12 ELA and math standards on nine pages.

These are not objective criteria. These are broad, loosely defined criteria. In fact, it ought to embarrass Finn and Petrilli to have their names attached to this fog. However, these "criteria" do allow for the speedy branding of most states as deficient when compared to CCSS. . . .

In fact, Fordham's own review notes that in its opinion, CCSS was not superior in both math and ELA in all states (and DC) that adopted CCSS:

Based on our observations, the Common Core standards are clearly superior to those currently in use in thirty-nine states in math and thirty-seven states in English. For thirty-three states, the Common Core is superior in both math and reading.

However [according to Fordham Institute's own report], three jurisdictions boast ELA standards that are clearly superior to the Common Core: California, the District of Columbia, and Indiana. Another 11 states have ELA standards that are in the same league as the Common Core (or "too close to call").

Eleven states plus the District of Columbia have math standards in the "too close to call" category, meaning that, overall, they are at least as clear and rigorous as the Common Core standards [according to Fordham Institute's own report].

Nowhere does one read about Finn and Petrilli cautioning states that are either "too close to call" or superior to CCSS to think carefully about scrapping their state standards and embarking upon unnecessary disruption of their educational systems for no gain by adopting CCSS. . . .

Why say nothing? . . . Because the goal of CCSS is not "excellence." It is standardization.

According to Fordham Institute, CCSS is the vehicle necessary for standardizing the entire American education experience.

In 2010, Finn clearly admits as much:

> For these standards to get traction in classrooms with kids and teachers, a whole bunch of other things need to happen. Curriculum needs to happen, textbooks need to be aligned with the curriculum, teacher preparation and professional development needs to be aligned, tests need to be aligned, the accountability system that is built on those tests needs to make sense and be workable—without all of those other things, and this is just skirting the surface—the standards are toothless tigers.[67]

Finn "wants to make good use of" 2010 through 2015 for the sake of standardizing American public education.

The "Bottom Line" and the 2009 NAEP

If one "tests" the Fordham state-standards-grading system by comparing it with 2009 national test results, the 2010 Fordham report (dare I write it?) earns an F.

For each of the states' "report cards" on its standards, Fordham Institute includes a brief ending statement it calls the "bottom line." Now, the entire 373-page Fordham report is readily available for the media to publish. However, the media are not likely to critically read Fordham Institute's report or have the expertise to critically appraise the subjectivity of the rubric used to grade the states. Finally, the media may overlook the fact that some states outscored CCSS in Fordham's own report. . . .

Consider the following "bottom line" info:

> With their grade of F, Wyoming's mathematics standards are among the worst in the country, while those developed by the Common Core State Standards Initiative earn an impressive A-minus.

Sure sounds like one might expect some really low national test scores out of Wyoming.

Not so.

In 2009,[68] the average National Assessment of Educational Progress (NAEP) math score for Wyoming eighth graders was 286. The national average was 282. The average NAEP math score for Wyoming 4th graders was 242. The national average was 239.

Yet Finn and Petrilli's Fordham has branded Wyoming as a failure in math. . . .

Let's consider Mississippi. Here's what Finn and Petrilli's Fordham has concluded as Mississippi's "bottom line":

> With their grade of C, Mississippi's mathematics standards are mediocre, while those developed by the Common Core State Standards Initiative earn an impressive A-minus.

According to Fordham, Mississippi's standards are better than Wyoming's. This does not play out in the 2009 NAEP scores; Mississippi math NAEP for 4th-graders was 227 (compared with the national average of 239). For 8th grade, Mississippi's math NAEP was 265 (versus the national average of 282).

Let's look at another—Minnesota:

> With their grade of B, Minnesota's mathematics standards are decent, while those developed by the Common Core State Standards Initiative earn an impressive A-minus.

On the 2009 NAEP, Minnesota was more than "decent" in math. Minnesota 8th-graders scored 294, second only to Massachusetts' 299 (national average is 282). Minnesota 4th-graders scored 249, again second only to Massachusetts' 252 (national average is 239).

Sure looks like there is a major disconnect between Fordham Institute's state standards evaluations and statewide student performance. It also sounds like Finn and Petrilli want to be certain that the press promotes CCSS at the expense of most states. Here is their conclusion:

> As should be clear by now, most state standards are woefully inadequate. . . .

I wonder how many journalists took the time to compare the 2010 Fordham Institute letter grades to the 2009 NAEP scores. I'm thinking none. . . . Here are some ELA comparisons:

> Kansas: Fordham Institute gave a "mediocre" C; 4th-grade 2009 ELA NAEP[69] was above average (224, compared with the national average of 220). For 8th grade, ELA NAEP was 267, above the national

average of 262. Nevertheless, Finn and Petrilli's Fordham is trying to sell CCSS, so they brand Kansas' standards as "mediocre."

Illinois: Fordham Institute branded Illinois with a D, "among the worst in the country"; however, Illinois' 4th-graders scored only one point below average (219, versus the national average of 220), and 8th-graders scored above average on the 2009 ELA NAEP (265, compared with the national average of 262).

In its "bottom line," Fordham Institute is careful not to assign a letter grade for states that equal or outrank their CCSS assessment of B-plus in ELA and A-minus in math.

Here's the "bottom line" for Louisiana's ELA, which Fordham graded as a B-plus:

Louisiana's standards treat both literary and nonliterary texts in more systematic detail than the Common Core, addressing specific genres, sub-genres, and characteristics of both type texts. Louisiana also more clearly prioritizes grade-appropriate genres in its writing standards and provides more detailed expectations for oral presentations.

On the other hand, Common Core includes samples of student writing to clarify grade- and genre-specific writing expectations. . . .

So, according to Fordham Institute's own assessment, Louisiana is "breaking even" by disrupting all of its ELA classrooms in order to move laterally to CCSS ELA.

Notice that Fordham never writes as much. . . .

Now here's the rub: Louisiana fared poorly on the 2009 ELA NAEP (4th grade: 207 versus national average 220; 8th grade: 253 versus national average 262).

The 2010 Fordham Institute ratings of standards are all over the map. Fordham Institute rates some standards as "worst in the country" or "mediocre," yet the previous year's NAEP results are high. It rates some standards as wonderful (no letter grades in the "bottom line," though—perhaps the press will not look elsewhere). Moreover, the 2009 NAEP results do not come close to matching some of Fordham Institute's glowing ratings. California and DC are stark examples: A ratings from Fordham Institute; obviously below-average 2009 NAEP scores in both ELA and math.

The Great Propaganda of the Fordham "Bottom Line"

The central element of the Fordham Institute "bottom line" is its biased judgment of what its letter grades mean. Traditionally, the A–F letter grades hold the following meanings:

A = excellent or outstanding
B = very good or above average
C = average or satisfactory
D = below average or needs improvement
F = failing or unsatisfactory

However, in Fordham Institute's "bottom line," traditional letter grade meaning is replaced with the following biased terminology (or is not discussed at all):

A = letter grade not included in "bottom line" (A-minus, B-plus, and sometimes B are also not included in "bottom line")
B = "decent"
C = "mediocre"
D = "among the worst in the country"
F = "among the worst in the country"

Fordham Institute's "bottom line" letter-grade setup allows for no state to outdo CCSS—not even California, Indiana, or DC—which Fordham gave A's in both ELA and math in the body of each state's report but did not dare list those two A's in the "bottom line" discussion. Instead, CCSS is compared to California, Indiana, and DC in a manner that makes CCSS appear comparable rather than inferior.

(Massachusetts' ELA standards are the exception: Fordham Institute includes no letter grade in its "bottom line" for Massachusetts and also does not state any "on the other hand" for Massachusetts' ELA. However, this is a safe bet because CCSS "outscores" Massachusetts' math standards.)

In other words, what California, Indiana, and DC need, according to Fordham's own assessment, is to go backwards and trade those two A's for Fordham's A-minus and B-plus, in order to take one for the pro-privatizing team and enable complete national standardization of American public education.

What I Learned from Reading True Crime

I enjoy reading true crime; it appeals to my analytical bent. Here is a lesson that I have learned from that interest: Sophisticated criminals manipulate their victims by utilizing a two-pronged strategy: Offer the victim an enticement to draw him toward a desired exploitation, but also introduce some element of fear in order to drive the victim away from some dreaded worst-case scenario (and again, toward the exploitation).

In offering billions to states willing to sign on for CCSS as part of the ultimately underfunded contest that is Race to the Top (RTTT)—even before the actual CCSS standards had been written, much less shared—President Obama and U.S. Secretary of Education Arne Duncan offer the enticement.

In grading the states' standards—and having the power to negatively publicize such results—Fordham provides the fear, combined with fear of giving up federal funds, from which governors and state superintendents have run—right into signing over their states (to CCSS) as part of RTTT....[70]

That the Fordham Institute is biased in favor of promoting CCSS is undeniable. One month following CCSS completion, in July 2010, the Fordham Institute produced the above-mentioned "analysis" of state standards and CCSS in order to reinforce the CCSS sale that Achieve has already noted happened in at least 46 states—before there was a *completed* CCSS—by way of state officials' signatures on the CCSS MOU in 2009.

Of course, Fordham had financial assistance in producing that 2010 state standards report—and it just happens to have come from the same major financial supporter who aided most of the CCSS push—billionaire Bill Gates. More on that to come.

On November 17, 2014, Fordham Institute issued a press release noting its plans to evaluate the CCSS-aligned tests (including those produced by both federally funded testing consortia—see Chapter 10) and publish the results in spring 2015. New Fordham Institute president Petrilli purports that the study—funded in part by major CCSS financial underwriter Gates (see Chapter 9)—will offer states "reliable information about the new tests."[71]

Once again, the Fordham Institute positions itself as *the* American public education arbiter.

To summarize the content of the previous two chapters: The CCSS idea was planted via the influence of three organizations—Achieve, Education Trust, and the Fordham Institute—as they began work on the American Diploma Project (ADP). In 2008, Achieve produced a review of ADP progress that just happened to be less of a report than a sales brochure for a "common core of standards" in ELA and math. That 2008 report placed American education on the brink of CCSS.

Achieve is controlled by two primary groups represented on its board of directors: state governors and business CEOs. So, one can rightly note that the National Governors Association (NGA) was "hidden" in the organization Achieve in promoting CCSS as a "stakeholder-originated" idea that came from the ADP. Likely, only a handful of individuals concocted the "common core" promotional that became the focus of

Achieve's 2008 *Out of Many, One* report. In promoting the CCSS concept, Achieve does not identify exactly who advanced the idea of a "common core of standards." However, it turns out that Achieve produced the report that would provide a template for the document that governors and state superintendents would sign tying their state education systems to an as-yet-uncreated CCSS.

That document—the CCSS MOU—is the focus of the next chapter.

CHAPTER 5

The "State-led" Lock-in

The Common Core Memorandum of Understanding

In July 2008, Achieve published its *Out of Many, One* report, which focused on a "common core of standards." Though the report was supposed to center on the progress of Achieve's (and the Education Trust and Fordham Foundation/Institute's) American Diploma Project (ADP), the report's purpose subtly shifted toward promoting K–12 "common" standards.

In its 2008 reporting, it seems that Achieve viewed the grade 9–12 standards devised for ADP as the given, high school component of the newly introduced idea, "state-led" "common core" (though few states had chosen to align with ADP in the first place):

> It is essential that states anchor standards in real world expectations. This led Achieve and the ADP states to focus initially on what students must know and be able to do when they complete high school. *States must now follow through and review and revise, as necessary, their K–8 standards* to create a focused, clear and rigorous set of grade-by-grade standards that provide a clear progression toward high school.[1] [Emphasis added]

Although Achieve was careful to note that this kind of "common" standards effort need not involve the federal government and could truly happen by being "state-led," the reality was that it would be quite a feat to get the governors of 50 states plus a number of U.S. territories not only to agree on what comprised a "common core of standards" but also to commit to the effort.

Plus, it would require *a lot* of money. Millions, at least. Perhaps billions.

Asking the federal government to foot the bill would be "common core" crib death.

So, how about asking the wealthiest man in the world to foot the bill?

During the same summer that Achieve published *Out of Many, One*, two individuals approached billionaire Bill Gates and his wife, Melinda, with the idea for a single set of K–12 "common standards." Those two individuals were then–Council of Chief State School Officers (CCSSO) President Gene Wilhoit[2] and national-standards-writing-company-turned-nonprofit Student Achievement Partners (SAP) founder and CEO David Coleman.[3, 4]

I discuss Gates's funding of CCSS and Coleman's involvement in subsequent chapters. However, for our current purpose, let us note a question that Gates asked of Wilhoit about the return on this democracy-purchasing Gates investment, a question regarding whether Wilhoit et al. could really pull off the likes of CCSS. Wilhoit said that there were no guarantees.[5]

Weeks later, Gates agreed to fund CCSS.

Funding for a major overhaul of American public education was initially tied to one man's wallet. However, as this chapter will reveal, the federal government would also become involved within a year.

Though Wilhoit told Gates that there were no guarantees, asking one man to invest millions in this "common core" idea arguably contributed to the need to secure a formal commitment from states regarding CCSS.

In December 2008, the National Governors Association (NGA), CCSSO, and Achieve produced a report that was clearly aimed at justifying a single set of K–12 standards for all U.S. states and territories: *Benchmarking for Success: Ensuring U.S. Students Receive a World-Class Education*.[6] Interestingly, both the Fordham Institute's Chester Finn and the Education Trust's Kati Haycock served on the report's "international benchmarking advisory group."

The *Benchmarking* report was the sales brochure for the Gates-invested CCSS. Indeed, Gates funded the report (as he had Achieve's July 2008 ADP report, but that was produced prior to the Wilhoit-Coleman request for Gates to fund CCSS). In it, adoption of these "common standards" was assumed to be an upgrade over all state standards. However, the report was much more than that, for it outlined a standards-dependent *package* of reforms in the form of five "action steps":

Action One involved states' adopting the assumed upgrade that was the as-yet-unwritten CCSS.

Action Two aimed to bring all textbooks, digital media, curricula, and assessments in line with CCSS.

Action Three involved "revising state policies" regarding teacher and administrator recruitment and preparation "to reflect the human capital practices of top-performing nations and states around the world."

Action Four concerned "hold[ing] schools and systems accountable" . . . "to ensure consistently high performance"—the clear implication being performance on standardized tests.

Action Five involved using international standardized tests to "ensure" U.S. superiority "to compete in the 21st century economy."[7]

CCSS was never intended to stand alone. It was created to drive curriculum and assessment. Some influential CCSS proponents who push for CCSS without high-stakes testing, such as American Federation of Teachers (AFT) president Randi Weingarten and Smarter Balanced Assessment Consortium senior advisor Linda Darling-Hammond, are missing this reality.[8]

The December 2008 *Benchmarking* report was "Achieve-led." As noted in its July 2008 *Out of Many, One* report, Achieve (along with NGA and CCSSO) indeed advocated that the ADP standards, which previously received an unimpressive national embrace, serve as a "framework" upon which to construct CCSS because, well, Achieve decided that the "state-led" CCSS should be constructed based on the ADP it had already created. Sure enough, ADP was determined by the leaders of the CCSS initiative (not "state-led" but instead "organization-led") to be *the* standards from which CCSS would launch:

> To upgrade state standards, leaders will be able to leverage the Common State Standards Initiative, an upcoming joint project of NGA, CCSSO, Achieve, the Alliance for Excellent Education, and the James B. Hunt, Jr., for Educational Leadership and Policy. *The initiative will enable all states to adopt coherent and rigorous standards in K–12 math, reading, and language arts that are fully aligned with college and career expectations and also benchmarked against leading nations.* [emphasis added][9]

Wow. Quite the promise for what had yet to be fully developed and what were, as of the December 2008 writing, only words on a report page. Never mind that the states are supposed to be creating what Achieve, NGA, and CCSSO are marketing in this December 2008 metaphorical "glossy brochure." Continuing:

> Achieve is developing an important initiative: a set of voluntary, globally competitive reference standards based upon the existing American Diploma Project (ADP) framework. Because of how it was originally developed, the ADP

framework already reflects the skills necessary to succeed in college and in well-paying jobs in today's labor market. Achieve is now working to further calibrate the framework to reflect international expectations as well as recent research on college and career readiness.[10]

Notice the language: These ADP-based anchors are still to be developed, yet they are guaranteed to be fine because they will be based upon what Achieve, the Fordham Institute, and the Education Trust *already* developed. Just take our word for it. After all, we are the CCSS initiative *leaders,* and you governors are being invited to *our* initiative—but we'll call it "state-led."

Using Achieve's beloved ADP as the CCSS framework for the high school level was not a state-led decision; it was a predetermined, prepackaged starter kit for CCSS construction that a handful of organizations intended to convince state governors to adopt—all in the name of global competition.

In 2014, I wrote a three-part series on this 2008 *Benchmarking* report.[11-13] The primary gist of the report is the now-too-familiar panic line that American education needs a test-driven overhaul in order to keep up globally. The underlying message is: "We need to see what other nations are doing because we think we can isolate what causes them to score higher than us on international tests. Then, we can pay attention to select issues, the ones that the experts named in this report perceive as those that produce higher test scores and graduation rates. By emulating these select qualities, we are trying to beat the other nations on international tests, which will prove our superiority and therefore translate into international economic security."

That, my friends, is "U.S. benchmarking to beat the rest of the world."

It took a 52-page report to spew this "U.S. domination" nonsense. However, according to NGA in its 2011 *Realizing the Potential* report, the December 2008 *Benchmarking* report served its purpose—it lured 51 states and U.S. territories into signing a CCSS MOU:

> In 2008 the NGA Center, CCSSO, and Achieve, Inc. jointly released the report *Benchmarking for Success: Ensuring U.S. Students Receive a World-Class Education,* which called on states to "upgrade state standards by adopting a common core of internationally benchmarked standards in math and language arts for grades K through 12 to ensure that students are equipped with the necessary knowledge and skills to be globally competitive."
>
> Following the release of that report, the NGA Center and CCSSO convened governors' advisors and chief state school officers to gauge interest in developing a set of common, internationally benchmarked academic standards. Fifty-one

states and U.S. territories signed a memorandum of understanding (MOU) committing them to participate in the development process.[14]

As Wilhoit had told Gates months earlier, there would be no guarantees regarding states' buying into a single set of K–12 standards. However, having governors and state superintendents sign what qualifies as a legally binding agreement[15] certainly provided Gates's millions some degree of "investment security"—and provided the U.S. Department of Education with a convenient document to include as part of its upcoming Race to the Top (RTTT) funding competition—one in which states were expected to show evidence of "common standards" and associated, consortium-developed assessments in vying for possible millions in federal education dollars.

According to NGA, 51 states and territories signed the CCSS MOU in spring 2009.[16] Most of these MOUs can be found as part of the Obama administration's Race to the Top (RTTT) application appendices (on file with the U.S. Department of Education).[17] Indeed, the Obama administration specifically named the CCSS MOU as an acceptable verification of a state's commitment to needed reform.

More to come on this federally arranged political opportunism.

The MOU is three pages long. In October 2013, I wrote a blog post[18] detailing the contents of the CCSS MOU. I used Delaware's CCSS MOU as my document of reference (pages 128–130 of the state of Delaware's *RTTT Application for Initial Funding*), which is publicly available on the U.S. Department of Education website. I will use that post as the basis for the remainder of this chapter, with additional commentary added.

MOU TITLE AND PURPOSE

The copyrighted "owners" of CCSS are named in the title of the MOU:

> The Council of Chief State School Officers and the National Governors Association Center for Best Practices Common Core Standards Memorandum of Agreement.

Section One is the MOU "purpose." The very first statement of the CCSS MOU is problematic:

> **Purpose:** This document commits states to a state-led process . . . that will lead to the development and adoption of a common core of state standards.[19]

If the state is leading itself, how is it that the standards will be common to other states? Simple: This MOU tells the states how they are to "lead themselves" in matters of CCSS. Here is the entire "purpose" paragraph:

> **Purpose:** This document commits states to a state-led process that will draw on evidence and lead to the development and adoption of a common core of state standards (common core) in English language arts and mathematics for grades K–12. These standards will be aligned with college and work expectations, include rigorous content and skills, and be internationally benchmarked. *The intent is that these standards will be aligned to state assessment and classroom practice. The second phase of this initiative will be the development of common assessments aligned to the core standards developed through this process.*[20] [Emphasis added]

Not only was the product, CCSS, not up for review via a conditional agreement; in signing this MOU, states agreed to an as-yet-undeveloped second phase of common assessments. Moreover, the alignment to classroom practice belies intent to standardize curriculum.

In signing this MOU, states are blindly agreeing to an outcome that requires the lining up of standards, curriculum, and assessments. And in all of this, signators (state governors and education superintendents) are following, not leading.

MOU BACKGROUND

Section Two is entitled "Background." It includes information on previous efforts to develop some set of common standards and assessments, including the ADP and the New England Common Assessment Program (NECAP).[21] NECAP has been misused as a graduation requirement in Rhode Island. Even the corporation that designed NECAP agrees that it should not be used as such.[22]

Here is the full text of the CCSS MOU "Background":

> **Background.** Our state education leaders are committed to ensuring all students graduate from high school ready for college, work, and success in the global economy and society. State standards provide a key foundation to drive this reform. Today, however, state standards differ significantly in terms of the incremental content and skills expected of students.
>
> Over the last several years, many individual states have made great strides in developing high-quality standards and assessments. These efforts provide a strong

foundation for further action. For example, a majority of states (35) have joined the American Diploma Project (ADP) and have worked individually to align their state standards with college and work expectations. Of the 15 states that have completed this work, studies show significant similarities in core standards across states. States have also made progress through initiatives to upgrade standards and assessments, for example, the New England Common Assessment Program.[23]

Let us consider some contradictory information noted above in the CCSS MOU. First, according to Achieve's July 2008 *Out of Many, One* report, 22 states "reported" completing the ADP standards process. However, the CCSS MOU has 15 states actually completing the process. Moreover, instead of Achieve's reported "critical mass" of state leaders arriving at "a common core of standards," only months later (from July 2008 to May 2009, at the latest), according to the CCSS MOU, "studies" are showing "significant similarities in core standards across the states." Finally, the same CCSS MOU apparently contradicts itself by maintaining that the "significantly similar" state standards also "differ significantly."

According to this MOU, state standards are both "significantly" the same and different.

Which is it: "significant" difference or sameness?

In the MOU "Background" section, the word *states* is used nine times—often as the subject of the sentence. This promotes the illusion that this CCSS magic originated as an idea of "the states"—and certainly not from Wilhoit and Coleman, who approached Gates for a CCSS initiative bankroll.

MOU BENEFITS TO THE STATES

In the third section, "Benefits to the States," NGA and CCSSO are making promises. But keep in mind that the states signing the MOU are committing to a process that they agree to implement in the future, not one that they themselves have already written or have even seen. To make promises about what CCSS is supposed to do in the future while calling it "state-led" for states just signing on is a contradiction.

Technically, if a single governor generated the idea for CCSS and all other governors followed, the "initiative" could still be called "state-led." Why not just call it what it is? In signing the MOU, states are agreeing to implement a set of standards and assessments that obviously originated after the date that most governors signed the MOU agreement, and with others, who are not state officials, in key leadership roles.

From the "Benefits to the States," it is clear that CCSS is "one-size-fits-all"—guaranteed:

> **Benefits to the States:** The time is right for a state-led, nation-wide effort to establish a common core of standards that raises the bar for all students. This initiative presents a significant opportunity to accelerate and drive education reform toward the goal of ensuring that all children graduate from high school ready for college, work, and competing in the global economy and society.[24]

Though here and elsewhere these goals might read well on the page, they represent a vision that is devoid of substance.

The One-Size-Fits-All Promise

The "Benefits" section also includes a list of what participating states will be able to do, including "articulating . . . general public expectations for students," "aligning textbooks . . . to the standards," "ensuring professional development . . . based on identified need and best practices," "develop[ing] and implement[ing] an assessment system to measure student performance against the common core," and "evaluat[ing] policy changes needed to help students and educators meet the common core standards. . . ."

It is not clear how this list connects to the promise that CCSS "ensures all children will graduate . . . ready for college. . . ." Nevertheless, the MOU "ensures" that *all* children will graduate with some unqualified, undefined "readiness" for whatever awaits beyond high school.

Interestingly, the 2014 CCSS website is more careful in qualifying what is "ensured" than is the potentially legally binding 2009 MOU, a document used by states to vie for RTTT money:

> To ensure all students are ready for success after high school, the Common Core State Standards establish clear, consistent guidelines for what every student should know and be able to do in math and English language arts from kindergarten through 12th grade. . . . The standards . . . ensure students are prepared for today's entry-level careers, freshman-level college courses, and workforce training programs.[25]

Although the language on the CCSS website is more precise, NGA and CCSSO still offer no proof to support this assertion that CCSS is indeed what "all" students "should know" in math and English language arts (ELA). The CCSS MOU changes the American classroom into a laboratory for testing unproven CCSS. However, the promoters promise it will work, so therefore it must . . . right?

On the heels of one unjustified promise comes another: According to the CCSS MOU, CCSS is guaranteed to match or outdo current state standards:

> *No state will see a decrease in the level of student expectations* that exist in their current state standards.[26] [Emphasis added]

NGA, CCSSO, Achieve, and the other organizations leading CCSS (let's just drop the "state-led" charade for a moment) failed to assess their own guarantee prior to the June 2010 unveiling of the CCSS. However, the Fordham Institute "graded" CCSS and publicized these results 1 month later, in July 2010—and found that CCSS was *not* superior to all state standards. Nevertheless, the Fordham Institute and all other CCSS-endorsing organizations chose to disregard the issue.

Promise broken.

MOU PROCESS AND STRUCTURE

Leadership

And now, on to the CCSS MOU section "Process and Structure." This section is the heart of the CCSS development process. It opens with a subsection entitled "Common Core State-Based Leadership" and includes a statement akin to the CCSS being "state-led" because NGA and CCSSO are in charge. It seems that NGA and CCSSO were trying to trademark the term *state-led* by noting that their organizations—made up of state leadership—"will facilitate a state-led process."[27] This is quite the stretch in logic, since it only serves to establish CCSS as being led by state bureaucracy. And so far, this leadership is only a sign-on, not actual development of standards.

There is another outcome related to NGA's and CCSSO's taking the lead: In an action that defies states' long established and legally protected autonomy over educational matters, it turns out that NGA and CCSSO own CCSS, as legally noted in a CCSS license.[28, 29] Notably, the licensing of CCSS to NGA and CCSSO—and the potential for revenue production associated with licensing—is not discussed in the MOU.

National Validation Committee

The next "Process and Structure" subsections are curious for their order-ing. First comes the national validation committee, a group of "national and international experts on standards." However, their role was not to *develop* CCSS—it was to *review*:

> CCSSO and the NGA Center will create an expert validation group that will serve several purposes, including validating end-of-course expectations, pro-viding leadership for the development of K–12 standards, and certifying state adoption of the common core. The group will be comprised of national and international experts on standards. Participating states will have the opportunity to nominate individuals to the group. The national validation committee shall provide an independent review of the common core. The national validation committee will review the common core as it is developed and offer comments, suggestions, and validation of the process and products developed by the stan-dards development group. This group will use evidence as the driving factor in validating the common core.[30]

The validation committee did not develop CCSS. It "reviewed" and "of-fered comments" to the standards development group. According to tes-timony of CCSS validation committee member Sandra Stotsky, the vali-dation committee was little more than a "rubber stamp" whose "requests were ignored" for the "supposed body of research evidence" on which CCSS was based.[31] In other words, when the validation committee asked for underlying research basis to support the standards as written, it was not produced, even though the MOU states that evidence will be used to validate CCSS.

The validation committee is listed first on the CCSS MOU, yet the validation committee did not write the standards.

Why list the validation committee first?

Because it looks good to list the expected education standards experts and teachers first, even if their role is superficial. On September 24, 2014, NGA and CCSSO released the list of 29 validation committee members (17 university professors, one university president, four K–12 administra-tors, four individuals in assessment, and three classroom teachers).[32] The NGA release also included biographical information on each committee member.

These individuals met as a committee twice: in December 2009 to re-view the CCSS "anchors"—the College and Career Readiness Standards

(CCRS), and in April 2010, to review CCSS. Two days of face-to-face meetings to set the standards that were to drive the education systems in a supposed 46 states and three U.S. territories (as noted in the 2009 NGA symposium report). Aside from conference calls and emails, that was it.

In May 2010, these committee members received an embargoed copy (not to be shared publicly) of CCSS "for review and certification." Twenty-four validation committee members signed off on CCSS. Five did not.[33] And there we have the pan-flash that was the "advisory" role of the CCSS validation committee.

Develop End-of-High-School Expectations

Let us continue our travels into the inner sanctum of CCSS "development." The next "Process and Structure" subsection, "Develop End-of-High-School Expectations," concerns the development of the CCRS, the supposed "anchors" for CCSS. Most individuals who are familiar with CCSS do not realize that there was supposed to be a CCRS to precede CCSS development. Though the MOU states that CCRS (and the subsequent CCSS) development is to be an "open" and "inclusive" process, it also states that it is to be an "efficient" process. Large groups do not lend themselves to efficiency—smaller groups within those large groups do. However, it does not look good to identify a smaller, inner group that actually is doing the "developing" as the greater group stands by and waits to approve some product. So, let's keep the details of exactly who is writing what a secret. A secretive "open" process—how about that! So the question is: Who wrote the now-national standards?

Recall that in the December 2008 *Benchmarking* report, the CCSS "anchors" for high school were assumed to be a finessed version of ADP worked out by Achieve. However, these anchor standards needed to be expanded to K–12 in both ELA and math. The CCSS MOU outlines the qualifications of the group that was supposed to develop these CCRS:

> CCSSO and the NGA center will convene *Achieve, ACT and the College Board* in an open, inclusive, and efficient process *to develop a set of end-of-high-school expectations in English language arts and mathematics* based on evidence. We will ask all participating states to review and provide input on these expectations. This work will be completed by July 2009.[34] [Emphasis added]

A couple of observations: First, NGA and CCSSO determined that Achieve and two testing companies, ACT and College Board, would be the ones to determine the CCRS, the CCSS "anchors." This is no open process. Achieve developed ADP. And ADP is already an assumed component of the CCSS-anchoring CCRS. Second, the inclusion of two testing companies in the development of what will ultimately be CCSS attests to the fact that CCSS was meant to be inseparably tied to high-stakes testing. Third, there is zero mention of including classroom teachers—and especially not current classroom teachers—in this CCRS process.

As it turns out, this first work group was not even announced until July 1, 2009, and that was as a result of public pressure. NGA and CCSSO wanted to keep the membership of this group a secret. Stotsky testified as much:

> After the Common Core Initiative was launched in early 2009, the National Governors Association and the Council of Chief State School Officers *never explained to the public what the qualifications were for membership on the standards-writing committees* or how it would justify the specific standards they created. Most important, it never explained why Common Core's high school exit standards were equal to college admission requirements without qualification, even though this country's wide ranging post-secondary institutions use a variety of criteria for admission.
>
> Eventually responding to the many charges of a lack of transparency, the names of the 24 members of the "Standards Development Work Group" were revealed in a July 1, 2009 news release.[35] The vast majority, it appeared, work for testing companies. Not only did CCSSI give no rationale for the composition of this Work Group, it gave no rationale for the people it put on the two three-member teams in charge of writing the grade-level standards.[36] [Emphasis added]

As the CCSS MOU notes, this "Standards Development Work Group" is overwhelmingly comprised of Achieve, ACT, and College Board members (five from Achieve, seven from ACT, and six from College Board). But there are others whose affiliations remain unacknowledged in the CCSS MOU—including David Coleman and his seeming-standards-writing company that became a nonprofit, Student Achievement Partners (SAP). (More on SAP in the next chapter.)

NGA and CCSSO added yet another group, a "feedback group," in order to provide (as its name states) feedback on CCRS development. Moreover, the July 2009 press release refers to a "national policy forum of education experts to share ideas, gather input and inform the common core state standards initiative."[37] The national policy forum is introduced in a latter section of the CCSS MOU.

In its July 2009 press release, NGA made it clear that the work group was to develop the CCRS—not the feedback group, not the national policy forum, and not the validation group—which really amounted to a total of six people writing all of the grade-level standards:

> The Standards Development Work Group is currently engaged in determining and writing the college and career readiness standards in English-language arts and mathematics. This group is composed of content experts from Achieve, Inc., ACT, and the College Board. This group will be expanded later in the year to include additional experts to develop the standards for grades K–12 in English language arts and mathematics. Additionally, CCSSO and the NGA Center have selected an independent facilitator and an independent writer as well as resource advisors to support each content area work group throughout the standards development process. The Work Group's deliberations will be confidential throughout the process. States and national education organizations will have an opportunity to review and provide evidence-based feedback on the draft documents throughout the process. . . .
>
> Also, as a step in the standards development process, the NGA Center and CCSSO are overseeing the work of a Feedback Group. The role of this Feedback Group is to provide information backed by research to inform the standards development process by offering expert input on draft documents. *Final decisions regarding the common core standards document will be made by the Standards Development Work Group. The Feedback Group will play an advisory role, not a decision-making role in the process.* [emphasis added][38]

Unlike for the validation committee members, NGA offered no biographical information for the CCRS work group members (or for feedback group members, for that matter). Why would it, if NGA really wanted to keep this 24-member group's particulars a secret? In its press release, NGA even states that "deliberations" will be "confidential." Contrast this with the "open, inclusive" language in the CCSS MOU. Again with the "open, inclusive" secrecy.

Regarding openness, I guess NGA and CCSSO changed their minds. Shut America out of the inner circle of decisionmaking. It's more "efficient"—which must mean "fast."

Nevertheless, appearances *are* important; so, let's offer a number of fringe "advisory" groups. Stakeholders will *look* involved; they will *feel* involved, but there will be a whole lot less of that messy, democratic "inefficiency" than there would be if they were *truly* involved.

Returning to the insiders:

In April 2014, I wrote a post in which I examined the credentials of the twenty-four July 2009 CCRS work group individuals to determine who had classroom experience. Here are my findings:

Among the math group:

- Only 3 of the 15 individuals on the 2009 CCRS math work group had held positions as classroom teachers of mathematics.
- None was a classroom teacher in 2009. None taught elementary or middle school mathematics. Three other members had other classroom teaching experience in biology, English, and social studies.
- None taught special education or was certified in special education or English as a Second Language (ESL).
- Only one CCRS math work group member was not affiliated with an education company or nonprofit.

In the ELA work group:

- Five of the 15 individuals had classroom experience—teaching English. None was a classroom teacher in 2009.
- None taught elementary grades, special education, or ESL, and none held certifications in these areas.

Overlapping group membership:

Five of the 15 CCRS ELA work group members also served on the CCRS math work group. Two are from Achieve; two from ACT, and one from the College Board.[39]

This first 24-member group was supposed to be in place for CCRS development scheduled to end in July 2009 with the completion of the CCRS, the CCSS "anchors." However, the process did not go according to its unrealistically tight schedule. Here is what the CCSS MOU stated would be the next part of the CCSS development process: moving from establishing the CCRS to writing the CCSS. In a world in which the theoretical transpires according to plan, CCRS development would have occurred as scheduled and would have smoothly and gracefully transitioned into CCSS development.

Alas, 'twas not to be.

Let us now contrast supposition with reality.

Develop K–12 English Language Arts and Math Standards

The CCSS MOU does not indicate any change of work group membership in the move from developing CCRS to developing CCSS:

> CCSSO and the NGA center will convene Achieve, ACT and the College Board in an open, inclusive, and efficient process to develop K–12 standards that are grounded in empirical research and draw on best practices in standards development. We will ask participating states to provide input into the drafting of the common core and work as partners in the common core standards development process. This work will be completed by December 2009.[40]

The expectation appears to have been that the group of individuals first publicly revealed in the July 2009 NGA press release would finish that same month with developing initial drafts of CCRS anchors; that those drafts would be "reviewed" and solidified in time for an "expanded" work group to write K–12 standards based upon these ELA and math "anchors;" and that the K–12 standards would be completed by December 2009, as the CCSS MOU indicates.

CCSS development did not happen according to schedule. Moreover, with the July 1, 2009, press release, NGA and CCSSO apparently anticipated the criticism over the absence of classroom teachers in the CCSS development process. So, they decided in their "forced" (according to Stotsky's previously cited testimony) July 2009 work group announcement to include a statement indicating that the work group was to be expanded following CCRS completion and before CCSS development was to begin. This yielded a second NGA work group press release, in November 2009:

> WASHINGTON—The National Governors Association Center for Best Practices (NGA Center) and the Council of Chief State School Officers (CCSSO) today announced the individuals who will develop the K–12 standards for English-language arts and mathematics in the Common Core State Standards Initiative (CCSSI). Fifty-one states and territories have joined this state-led process. The draft college and career-readiness standards, the first step in this initiative, were released in September. . . . The K–12 standards for English-language arts and mathematics will align with the college- and career-readiness standards. . . .[41]

It seems that between July and November, CCSS picked up two more states/territories. Also note that in this November 2009 press release,

NGA and CCSSO state that the "feedback" group was to remain in place and that an "advisory" group was to be added.

The NGA states that the first part of the CCSS development process—the development of CCRS (the CCSS "anchors")—was completed in September 2009. What this press release does not indicate is that the CCRS in math were considered a failure and were dropped. No math anchor standards (i.e., no CCRS) exist for CCSS. They simply vanished with no explanation.[42]

In its November 2009 press release, NGA also fails to acknowledge that the first 24-member group actually wrote the first draft of CCSS.[43] They were not supposed to; per NGA's July 2009 press release, the writing of the CCSS was to be done after this group of 24 was "expanded."

Why sneak and attempt to write CCSS prior to expanding the work group?

One possibility is that fewer people means better "efficiency." Recall that the first group included no elementary teachers, no ELL, no special ed teachers. Likely, not many of those work group members were actually composing CCSS.[44] Another possibility is that CCRS and CCSS development was rushed, and as a result, transitioning from the CCRS work group to the "expanded" CCSS work group was not well planned and executed. Nevertheless, according to work group member Sue Pimentel, the first draft of CCSS was developed between September and November 2009—before work group expansion officially occurred—and it was "a flop."[45] (More to come on Sue Pimentel and her role in this process in Chapter 6.)

Given Pimentel's statement above, by the time the second, "expanded" work group was announced, it appears that members were working on what was at least the second try at CCSS. It seems that the discrepancy in work group tasks was not one of efficiency and that keeping to the NGA- and CCSSO-prescribed tight timeline proved messy. Of course, it wasn't supposed to be that way, according to details from the November 2009 NGA press release:

> The K–12 standards development process has a parallel structure to the college- and career-readiness standards, with a work group drafting the standards and receiving continual input from outside experts and practitioners.
>
> The Work Group for K–12 standards development is composed of individuals representing multiple stakeholders and a range of expertise and experience in assessment, curriculum design, cognitive development, early childhood, early numeracy, child development, English-language acquisition and elementary, middle, and postsecondary education.[46]

(Note: The "work group" can be understood as a single group, or it can be described in more specific terms as an ELA work group and a math work group.)

Timing issues aside, in expanding the original work group (comprised of one ELA work group and one math work group), NGA and CCSSO were obviously trying to make the work group appear more credible. Members with experience in curriculum design. Early childhood. English-language acquisition. Those do sound impressive.

In April 2014, I examined the credentials of the 101 members[47] of the expanded CCSS development ELA and math work groups. Examination of this second work group betrays a convenient membership, overwhelmingly comprised of university professors and state department of education employees and including others who could benefit financially from there being a CCSS. Below are more details, as originally posted on my blog:

> The November 2009 press release lists 51 individuals on the CCSS math work group. Seven of the members remain from the July 2009 list (of these, one is listed from College Board; two, from Achieve; one, from ACT, and one, from SAP). Sixteen work for state departments of education. Twenty work for colleges or universities.
>
> Only two identified themselves as current (2009) classroom teachers: one elementary teacher; one middle school teacher.
>
> As to the November 2009 CCSS ELA work group list: It includes 50 members. Seven remain from the July 2009 list (three are listed from Achieve; two, from ACT; one, from College Board, and one, from SAP). Seventeen work for state departments of education. Twelve work for colleges or universities.
>
> Three identified themselves as current (2009) classroom teachers: two elementary, and one high school teacher in ESL (English as a Second Language). Some other notable observations about these November 2009 CCSS work groups:
>
> Two other individuals on the CCSS ELA work group . . . identify themselves as ESL, though it seems they are not currently in the classroom. [One of these individuals] was involved with Fordham [Institute's] grading of state standards. Laura McGiffert Slover, now the CEO of PARCC (Partnership for Assessment of Readiness for College and Careers) remained on both CCSS ELA and math work groups.
>
> All three Student Achievement Partners (SAP) CCSS "lead writers"—David Coleman, Susan Pimentel, and Jason Zimba—remained from the July 2009 CCSS work groups. [More on Student Achievement Partners in Chapter 6.]

Matt Davis, director of the reading program for E. D. Hirsch's Core Knowledge, an ELA curriculum later marketed as CCSS-aligned, was on the CCSS ELA work group. . . . Thus, CCSS served as a convenient vehicle for Core Knowledge promotion. . . .

Laura Mongello, member of the CCSS ELA work group, is in "product development" for the Quarasan Group. Here is a description of her "services" from the Quarasan website:

> *Laura's team enhances this blueprint, adding grade-level appropriate content, visual value, and substance to every paragraph and learning object.*

It appears that Mongello's job is to "enhance" CCSS by "adding . . . substance" (??).

David Liben, listed as affiliated with Liben Education Consulting in 2009 is now with . . . Student Achievement Partners (SAP). . . . It is possible that Liben was with SAP during 2009. . . . His wife [Meredith Liben] was employed by SAP even as they both served on the November 2009 CCSS ELA work group.[48]

Much of the public controversy surrounding CCSS development concerns the lack of current classroom teachers involved in decisionmaking roles. From the brief biographical information presented above, one can see that practicing teachers did not develop CCSS but that a variety of education- and business-related individuals were accorded access to the CCSS development "inside track." Furthermore, the presence of so many state department of education employees serving on the CCSS work group enabled those wishing to do so to say that "teachers" were involved in developing CCSS. Technically, such a statement about "teacher involvement" is correct because many of the state department of education work group members were once teachers. However, it is clear that the overwhelming majority of these work group members looked impressive on paper yet they were removed from the reality of teaching in this atmosphere of test-driven "reform."

There is another issue concerning state department of education employees more so than for the university professors: Employment with state departments of education places these work group members in a precarious position to serve on this controversial CCSS work group under the close watch of state superintendents who want to advance CCSS. As a result, perceived freedom to express concern regarding CCSS becomes less likely if one believes one's employment might somehow be affected.

Recall that CCSSO—a collection of state superintendents—is deeply invested in the CCSS effort.

Many state department of education employees might have even been told that as part of their job duties, they had to serve.

My suspicions regarding the possibility of coerced service on the CCSS work group come from a couple of experiences. The first concerns "three [Louisiana] teachers" who were touted as "developing" CCSS. Although I heard these three teachers mentioned in two venues in defense of CCSS—once when I was involved in a CCSS debate in November 2013 for a public policy awareness group, Leaders with Vision in Baton Rouge, Louisiana, and once on an April 2014 video clip of a Louisiana House Education Committee meeting—in neither venue were these three teachers named.

It turns out that the three Louisiana "teachers" who "developed" CCSS all hailed from the Louisiana Department of Education. None was a current classroom teacher. One even erased her CCSS work group experience from her LinkedIn bio.[49] All three names were carefully guarded by those promoting CCSS in Louisiana.

The second experience that makes me suspicious of this November 2009 work group membership is the secrecy. In its July 2009 press release, the NGA wrote that deliberations surrounding CCSS would be confidential. Though there was no such language used in the November 2009 press release, the overwhelming silence of the work group members on the issue of CCSS development made me wonder if these individuals were under some sort of gag order.

In late April 2014, I attempted to contact more than a dozen November 2009 work group members, mostly by email. I was able to locate current email addresses for six of them. I tried to contact an additional individual via Facebook messaging and another in the comments section of my blog. Below is the text of my email/Facebook message:

(Recipient name), my name is Mercedes Schneider.

I am a Louisiana public school teacher and education writer. I blog at deutsch29.wordpress.com: deutsch29.wordpress.com/about/

I also just had a book published on key individuals and organizations exploiting public education: deutsch29.wordpress.com/2014/04/29/the-table-of-contents-to-my-book/

The reason I am writing to you is that I read your name on the November 2009 NGA press release of Common Core work group members.

I have a question about the CC work group:

Were you required to sign a confidentiality agreement regarding CC work group discussions?

Thank you for your time.

Regards—

Mercedes Schneider

Of the eight work group members I attempted to contact, I heard back from only two. The first replied on April 29, 2014: It was someone who served as a member of the CCSS math work group. (Gender deliberately concealed.)

Ms. Schneider,

This is so long ago that I have to say that I don't remember [if I signed a confidentiality agreement]. It was a lot of work, especially in my case, so my only memory is the hard work I had to put in.

I wondered why this person wrote that (s)he had to work "especially" hard. This work group had 50 other members. So, I asked:

If I might ask, why hard work "esp in your case"?

His/her response (with typo):

A had a lot of input in the CCSSM (math CCSS).

This lent credence to my belief that only a handful of individuals truly wrote CCSS. However, I wanted to clarify my thinking. So, I asked:

Would you mind discussing your CC experience with me via phone sometime in the next month?

The next day, April 30, 2014, this work group member's response was as follows:

Ms. Schneider,

I should apologize for not having read your original email carefully. I was never a member of the 2009 work group that produced the disastrous first draft of the 2009 college and career readiness standards. I only worked on the 2010 CCSSM.

In my original email, I did not ask if this person were a member of the first group. So, it seems that (s)he was "misunderstanding misunderstanding me." His/her "disastrous" reference is to the CCRS math "anchors" that "disappeared." I knew that this person was a member of the second group, the one supposed to draft CCSS.

I sent this reply:

Would you mind if I interview you, a question at a time, via email?

His/her response:

If you want to use it in a public forum, I am sorry I won't do it because it is not the right time.

This person's words surprised me. "Not the right time?" I thought, "This person is invested in his/her creation. Whether CCSSM translates into what teaching practitioners can use is not of utmost importance. Saving CCSSM is." So I asked:

When is the right time?

No response for a couple of days. Then, on May 2, 2014, I received this email:

When the CCSSM stabilizes, then we can talk.

What can I do except shake my head? CCSS was a hot issue in statehouses across the country—evidence that the top-down creation and imposition of CCSS upon America's schools produced a poor, unwelcome fit with educational needs as determined by those closest to students: their parents, teachers, and local administration. This dissatisfaction had moved into state legislatures, and rightly so. "Top-down" CCSS and its looming assessments are a nondemocratic means to an ill-fitting, ultimately punitive educational end.

The CCSS MOU states that CCSS development was to be "open" and "inclusive."

Ha!

In preparing to publish this book, I emailed the above-cited CCSS work group member for permission to publish our email exchange. This person declined to be identified and included the following explanation:

Mercedes,

Sorry to disappoint you, but having thought about it, I will stick to my original decision not to be involved in any "history of the CC" at all at this point.

Please do not mention my name in any shape or form.

Such unwillingness to be identified does nothing to promote the façade of "open and inclusive" CCSS development.

Just as I had finished drafting this chapter, on June 11, 2014, I received a response to my April 29, 2014, email from another work group member—again, one whom I am not at liberty to identify:

Hello Ms Schneider,

Sorry your message got lost in the stack. I don't remember signing a confidentially [sic] agreement but I did sign a bunch of documents. I will research it. Also please feel free to contact me via my cell phone.

What immediately captured my attention was this person's statement about signing "a bunch of documents." It seems that some of these documents must have concerned surrendering intellectual property rights to NGA and CCSSO, the CCSS owners (see Chapter 8). I was curious to know the details of the "bunch" of documents this person was required to sign regarding his/her role as a CCSS work group member. I did not phone him/her because I wanted to have a written record of our correspondence. Instead, on June 11, 2014, I emailed the following response:

Thank you for responding.

If you would not mind describing to me the documentation you had to sign, I would appreciate it.

Thank you.

Mercedes

I did not hear back from this person, so I resent the same email on July 12, 2014. No detailed accounting of the signed documentation ever came.

In January 2014, one of the CCSS work group members, Louisa Moats, was interviewed in the *Huffington Post* regarding her change in position from supporting CCSS to opposing it. (Moats is not one of the two anonymous work group members previously discussed. She has an established career as a reading and language specialist and psychologist.[50])

If Moats signed an agreement in 2010 not to speak negatively against CCSS, she decided in 2014 that it was time to publicly register her dissatisfaction.

Below is a rather pointed excerpt from her *Huffington Post* interview with Mark Bertin in which Moats notes her "naivete" regarding the purpose of CCSS as a nucleus for test-driven "reform":

> Marilyn Adams and I were the team of writers, recruited in 2009 by David Coleman and Sue Pimentel, who drafted the Foundational Reading Skills section of the CCSS and closely reviewed the whole ELA section for K–5. We drafted sections on Language and Writing Foundations that were not incorporated into the document as originally drafted. I am the author of the Reading Foundational Skills section of Appendix A. . . .
>
> *I never imagined when we were drafting standards in 2010 that major financial support would be funneled immediately into the development of standards-related tests. How naïve I was.* The CCSS represent lofty aspirational goals for students aiming for four year, highly selective colleges. Realistically, at least half, if not the majority, of students are not going to meet those standards as written, although the students deserve to be well prepared for career and work through meaningful and rigorous education.
>
> Our lofty standards are appropriate for the most academically able, but what are we going to do for the huge numbers of kids that are going to "fail" the PARCC (Partnership for Assessment of Readiness for College and Careers) test? We need to create a wide range of educational choices and pathways to high school graduation, employment and citizenship. The Europeans got this right a long time ago.
>
> If I could take all the money going to the testing companies and reinvest it, I'd focus on the teaching profession—recruitment, pay, work conditions, rigorous and on-going training.[51] [Emphasis added]

A couple of observations. First, Moats was on the inside of CCSS development, and she seems unaware that the CCSS she was helping to create was intended to be a vehicle for test-driven "reform." Thus, at least one CCSS work group member appears not to have been apprised of the "big picture" regarding the standards the group helped create. Second, the duo who recruited Moats—David Coleman and Susan Pimentel—were obviously in charge and could have fully informed Moats of the 2009 NGA plan to develop both CCSS and associated assessments—yet they apparently chose not to. Thus, what Moats created in the name of "aspiration" instead became the "standardized" expectation.

Never mind any rift. Time to adopt.

Adoption

Under "Adoption," states are given 3 years to fully institute CCSS. That brings us to the 2014–2015 CCSS implementation deadline shared by most CCSS states (and three U.S. territories).

This section also includes the statement, "This effort is voluntary for states . . . ," a convoluted statement given the requirement of states to commit to CCSS prior to judging the finished product—and without field testing. States also agree to use the complete CCSS, even though NGA and CCSSO "fully intend that states . . . choose to include additional state standards beyond the common core" such that 85% of a state's total standards are comprised of the CCSS package. This is the place in the MOU in which Achieve's 2008 *Out of Many, One* report's statement that "common does not mean identical standards"[52] is loosely accommodated. *Technically,* states can add to CCSS; therefore, *technically,* "state" standards can still differ. Thus, all states could have CCSS plus a wee bit of "individuality" dressing.

In the "Adoption" subsection, NGA and CCSSO note that they want to foster a process of continued improvement to "this first version of the common core. . . ."

By definition, "common" means no "state-led" modifying of CCSS on an individual state basis. States might declare an intention to modify CCSS; however, individual states do not own CCSS; two nonprofits do: NGA and CCSSO. If there is any "modifying" to be done, NGA and CCSSO will direct the effort. Again, *technically,* this meets Achieve's 2008 *Out of Many, One* assertion that "real world standards must be dynamic, not static."[53]

National Policy Forum

We're traveling further down the ladder of CCSS influence. Time for that token teacher input. This is where organizations like the National School Boards Association, National Education Association, and American Federation of Teachers are allowed into the CCSS clubhouse. It is a token role to "inform the common core initiative," a "place for refining our shared understanding of the scope and elements of a common core."

The national policy forum was created with an additional goal: to advertise and implement CCSS:

CCSSO and the NGA center will convene a National Policy Forum comprised of signatory national organizations (e.g., the Alliance for Excellent Education, Business Roundtable, National School Boards Association, Council of Great City Schools, Hunt Institution, National Association of State Boards of Education, National Education Association, and others) to share ideas, gather input, and inform the common core initiative. The forum is intended as a place for refining our shared understanding of the scope and elements of a common core; providing a means to develop common messaging between and among participating organizations, and building public will and support.[54]

Teachers and other traditional educators (i.e., the ones not affiliated with education companies or standards-writing nonprofits) are invited late to the CCSS party. And why are they invited, really?

To form a CCSS sales network.

To those teachers who say, "I know that CCSS was developed by teachers; I was there," I say:

You have been used to promote the CCSS image.

Federal Role

There is no getting around it; according to the CCSS MOU, the federal government was intended to be connected to CCSS. In this section, NGA and CCSSO try to walk the tightrope between promoting CCSS and "state-led" standards and acknowledging that the U.S. Department of Education will be contributing money to the CCSS effort—but not to CCSS per se—to CCSS *implementation* and the CCSS *assessments*. Yes, as CCSS work group member Louisa Moats learned, CCSS was designed to be assessed. Never forget, CCSS is birthed out of test-driven, federally created NCLB. The point of having CCSS is to bring states under uniform standards tied to uniform assessments. In the "Federal Role" section, NGA and CCSSO declare that ponying up the dough for both CCSS implementation and assessments is an "appropriate role" for USDOE:

> **Federal Role.** The parties support a state-led effort and not a federal effort to develop a common core of state standards; there is, however, *an appropriate federal role* in supporting this *state-led effort*. In particular, *the federal government can provide key financial support* for this effort in developing a common core of *state standards* and in *moving toward common assessments,* such as through the Race to the Top Fund authorized in the American Recovery and Reinvestment Act of 2009. Further, the federal government can incentivize this effort through

a range of tiered incentives, such as providing states with greater flexibility in the use of existing federal funds, supporting a revised state accountability structure, and offering financial support for states to effectively implement the standards. Additionally, the federal government can provide additional financial support for the development of common assessments, teacher and principal professional development, and other related common core standards supports, and a research agenda that can help continually improve the common core over time. Finally, the federal government can revise and align existing federal education laws with the lessons learned from states' international benchmarking efforts and from federal research.[55]

So, the "appropriate" federal role is for USDOE to pour money into everything *except* the actual creation of CCSS. Notice the federal input via the federal wallet is on all other aspects of CCSS as captured in the phrase "the federal government can provide additional financial support for . . . other related common core standards supports." Assessments. Professional development. Research. And "Other Related CCSS Supports."

The word *curriculum* is conspicuously absent from this list. However, curriculum most certainly is a "CCSS support." Thus, beyond CCSS creation, the federal government can offer money for the entire CCSS enterprise.

Technically, the federal government did not create CCSS. However, the federal government's role in controlling the CCSS venture by offering money for related aspects places USDOE firmly in the driver's seat over state education affairs.

It is interesting how well the "Federal Role" section of this pre-RTTT, CCSS MOU summarizes much of what would be included in RTTT, which would be unveiled in the months following the creation of the CCSS MOU, in July 2009.[56] (More on RTTT and the CCSS in Chapter 10.)

So, you see, the federal government has not written CCSS.

(Neither have NGA and CCSSO, but I digress.)

Still, the federal government has helped pay for CCSS, and NGA and CCSSO (themselves, ironically, national-level organizations pushing for "state-led" involvement) have generously invited the federal government to pay for as much that is connected to CCSS as is possible to pay for and to funnel federal money earmarked for states to use for other purposes into CCSS.

Certainly, the federal government would not use federal funding to hold states hostage to CCSS. . . . (See Chapter 10 on RTTT for the answer to this uncertainty.)

Agreement

We have arrived at the end of the CCSS MOU. Time to sign on the dotted line. Just two signatures requested and required: those of a state's governor and education superintendent.

> The undersigned state leaders agree to the process and structure as described above and attest accordingly by our signature(s) below.[57]

Two officials making a decision with profound consequences for thousands of people.
"State-led."

CHAPTER 6

The Invisible Architects and Visible PR Machine

Student Achievement Partners

The Common Core State Standards (CCSS) memorandum of understanding (MOU) outlined who would be involved with the actual development of CCSS and who would be on the fringes in the roles of reviewer and promoter.

The CCSS MOU directly identifies Achieve, ACT, and the College Board as the key developers of CCSS.[1]

The word *teacher* was never used in the CCSS MOU naming of CCSS developers. In fact, if teachers had been leading this effort, they would not have agreed to form a set of standards that were to be a rigid template for test-driven reform "voluntarily" adopted by two state officials before the product was produced—and that without any pilot testing.

That does not mean teachers were not permitted on the fringes of this national effort. However, the CCSS *developers* were chiefly those in the "in crowd" of American Diploma Project (ADP) development and those working for national assessment companies, and that "in crowd" had decided that CCSS was to be a vehicle for test-driven reform. As per the CCSS MOU, the National Governors Association (NGA) and the Council of Chief State School Officers (CCSSO) provided explicit directions regarding the controlled "work group" center upon which to drape the "evidence" of supposedly democratic teacher and public involvement in "creating" the CCSS test-driven-reform hub.

In the July 2009 press release regarding the original 24-member work group (the group whose membership NGA and CCSSO wanted to keep secret from the public but eventually released under pressure), the CCSS owners, NGA and CCSSO, offered a concession to include additional work group members from outside Achieve, ACT, and the College Board:

The Standards Development Work Group is currently engaged in determining and writing the college and career readiness standards in English-language arts and mathematics. This group is composed of content experts from Achieve, Inc., ACT, and the College Board. This group will be expanded later in the year to include additional experts to develop the standards for grades K–12 in English language arts and mathematics. Additionally, CCSSO and the NGA Center have selected an independent facilitator and an independent writer as well as resource advisors to support each content area work group throughout the standards development process.[2]

There is still no specific inclusion of teachers among these "experts"—only an "independent facilitator," "independent writer," and "resource advisors." Moreover, according to the NGA and CCSSO, these additional individuals would be added following the development of the College and Career Readiness Standards (CCRS), the CCSS "anchors."

Or would they?

As noted in the previous chapter, the first 24-member work group did include some individuals who were not affiliated with Achieve, ACT, or the College Board. Two of those individuals identified themselves as the founder and cofounder of Student Achievement Partners (SAP). Neither one was ever a classroom teacher.

They are David Coleman and Jason Zimba.

Writing about SAP founder Coleman and cofounder Zimba separately one from another proves to be a challenge because their professional backgrounds are intertwined. Both are "edupreneurs"—individuals with zero K–12 classroom teaching experience who began businesses in education and received financial backing from other edupreneurs serving in influential roles.

There is a third noted name associated with SAP—Susan Pimentel. Pimentel is also an edupreneur—she has no recorded classroom teaching experience yet she has built a career advising on educational issues. She was involved with the American Diploma Project (ADP) as a paid consultant with Achieve and moved on to involvement with CCSS as one of the original 24-member work group as a member of Achieve. However, Pimentel has also become associated with SAP; in fact, its founder and cofounder, Coleman and Zimba, insist that Pimentel, too, was another cofounder of SAP in 2007. Archived documentation directly contradicts Pimentel's involvement with SAP prior to 2011. Nevertheless, following CCSS completion in 2010, both Coleman and Zimba began to advertise that Pimentel was a "cofounder in 2007" of SAP. It seems likely that

Pimentel was retroactively identified as a cofounder to leverage her teacher-friendly female presence for purposes of relating positively to teachers in a grand effort to promote CCSS.

SAP also has two other individuals who served as members of the second, 101-member work group: husband and wife David and Meredith Liben. Meredith Liben concealed her association with SAP during her tenure as a CCSS work group member, instead listing her affiliation as Liben Education Consulting. Her husband, David, might have also been with SAP during his time on the CCSS work group; however, his later employment with SAP (by April 2012) is verifiable.[3]

In addition to these five are another two members of the second, 101-member work group: Phil Daro and William McCallum. They co-led the CCSS math writing with Zimba and later became members of the SAP "board and advisors."[4]

And if those seven are not enough, let us add Council of Chief State School Officers (CCSSO) former CEO Gene Wilhoit, who joined the SAP board in January 2013 to "directly support SAP's core mission of helping teachers successfully implement the Common Core."[5]

CCSS: Providing endless career-enhancing opportunities for those running the show.

In sum, eight individuals exerting influence over CCSS were associated with SAP by 2013. Seven of those were involved in the inner circle of actual CCSS development: Three were formally associated with SAP during CCSS development (Coleman, Zimba, and Meredith Liben) and four (Pimentel, McCallum, Daro, and David Liben) joined SAP afterward. Of these seven, Coleman and Pimentel have become the chief spokespeople—the public face—for CCSS. Zimba also does some public relations regarding CCSS but is not nearly as visible as Coleman and Pimentel. Daro has been actively overseeing and promoting a CCSS-aligned math curriculum known as Eureka Math.[6] The Libens have no overt public role in promoting CCSS. And whereas McCallum does produce a blog with Zimba called *I Support the Common Core* and has even traveled with Fordham Institute's Michael Petrilli to testify on behalf of CCSS,[7] his public role in promoting CCSS is rather limited nationally.

In this chapter, I examine the backgrounds and CCSS-promoting roles of Coleman, Zimba, and Pimentel. I begin with Zimba because his public role is minor compared with the roles of Coleman and Pimentel. However, as previously noted, the professional worlds of Coleman and Zimba overlap.

JASON ZIMBA (AND COLEMAN INTERTWINED)

Aside from his SAP association in the July 2009 NGA press release, SAP cofounder Jason Zimba is also listed as "faculty member, physics, mathematics, and Center for the Advancement of Public Action, Bennington College."[8] In my April 2014 blog post examining the credentials and backgrounds of the original 24 work group members, I wrote the following regarding Zimba:

> Jason Zimba, another "lead writer" of the CCSS math, holds a bachelors and masters in mathematics and another masters plus a doctorate in physics. Zimba once taught physics and mathematics at Bennington College; however, he is no longer there, and the link to his vita is dead. According to Zimba's bio on the Student Achievement Partners (SAP) website (the company-gone-nonprofit that directed CCSS), Zimba has taught "disadvantaged high school students, and children of non-English speaking immigrants"; however, no details are provided regarding Zimba's having any specific K–12 classroom teaching experience.
>
> The *Baton Rouge Advocate* includes this very telling observation by Zimba regarding the suitability of CCSS math for "college readiness."
>
> > Jason Zimba, a professor of physics and math at Bennington College in Vermont and lead writer of the math standards, says they include "an awful lot of algebra before eighth grade," even though the first full course doesn't come until high school.
> >
> > But Zimba also acknowledges that ending with the Common Core in high school could preclude students from attending elite colleges. In many cases, the Core is not aligned with the expectations at the collegiate level. "If you want to take calculus your freshman year in college, you will need to take more mathematics than is in the Common Core," Zimba said. [9, 10]

It is very telling that CCSS is being promoted in the media as "superior," and a guarantee of college readiness, yet one of the "lead writers" of CCSS math admits that it has its problems and that it does not prepare students for elite college requirements. Despite his public admission of CCSS shortcomings, Zimba continues to sell CCSS.

In February 2013, American Enterprise Institute (AEI) scholar (his own chosen title) Frederick Hess interviewed Zimba regarding CCSS. Hess introduces Zimba as follows:

> You didn't think the ferment around Common Core could keep building? Hah! Prepare for several more years of increasing wackiness. In the middle of it all is

Jason Zimba, founding principal of Student Achievement Partners (SAP) and the man who is leading SAP after David Coleman went off to head up the College Board. SAP is a major player in Common Core implementation, especially with the aid of $18 million in support from the GE Foundation. Zimba was the lead writer on the Common Core mathematics standards. He earned his doctorate in mathematical physics from Berkeley, co-founded the Grow Network with Coleman, and previously taught physics and math at Bennington College. He's a private dude who lives up in New England and has not been part of the Beltway policy conversation.[11]

In the interview, Zimba names himself and two other individuals, Phil Daro and William McCallum, as the "the writing team" for CCSS math.[12]

Also in his February 2013 AEI interview, Zimba is credited as the leader of SAP since Coleman moved on to the College Board following CCSS completion in June 2010. (More to come on Coleman.) When Hess asks how Zimba came to be involved with CCSS, Zimba notes that the NGA "named" him to the writing team following being on the CCRS writing team for math (i.e., those missing CCRS in math "anchors").

The "writing team" is apparently the inner circle inside the inner circle—the few work group members who actually did the writing of CCSS. Recall that in a brief email exchange that I initiated, another mathematics professor implied that (s)he, too, was a major writer of CCSS for math.

Here is what Zimba offers as his justification for being in that inner circle of writers of the CCSS math standards:

At the time, I was a faculty member in physics and mathematics at Bennington College. But I'd had a lot of experience working with math standards prior to academia because I had co-founded an education technology company, and I'd never really stopped thinking about those issues. In 2008 I co-authored a paper with David Coleman about standards for the Carnegie Commission. But I didn't just want to write a position paper—I wanted to help address some of the problems we had identified.[13]

One note about the language of the 2008 Carnegie Commission paper to which Zimba alludes: That paper introduced the phrase "fewer, clearer, higher,"[14] which is now tied to CCSS.[15]

Zimba assumes that he is qualified to write standards for K–12 education because he has a history in education technology. He does not mention having any classroom experience or even being employed in any capacity in a K–12 public or private school system.

Given my background as a teaching practitioner, the break between Zimba's (and Coleman's) ideology about standards and how classrooms function is obvious. For example, in their 2008 Carnegie-commissioned paper on standards, Coleman and Zimba write the following:

> This [independent practice] focus need not be seen as multiplying a teacher's workload. If students spend more time during the school day independently creating work, teachers will have more time during the day to evaluate it. Teachers in other countries spend less time in front of the classroom, leaving more time for evaluating student work and collaborating with other teachers on lesson development and planning.[16]

What Zimba does not note is that teachers in other countries don't have more time by virtue of giving students independent work. They have more time because teachers in leading countries like Finland have fewer hours in classrooms during the school day so that they can better collaborate and prepare.[17] Coleman and Zimba also assume that all students will take the initiative to work independently, that none will resist, and that none will require teacher assistance. In addition, they assume that because students are "working independently," American teachers will have their time freed to collaborate and grade.

Coleman and Zimba have at best incidental K–12 classroom teaching experience from which to draw in America, let alone in other countries.

America is not like "other countries." Education systems are not easily divorced from the cultures in which they function. In America, I am required to be with my students during the time that they are assigned to my class. I am legally responsible for them. I cannot leave my room to go collaborate with others. If I have students, I am not allowed to use my class time to grade while they "work independently." Furthermore, my students are for the most part average American teenagers. They desire to socialize, and eat, and sleep. They do not enter my room asking if they might work. They want to sit by friends and talk; they want to listen to music and text. They are grade-conscious by degrees. Some will do as little as possible to pass. Others will work fast so that the assignment is done and they might socialize. Still others value the socializing above any threat of failing a class. And yet others will work for the intrinsic reward of doing well, but these are few. As their teacher, I must keep them on task and assist them when they need help. I often assign independent work, but I still help when assistance is needed. I often have to prod students to apply themselves before approaching me for help.

Thus, assigning "independent work" is still labor-intensive for me as an American public high school teacher. Zimba cannot know this classroom reality because his education "experience" is only theoretically based.

The absence of any documented, sustained K–12 classroom teaching career makes Zimba like scores of other edupreneurs. They form education companies and subsequently push to influence classroom procedure based upon their ideological position on what they see as proper classroom functioning.

Indeed, aside from his brief stint as a college faculty member at Bennington, Zimba is a man in the education business. He and David Coleman founded Grow Network in 2000.[18] And in stepped well-positioned education nonpractitioner, Chicago Public Schools CEO Arne Duncan. In 2002, Duncan awarded Grow Network a $2.2 million, noncompetitive contract (renewed in 2003 for $2.1 million) for "use of assessments, skills analyses, and professional development." The Grow Network provided test reports to teachers and administrators.[19] In short, Grow Network was a company specializing in test-driven reform.[20]

Long before CCSS, Jason Zimba and David Coleman had a test-driven business history with CCSS promoter Arne Duncan.

In January 2009, Duncan was confirmed as U.S. secretary of education;[21] in July 2009, he announced Race to the Top (RTTT), of which CCSS is a key component;[22] that same month and year, Coleman and Zimba became part of the NGA-publicized, 24-member CCRS work group.[23]

Back to Zimba's (and Coleman's) Grow Network:

In July 2004, Coleman (and Zimba) sold Grow Network to McGraw-Hill. From McGraw-Hill's press release on the acquisition:

NEW YORK, July 19 /PRNewswire-FirstCall/—McGraw-Hill Education, a division of The McGraw-Hill Companies, Inc. (NYSE: MHP) today announced the acquisition of Grow Network (Grow.net, Inc.), a privately held company that is a leading provider of assessment reporting and customized content for states and large school districts across the country. Terms of the acquisition were not disclosed.

. . . "Its unique and proven reporting services help educators respond thoughtfully to the increased accountability and Adequate Yearly Progress requirements associated with No Child Left Behind," said Harold McGraw III, chairman, president and chief executive officer of The McGraw-Hill Companies. . . .

Grow will become a unit of the School Education Group of McGraw-Hill Education and will be renamed Grow Network/McGraw-Hill. It will continue to be based in New York, and David Coleman, its chief executive officer, and his team will remain in place.[24]

Thus, Zimba and Coleman continued to work for Grow even after McGraw-Hill owned it. Assessment was big business, especially in this time of test-driven No Child Left Behind (NCLB).[25]

Zimba and Coleman remained with McGraw-Hill until they decided to form another education-styled business, SAP, in 2007. It seems that Coleman led the founding of SAP,[26] with Zimba tagging along. Here is how Zimba recounts the founding in his February 2013 AEI interview:

> [SAP is] a nonprofit organization dedicated to helping states and districts implement the [CCSS] standards. We work with teachers to develop implementation tools and offer them free on our website, www.achievethecore.org. I founded the organization (SAP) in 2007 with Sue Pimentel and David Coleman, so I've been involved from the start.[27]

A couple of points regarding Zimba's words: First, in discussing his role as a "founder with" Coleman and Pimentel, Zimba promotes the idea that all three are equals in this SAP venture. However, whereas Coleman is often referred to as the SAP "founder," when Zimba is referred to at all, he is referred to as "cofounder." (This is true even in the July 2009 NGA CCSS work group press release.)[28] Coleman is clearly the leader and he often refers to himself as "founder" with no mention of Zimba even as "cofounder."[29-33] This only underscores Coleman's more dominant role as CCSS spokesperson over Zimba—even after Coleman became president of the College Board and left Zimba as the supposed president of SAP.

A second point regarding Zimba's words on the founding of SAP concerns his referring to SAP as a "nonprofit." However, when SAP was founded, it was not a nonprofit. It was a company. In fact, SAP was not registered as a nonprofit until 2011.[34] That same year, SAP the nonprofit received $4 million from the GE Foundation.[35, 36] Changing from a profit to a nonprofit allows SAP to pay no taxes and allows its donors to claim tax exemption for their donations.

Third, notice that Zimba states that the role of SAP is dependent on there being a CCSS to "implement." SAP was involved in CCSS as an entity that was financially dependent on CCSS panning out, not only in the short term but also in the very long term. So long as CCSS exists, SAP can be there to "assist with implementation." Though CCSS are not considered by creators such as SAP as "national," the idea of convincing most states to adopt CCSS surely brings CCSS to national scale. Thus, SAP can draw in millions in nonprofit cash to promote ongoing, national-level CCSS implementation. As a result, SAP is in a fine position to steer the CCSS ship—to promote CCSS in the media, including endless potential CCSS classroom "innovations."

Finally, in his SAP origins statement to AEI, Zimba is creating a history in which Pimentel supposedly helped "found" SAP. Grafting her into SAP from its outset serves two key purposes for SAP's credibility in the public eye. Stay tuned.

For now, let us shift attention to SAP founder David Coleman.

DAVID COLEMAN, CCSS "ARCHITECT"

Below is Coleman's oft-presented bio:

> David Coleman is founder and CEO of Student Achievement Partners, LLC, an organization that assembles leading thinkers and researchers to design actions to substantially improve student achievement. Most recently, David and Jason Zimba of Student Achievement Partners played a lead role in developing the Common Core State Standards in math and literacy. David and Jason also founded the Grow Network—acquired by McGraw-Hill in 2005—with the mission of making assessment results truly useful to teachers, school leaders, parents, and students.
>
> David spent 5 years at McKinsey & Company, where his work focused on health care, financial institutions, and pro bono service to education. He is a Rhodes Scholar and a graduate of Yale University, Oxford University, and Cambridge University.[37]

The particulars on Coleman's postsecondary education are a haze. He offers no details regarding years attended at the institutions he names, and no comprehensive vita noting majors and degrees attained.

Coleman's mother, Elizabeth Coleman, was president of Bennington College (yes, the same institution where Zimba briefly belonged to the faculty). After 25 years as Bennington's president, Elizabeth Coleman retired in 2013.[38]

Coleman was in England on a Rhodes scholarship; he returned to New York and tried to land a high school teaching position despite his having no teaching certificate on file. It seems he just thought he would somehow qualify to teach without having attained the proper credential. Following his failed attempt to teach high school in New York, Coleman went to work for McKinsey and Company,[39] formed Grow Network with Zimba in 2000, sold Grow Network to McGraw-Hill in 2004, and stayed on with McGraw-Hill until 2007, at which time he founded SAP.

The rest is CCSS history.

Let us put the microscope to that history.

It is quite the coincidence that David Coleman decided to form a nebulously defined education company[40] the very same year that CCSSO decided in its annual education policy forum to focus on national standards—2007. (Even in 2014, the "mission" of SAP as noted on its tax forms remains nondescript: "assemble educators and researchers to design actions based on evidence that will substantially improve student achievement."[41]) As noted in the November 2007 minutes of the Illinois State Board of Education:

> Dr. Koch [Illinois superintendent of education] commented that the CCSSO conference reading material was all on National Standards, and they, as an organization, are trying to make changes voluntarily instead of being forced into changes by the (US) Department of Education.[42]

Now, this call to national standards presents some curious connections. David Coleman has a history tied to Arne Duncan, who was confirmed as U.S. secretary of education 14 months after the 2007 CCSSO annual meeting. Prior to his "deciding" to create SAP, Coleman was employed by McGraw-Hill and connected to NCLB state-level assessment assistance. McGraw-Hill has an established history of financially supporting the CCSSO annual policy forum.[43, 44] In November 2007, CCSSO promoted the idea of "state-led" national standards, arguably as a scare tactic to state superintendents. (*If you don't "volunteer," USDOE will force national standards on you.*) Finally, by summer 2008, then–CCSSO President Gene Wilhoit—accompanied by David Coleman—founder of a sparkling new company poised to write educational standards (SAP)—approached billionaire Bill Gates to fund the CCSS effort.

David Coleman might be more of a CCSS "architect" than he first appeared.

In May 2013, Coleman made the following statement at the Strategic Data Partners' "Beyond the Numbers Convening" conference in Boston:

> When I was involved in convincing governors and others around this country to adopt these standards, it was not "Obama likes them"; do you think that would have gone well with a Republican crowd?[45]

In winter 2009, approximately half of the states and U.S. territories had Republican governors.[46] It just so happens that in February 2009, the NGA voted to support a "common standards" effort.[47] On April 17, 2009, the NGA and CCSSO came together and formally committed to what is now called the Common Core State Standards Initiative. As for the "others" Coleman spoke of "convincing," they could have been any number of organizations that eventually garnered millions (billions?) in Gates funding toward promoting and "implementing" CCSS. (More on Gates's funding of CCSS in Chapter 9.)

It could have even meant "convincing" Coleman's longtime connection, Arne Duncan.

In 2007, Coleman started SAP arguably with an eye on writing national-level standards. He had been an inside presence in the CCSS process since CCSS' 2007 CCSSO inception. (Note: CCSS key player organization Achieve and its ADP were also represented at the 2007 CCSSO annual meeting *at least* via the presence of ADP creator, Education Trust's affiliated organization, the Data Quality Campaign [DQC].[48] I realize these connections can be difficult to follow, but Achieve is associated with Education Trust, which is associated with DQC, and all want CCSS.) Recall that Coleman also had a prior relationship with Arne Duncan, who needed to figure out what to do concerning the floundering NCLB. In April 2009—3 months after Duncan was confirmed as U.S. secretary of state and 3 months before the official USDOE RTTT announcement—the Broad Foundation convened a who's who in corporate reformers in order to advise states about the direction they should take with the American Recovery and Reinvestment Act's (ARRA) $100 billion (stimulus money) from the federal government:

> This paper lays out five big ideas for investing the one-time recovery funds that, if seized, will enable parents, educators, taxpayers, and students to see real educational results by 2012 and provide the base for more dramatic improvements in the future. If states and districts focus their funds on these ideas, we believe that it will be a down payment on excellence that lays the groundwork to produce breakthrough gains in what our students learn and achieve for the next generation.[49]

Whereas the advice in this report resembled NCLB for its test score–driven bent (e.g., closing and "turning around the poorest performing" schools and using "data" to evaluate teachers and "ensure timely dismissal" of teachers who didn't measure up), it also included a shiny new promise:

First, and most fundamental, by January 2012 Americans should expect to see a common core of fewer, clearer, higher, evidence-based, college- and career-ready standards adopted by at least 40 states representing the majority of the nation's students. These academic content standards, benchmarked internationally to the best in the world and linked to common, higher-quality assessments of student progress, will provide a foundation of clear goals and priorities to help teachers teach and students learn. The time for action is now. Our children deserve the chance to thrive in an increasingly interdependent world.[50] [Emphasis added]

There it is—the CCSS sales pitch[51] in the spring of 2009—the same month that the NGA and CCSSO met and the CCSS MOU appeared.

Coleman was a member of this Broad-sponsored group. So was Ellen Alberding of the Joyce Foundation (the Chicago foundation on the board of which Obama[52]—who also served as an advisor in relation to the Chicago education plan involving that $2.2 million contract to Coleman's Grow Network in 2002[53]—once sat); Byron Auguste and Michael Barber, both of former Coleman employer McKinsey and-Company (Barber was to become chief education advisor of Pearson[54]); Chester Finn of the Fordham Institute; Kate Walsh of the Fordham Institute–created National Council on Teacher Quality (NCTQ); Aimee Guidera of Ed Trust–associated DQC; and Lynn Olson, Stefanie Sanford, and Steve Seleznow, all of the Gates Foundation.[55]

It is hard to know which was the chicken and which was the egg: the April 2009 Broad report or the April 2009 NGA declaration of an official CCSS initiative. No matter which one came first, one issue is certain: David Coleman was connected to the action on both fronts. That much is evident in CCSSO's Wilhoit and Coleman approaching Gates to fund CCSS.[56] (An aside: Recall that after retiring from CCSSO in 2012,[57] Wilhoit went to work for SAP.[58] How about that?)

Instead of obvious federal funding (which the CCSS MOU introduced as the "appropriate" federal role), CCSS would have not-as-obvious Gates funding—not so obvious for years.

And so, CCSS did move forward, and Coleman was at its center. A man who has no background in classroom teaching and no background in writing educational standards is now the recognized "architect" of CCSS.

In 2011, Coleman spoke at the senior leadership meeting at the Institute of Learning at the University of Pittsburgh. Director Lauren Resnick introduced Coleman as follows:

Okay, so this is the kind of person we are going to be privileged to hear tonight. He has been involved in virtually every step of setting the national standards, and he doesn't have a single credential for it. He's never taught in an elementary school—I think. You know, I actually don't know. He's never edited a scholarly journal, but I think he has written scholarly papers. And a variety of other things that have, you know, everybody here has done some of, he hasn't done.[59]

Resnick then laughs.

Resnick had Coleman's publicized bio in her hand as she spoke, but she basically said that being a Rhodes scholar and attending Cambridge were nice but not relevant to standards writing.

In another amazing turn, Coleman agrees with Resnick and attests to his (and SAP's) utter lack of credentials for standards writing. However, he believes his lack of experience is irrelevant if he tells his audience that he "demanded evidence" for what others suggested be included in the standards. Nevertheless, these same standards are being peddled to the nation, and Coleman—admittedly unqualified—had been somehow powerfully positioned to direct this CCSS effort:

> *Student Achievement Partners, all you need to know about us are a couple things. One is we're composed of that collection of unqualified people who were involved in developing the common standards. And our only qualification was our attention to and command of the evidence behind them.* That is, it was our insistence in the standards process that it was not enough to say you wanted to or thought that kids should know these things, that you had to have evidence to support it, frankly because it was our conviction that the only way to get an eraser into the standards writing room was with evidence behind it, *'cause otherwise the way standards are written you get all the adults into the room about what kids should know, and the only way to end the meeting is to include everything. That's how we've gotten to the typical state standards we have today.*[60] [Emphasis added]

This, even though a member of the validation panel, Sandra Stotsky, never received relevant evidence even when she specifically requested it. The best evidence would have been to pilot test the final product, and to have done so before enticing states to sign a contractual agreement for standards that did not yet exist.

No matter for Coleman. Effective October 2012, he became president of the College Board—one of the few privileged organizations allowed to develop CCSS. In the *New York Times* article announcing his new position, Coleman is quoted as saying, "We have a crisis in education. . . ."[61]

Given that the likes of Coleman are time and again being placed in positions of power over the American classroom, I couldn't agree more.

SUSAN PIMENTEL

In addition to Coleman, Susan Pimentel has become a public face of CCSS. Below is the biographical tagline provided in the July 2009 NGA CCSS press release for Susan Pimentel:

> Sue Pimentel, Co-Founder, StandardsWork; English Language Arts Consultant, Achieve [62]

SAP was founded in 2007. Pimentel was scheduled to speak at an Arizona English Language Learners Task Force meeting on December 13, 2007. Even though Pimentel was unable to attend, the meeting minutes include her credentials:

> Ms. Pimentel is a nationally recognized educational analyst and standards consultant. She is a graduate of Cornell University and holds degrees in early childhood education and law. She was special counsel to the Maryland governor and has worked on education standards and other education issues with the following states: Oklahoma, Pennsylvania, South Carolina, North Carolina, Illinois, Arkansas, Wyoming, Missouri, Wisconsin, Delaware, Arizona, California, Ohio, and Maryland. *Ms. Pimentel is involved in several national efforts, including the American Diploma Project.* The Fordham Foundation recently rated states in which Ms. Pimentel has coordinated the development of standards as having among the best content standards. *As a result of her efforts working with the state of Maryland, the state raised its ranking from 43rd to 10th in 2000.* Ms. Pimentel is co-author of *Raising the Standard: an Eight-Step Action Guide for Schools and Communities.* In October 2007, U.S. Secretary of Education Margaret Spellings announced the appointment of Ms. Pimentel to the National Assessment Governing Board for a 4-year term.[63] [Emphasis added]

This biographical sketch does include some noteworthy information. First of all, Pimentel holds degrees in law and early childhood. However, there is no clear connection between her degrees and her establishing a career advising on education standards. Her law degree sounds impressive, and her early childhood education degree lends the illusion that Pimentel is suited to working in education. Absent from this bio is any hint that Pimentel darkened the doorways of a classroom in any capacity, so a classroom teaching career could not have provided Pimentel entrance into the world of education standards writing.

More details regarding Pimentel's legislative connections come in association with the company she says she cofounded, StandardsWork.

Here is Pimentel's archived bio sketch, dated November 25, 2010, from the StandardsWork website:

> Susan Pimentel, co-founder of StandardsWork®, specializes in standards-driven school reform and works as an education writer, analyst, and consultant. After earning a bachelor of science in early childhood education and a law degree from Cornell University, *Pimentel worked in the Maryland state legislature. She served as senior policy advisor for Maryland Governor William Donald Schaefer, and then as special counsel to former Superintendent John Murphy in Prince George's County, MD, the nation's sixteenth largest school district.* Her efforts resulted in the phase-out of student tracking, an enriched core curricula, advances in school-site management, *and a results-based school accountability program.* Subsequently, she was director of the World Class Schools Panel (impaneled to sculpt *a concrete plan of action for school transformation)* in Charlotte-Mecklenburg, NC.
>
> *In recent years, her work has focused on academic standards with corresponding work in principal evaluation, student assessment, and school accountability.* Her efforts stress standards-setting, constituency building, policy analysis and strategic planning in such varied jurisdictions as Beaufort, SC; Chicago, IL; Red Clay, DE; Jackson, TN, Ardmore, OK, Elaine and Marvell, AR; and the states of Arizona, California, Georgia, Maryland and Pennsylvania. She has also worked with individual charter schools in Massachusetts. Pimentel is co-author with Denis P. Doyle of the best-selling book and CD-ROM, *Raising the Standard: An Eight Step Action Guide For Schools and Communities.*
>
> In October 2007, Ms. Pimentel was appointed to the National Assessment Governing Board (NAGB).[64] [Emphasis added]

Pimentel was connected to the Maryland state legislature and state governor and worked for "results-based school accountability" and "school transformation" during the test-driven years of NCLB.

Her StandardsWork bio reports the same information as above, and also the following,[65] dated June 14, 2014:

> In addition to Co-founding StandardsWork, Susan Pimentel is the lead writer for the English Language Arts and Literacy Standards for the Common Core State Standards Initiative, Co-founder of Student Achievement Partners and Vice-Chair of the National Assessment Governing Board.[66]

History has been changed. "The lead writer" for the CCSS ELA, Pimentel has been grafted in as a cofounder of SAP.

Back to the noteworthy information gleaned from Pimentel's Arizona meeting bio. At some point, Pimentel became associated with Achieve and ADP. Achieve's tax forms for the years 2006–2009 and 2011 indicate that Pimentel was paid for "consulting." The 2008 and 2009 Achieve tax documents identify Pimentel as "Susan Pimentel, Inc."[67] She is also credited with improvements in Maryland's state standards, which were graded in 2000 by the Fordham Foundation/Institute. The Arizona meeting minutes note that Pimentel was instrumental in raising Maryland's standing in the Fordham Foundation/ Institute's ranking of state standards "from 43rd to 10th in 2000."[68] The problem with giving Pimentel such credit is that Fordham Institute/Foundation evaluated Maryland's English standards for the first time in 2000. There was nothing to "raise" them from.[69]

Pimentel is also credited with her work on standards as receiving high marks from standards-grading Fordham Foundation/Institute. However, of the 14 states named in the 2007 Arizona meeting minutes, in Fordham's report *The State of State Standards—and the Common Core—in 2010*, it rated the ELA standards in 11 of those 14 states as "clearly inferior" to CCSS ELA—which itself did not receive an "A"rating.[70]

One of those "clearly inferior" states was Maryland.

Apparently, Maryland and ten other Pimentel-assisted states were not as impressive on paper in 2010 as in 2007.

Perhaps this induced Pimentel to purge her state standards-writing history from her 2014 StandardsWork bio revision.

Her glowing 2011 National Assessment Governing Board (NAGB) reappointment (by Arne Duncan) bio sketch also includes no mention of cofounding SAP. The NAGB announcement does note that Pimentel now holds the title "curriculum specialist" (so hard to separate standards tied to tests from the curriculum that provides the connecting tissue) and is lauded for her work "to advance education reform and champion tools for increasing academic rigor." Pimentel is also identified as ADP's "principal architect."[71]

From Achieve "consultant" to ADP "principal architect" to CCSS ELA "lead writer."

Like her fellow CCSS ELA "lead writers" Coleman and Zimba, Pimentel has been positioned to implement education policy without any firsthand practitioner knowledge of the millions of classrooms she is influencing.

It is easier to advocate for an inflexible set of standards tied to high-stakes assessments if one will not know firsthand the damage such advocacy can and will produce on students, teachers, the teaching profession, schools, and communities.

Pimentel is like Coleman and Zimba in her complete inability to ground her promotions in her own teacher practitioner experience. However, there are key ways in which Pimentel differs from these true SAP cofounders: By the time CCSS was released in 2010, Pimentel had been "doing" standards for 25 years.[72] SAP sure could use that street cred. Also, the test-driven "reform" movement was obviously (White) male dominated, and teaching is primarily a female profession.

Time for a female face for SAP.

Enter Pimentel. Teachers would trust her because she is a pleasant personality and a woman speaking publicly to audiences comprised of mostly women. Teachers would see Pimentel and forget that she is not a teacher; they would identify with her because she is a woman.

Image is important in selling "voluntary" CCSS. Current classroom teachers were not in the decisionmaking positions in the CCSS venture. SAP—an organization that by 2014 existed almost exclusively to promote CCSS[73]—was thinking strategically years before, back in 2011.

And so, like Coleman, Pimentel speaks at venues nationwide promoting CCSS. It was in her 2013 NBC "Education Nation" speech that I noticed discrepancies between the July and November 2009 NGA press releases regarding the timing of the CCRS and CCSS work groups and actual CCSS development.

In order to be clear on Pimentel's CCSS timeline discrepancies, allow me to repeat some of my previous writing on the issue. According to the CCSS MOU, CCRS (the CCSS "anchor" standards) were supposed to be completed by July 2009. However, the group appointed to develop CCRS was not announced until July 1, 2009. So, the CCRS could not be finished by July. It is possible that the CCRS work groups were appointed prior to this press release[74] because NGA did not want these work group names to be made public in the first place. (See Chapter 5 on the CCSS MOU.) Indeed, the NGA did not announce the CCRS as being available for public comment until September 21, 2009.[75] Not that the public knew about the CCSS push in 2009. Many did not even know about CCSS several years later.

Public comment and feedback supposedly happened for CCRS in late September and October 2009.[76] According to the September 2009 NGA press release inviting comments, CCRS was supposed to be in place prior to "tak[ing] in the real work" of CCSS development,"[77] which meant the writing of the actual CCSS.

The CCRS were supposed to be the "anchors" for CCSS. Thus, they were to be completed before undertaking CCSS development.

Not so.

According to Pimentel in her 2013 Education Nation speech, CCSS writing began in September 2009—overlapping both CCRS completion *and* the official appointment of the second, "expanded" work group:

> This was September 2009, right? They told us that we had to have a draft ready by November 2009. So, I don't know if any of you have written standards before, but that's fast, and to give it to the nation, right? Well, so we did. . . .[78]

I'm assuming "they" were the NGA and CCSSO, the two organizations that legally "own" CCSS. (More to come on the CCSS copyright in Chapter 8.) As for the "we," Pimentel alludes to six principal writers, three for ELA and three for math. For ELA, Pimentel was listed on the November 2009 NGA press release as the ELA "lead" writer; Coleman is also widely recognized as a principal writer of CCSS ELA. The third ELA "lead" writer is unidentified.

Pimentel admitted that the first draft of CCSS had been written *by* November 2009—the time that this first, 24-member NGA CCRS ELA and math work group remained the "official" group—and too soon for the CCRS to be vetted and finalized in order to inform CCSS development.

By Pimentel's own admission, CCSS development was rushed. And based on the conflicting information offered in "official" NGA press releases, it is obvious that CCRS and CCSS development was little more than a hurried push to *get this thing finished.*

Pimentel describes the first, November 2009, draft of CCSS as "a flop."[79]

Meanwhile, even though CCRS ELA was completed, CCRS math disappeared. (The CCSS website includes ELA "anchors;[80] however, no similar "anchors" exist for CCSS math.)[81]

A second CCSS draft was developed and made available for (under-advertised) public comment in March 2010.[82]

It seems that in its announcements, the NGA and CCSSO failed to mention the as-yet-undeveloped, high-stakes assessments meant to accompany CCSS. They glorified CCSS without a word that CCSS was created as part of test-driven "reform." (In 2013, CCSS ELA work group member Laura McGiffert Slover of Achieve became CEO of CCSS testing consortium PARCC.)[83]

No matter. This train was moving forward. States had "voluntarily" signed on.

In June 2010, NGA and CCSSO released the official report of validation committee approval of CCSS.[84]

And with that, SAP—an organization created by two well-connected edupreneurs for the original, nebulous purpose of "assembling educators and researchers"[85]—now had a clear purpose: to promote CCSS.

Add a female face, and *voilà!* The SAP image is complete:

> *Student Achievement Partners was founded by David Coleman, Susan Pimentel and Jason Zimba, lead writers of the Common Core State Standards. We are a nonprofit organization* with one purpose: to help all students and teachers see their hard work lead to greater student achievement.
>
> *As educators, as researchers, and as citizens, we view the changes brought by the college and career readiness focus of the Common Core State Standards as a once-in-a-generation opportunity for kids of all backgrounds and ability levels to better fulfill their potential.* Like the standards themselves, we are evidence-based in our approach. *Our work is aimed at ensuring that teachers across the country are able to put the standards to work,* quickly and effectively, to help their students and colleagues aspire to a higher standard and reach it. Accordingly, the content available on this site is assembled by and for educators and is freely available to everyone to use, modify and share.
>
> We invite educators and people curious about the Common Core State Standards to explore what the site has to offer, including hundreds of math and literacy resources for teachers, resources for leaders who are putting college and career readiness standards into action in their own schools, and opportunities to become an advocate for the Common Core.[86] [Emphasis added]

Even though SAP is no longer officially registered as a business, make no mistake: Coleman, Zimba, and Pimentel are indeed in the business of education reform. And for them—three individuals whose careers are untouched by test-driven-reform consequences—business is *good.*

CHAPTER 7

America, "Stay the Course" (Don't Remove That Noose)

The Common Core Surveys

Selling the idea of the Common Core State Standards (CCSS) involves more than enlisting governors and state superintendents to agree to be state-led and having a billionaire and the federal government agree to finance the development of the CCSS and its assessments, respectively. And it involves more than National Governors Association (NGA) press releases and Achieve reports. The CCSS memorandum of understanding (MOU) includes a section that enlists committed investment from national organizations in order to solidify public relations for the CCSS campaign:

> **National Policy Forum.** NGA and CCSSO will convene a National Policy Forum (Forum) comprised of signatory national organizations (e.g., the Alliance for Excellent Education, Business Roundtable, National School Boards Association, Council of Great City Schools, Hunt Institute, National Association of State Boards of Education, National Education Association, and others) to share ideas, gather input, and inform the common core initiative. The forum is intended as a place for refining our shared understanding of the scope and elements of a common core; sharing and coordinating the various forms of implementation of a common core; *providing a means to develop common core messaging between and among participating organizations; and building public will and support.*[1] [Emphasis added]

The CCSS "initiative" was not "initiated" by either education practitioners or by public demand. Thus, it should come as no surprise that for years following the June 2010 NGA announcement of CCSS completion, the "initiative" was relatively unknown. (Achieve released a report on a poll it conducted in August 2011 and actually entitled it *Strong Support, Low Awareness.*[2] How the public supports an issue "strongly" unaware presents an interesting quandary.)

The year 2013 appears to have been *the* year for organizations utilizing survey research in order to fulfill the CCSS MOU call to "build public will and support." An indispensable component of the "building" of public will involves "confirming" that teachers and administrators support CCSS. In other words, if those utilizing CCSS approve, then certainly the public will be put at ease and will approve as well—undeniably a fantastic marketing ploy.

The public sell of CCSS is crucial for assuring The Core a fixed position in American public education. And what better way to advance the sale of CCSS than by broadcasting the supposed pro-CCSS results of surveys sponsored by national-level, education-related organizations?

Survey results are easy to manipulate. One can restrict the participant pool, use a nonrepresentative sample, bias question wording, limit item response choices, merge response categories, report incomplete results, emphasize some results at the expense of others, manipulate reporting graphics, or withhold the actual survey instrument from public view. The possibilities are numerous for an organization with a settled agenda to use survey results to advance that agenda. And so it goes with national organizations that support CCSS and that just happen to have conducted survey research on the matter.

In 2013, I examined five surveys purporting to offer proof that either teachers or administrators favor CCSS. These five surveys were produced by the American Federation of Teachers (AFT), the National Education Association (NEA), the Gates Foundation/Scholastic, Stand for Children Louisiana, and the National Association of Elementary School Principals (NAESP). In this chapter, I will briefly report my findings, which led me to the ultimate conclusion that teacher and administrator "support" for CCSS in survey research is overrated at best and fabricated at worst.

This chapter on slanted pro-CCSS surveys includes no excerpts from either the actual surveys or survey result reports. I realize that offering visuals would have aided in readers' understanding the problems I describe regarding survey construction and reporting. However, it is difficult to approach the creators of such surveys and ask permission to include excerpts in a chapter designed to drill holes in their pro-CCSS survey credibility. What I do offer is citation information for each of the five surveys examined in this chapter. Using such information, readers might view firsthand the surveys and associated reports as I saw them myself.

And now, for the five surveys purporting to demonstrate either teacher or administrator support for CCSS in 2013, beginning with the AFT survey.

AMERICAN FEDERATION OF TEACHERS (AFT)/HART CCSS SURVEY

In March/April 2013, Hart Research Associates conducted a poll of AFT members regarding opinions about CCSS, which has been declared "the solution" and "what kids need to learn." A finding publicized by AFT President Randi Weingarten is that "75% of AFT teachers polled support CCSS."[3] Much of my discussion on the AFT/Hart CCSS survey is taken directly from two blog posts I wrote in May 2013.[4] As teachers and public opinion have become more acquainted with CCSS, Weingarten is saying that standards can't be a straitjacket and need to be decoupled from tests.[5]

Opinion polling is a tricky business. Care needs to be taken in obtaining a representative sample. Gallup is an established name in opinion polls, and one of the standards used by Gallup is the *stratified random sample*.[6] A stratum is a subgroup; the random sampling happens within the defined subgroup. CCSS is a nationally promoted education agenda. However, it is adopted on the state level. There is no uniform, national protocol for adopting CCSS—a critical issue in the years of transition as states decide how to approach ultimate implementation. Thus, using the state as the unit of adoption of CCSS, some number of the 45 states (and DC) adopting CCSS should have comprised the strata used in the AFT poll. Yet Hart admits that 36% of the sample respondents were from a single state: New York.[7] That's 288 out of 800 individuals surveyed.

When the public hears Weingarten state that "75% of AFT teachers surveyed support CCSS," they do not get to hear that "over one-third of survey respondents live in New York State." The fact that CCSS had been differentially implemented in New York—and that Hart knew as much—lends support for the argument for survey stratification by state.

And here is another important sampling query: How many of those New York teachers are English language arts (ELA) and math teachers, those closest to CCSS?

In reporting that "75% teacher approval" of CCSS, AFT crossed a line in deceptive reporting in its use of a PowerPoint presentation that supposedly showed the AFT/Hart survey results. One slide in particular has the heading "Teachers Overwhelmingly Approve of the Common Core State Standards." AFT/Hart printed only the number "75%" above the approval bar and the general statement, "approve" beneath, and "22%" above the disapproval bar and the general statement "disapprove" beneath. Here is what the public does not get to know from the AFT/Hart presentation: The "overwhelming approval" is actually chiefly comprised of teachers who are "somewhat approving" of CCSS. In fact, the largest subcategory selected for the question, "Based on what you know about these standards and the expectations they set for children, do you strongly approve, somewhat approve, somewhat disapprove, or strongly disapprove of your state's decision to adopt the Common Core State Standards?" is "somewhat approve." In merging two categories (the larger "somewhat approve" with the notably smaller "strongly approve"), AFT/Hart manipulated the reporting of the less-than-impressive survey outcome.

The collapsing of categories is problematic in itself. It draws readers' attention away from the detail gleaned from the exact question. The slide proclaims that "75% of teachers approve of CCSS." AFT President Randi Weingarten openly promotes this shaped statistic [8]—which means the message that 75% of teachers approve of CCSS becomes uncritically accepted via popular media,[9, 10] and the public accepts the idea that teachers "overwhelmingly support CCSS" as the truth.

And the statistical shaping does not stop with AFT.

NATIONAL EDUCATION ASSOCIATION (NEA) CCSS SURVEY

Here we go again with the CCSS support propaganda from an organization that has accepted millions from Bill Gates to promote the Common Core State Standards (CCSS) (see Chapter 9). Much of the detail in this section comes from a blog post I wrote in September 2013 on the issue.[11]

The National Education Association conducted a survey in September 2013. AFT accepted Gates money for promoting the CCSS; so did NEA.[12] NEA now has its own survey in which it reports that its members "strongly support" CCSS.[13]

> According to a new poll by the National Education Association, the Common Core State Standards are strongly supported by its members. Roughly two-thirds of educators are either *wholeheartedly in favor of the standards (26%) or support them with "some reservations" (50 %)*.[14] [Emphasis added]

Don't miss this because this would have been the honest way to report: Strong support is *not* merely 26% "wholeheartedly in favor."

Half of NEA members surveyed expressed reservations regarding CCSS. Thus, the NEA survey result reflects only modest support. Furthermore, a notable 13% of their 1,200 members (teachers?) surveyed offered no opinion.

Both national teachers' unions accepted millions in "philanthropic" money toward implementing CCSS, and both just happened to produce surveys that were deceptively CCSS-favoring and have the fashioned result of "strong" teacher support.

In reality, both surveys yielded a similar result, with most teachers supporting CCSS "somewhat" or "with reservations"—hardly the spectacular foundation for "building public will and support" as expected in the CCSS MOU.

STAND FOR CHILDREN (SFC) LOUISIANA CCSS SURVEY

Stand for Children (SFC) is a well-financed national organization known for inserting itself into local and state elections in order to support candidates who are friendly to corporate reform. SFC founder Jonah Edelman actually bragged publicly about his work in attempting to cripple the Chicago Teachers Union. SFC is anti-union. It wishes to strip classroom teachers of their bargaining rights. As education historian Diane Ravitch writes:

> No one knows for sure when Stand for Children abandoned its original mission of advocating for public schools and seeking more equitable funding.
>
> But by 2011, Stand for Children had become a handmaiden of the hedge fund managers and super-rich, promoting their agenda of privatization. Its founder, Jonah Edelman, boasted at the Aspen Ideas Festival[15] of how he had outsmarted the teachers' unions and had bought up the best lobbyists.[16] He worked with like-minded legislators in Illinois to pass legislation to take away teachers' job protections. The legislation said that the Chicago Teachers Union would need a 75% approval to strike, and Edelman was certain this would never happen.
>
> He sat side by side with an equity investor from Chicago as he boasted of his triumph in crushing the teachers of Illinois, especially those in Chicago.
>
> It cost millions to achieve this "victory," and he had no trouble raising the millions.
>
> Stand for Children, with no roots in Massachusetts, went there to bully the teachers' union with the threat of a ballot initiative to strip them of hard-won rights, so the union conceded to avoid an expensive election battle.
>
> Flush with cash from equity investors, Stand is now operating in many states. It still pretends to be "for the children," but it uses its money to attack their teachers. It still pretends to be a supporter of better education, but cannot explain how to get better education if teachers are treated as at-will employees, lacking any academic freedom or collective voice.

Many of its former supporters now refer to Stand for Children with a different name: They call it Stand On Children.[17]

Since 2005, SFC has taken over $10 million in Gates money.[18] Gates money to SFC includes $750,772 in November 2013 "to support public understanding and successful implementation of college and career ready standards in states."[19] Also, just over $1 million is specifically earmarked for Louisiana in 2013 for "support[ing] a cohort of school district superintendents to advocate for . . . results in Louisiana public schools"[20] and "organiz[ing] supportive parents and teachers in Jefferson Parish, Louisiana, to implement reforms. . . ."[21]

Regarding its CCSS survey, SFC did not release a comprehensive survey result, only a report of select survey findings[22]—findings that were solicited from SFC-Gates-targeted Jefferson Parish.[23] In this age of computer ease, there is no (honest) reason for SFC to withhold the comprehensive survey result by not linking to it as part of its online report. The report did include a link to the Louisiana Department of Education (LDOE) website for additional information on CCSS.

SFC is an outspoken supporter of CCSS.[24-26] Therefore, it should come as no surprise that a CCSS survey sponsored by SFC reports "favorable" results. In publicizing such so-called results, consider what the SFC press release actually reports:

Stand for Children Louisiana released a new report this week proving that implementation of Louisiana's Common Core State Standards is well underway *and that teachers overwhelmingly feel prepared to teach the higher standards.*

Over 90% of respondents felt like they had some or comprehensive knowledge of the Common Core.

Ninety-three percent of teachers reported that they *had already incorporated the standards into their instruction to some degree.*

Over 70% of respondents believe that the Common Core State Standards *are more demanding and raise expectations* for students and teachers.[27] [Emphasis added]

Notice the jump in logic from "overwhelmingly feel prepared to teach" and the evidence that "over 90% of respondents felt like they had some or comprehensive knowledge of the Common Core." (Lumping "some" and "comprehensive" together is a convenient means of not disclosing exact percentages while allowing for the word *comprehensive* to be associated with the only number reported: 90%.)

In SFC language, "some or comprehensive knowledge" of CCSS must equal "overwhelmingly feel prepared."

Not hardly.

The fact that many teachers are using CCSS is a no-brainer: Teachers were required to do so as per the CCSS MOU signed by Governor Bobby Jindal and former state superintendent Paul Pastorek in May 2009, a year before CCSS even existed[28] (see Chapter 5). As for respondents "feeling like they have some knowledge of CCSS": This, too, is a no-brainer. In fact, State Superintendent John White moved full implementation of CCSS ahead by a year—from 2014–2015 to 2013–2014—to the shock of districts statewide. Louisiana teachers knew about CCSS by the time SFC Louisiana was conducting its survey (August 2013[29]) because they were blindsided by full implementation a year ahead of schedule. By the time SFC released its survey in December 2013, all Louisiana school districts were required to incorporate CCSS into their classrooms and had done so for a semester.

As for "70% of respondents" believing that CCSS is "more demanding and raises expectations": This is not necessarily a positive finding. I can be "more demanding and raise expectations" in a moment with my students. If I do so without carefully (and expertly) considering what constitutes a reasonable demand, I can damage them.

What SFC offers to readers as its online "survey results" is nothing more than a colorful brochure of incompletely reported survey information. For example, SFC offers "examples of survey questions" without providing the complete question, including all possible answer choices. Complete survey information is important to report, as responses can be shaped by the answer choices. If the public does not get to see the limited answer choices, then the public might assume that respondents arrived at these answers without any leading that might support an organization's agenda.

Recall that it is easy to shape a preferred outcome using structured survey responses.

Another graph has the heading "The CCSS benefit most students because they will/are. . . ." The problem here is with the item wording. CCSS has not been billed to "benefit most students." It has been promoted as benefiting *all* students.[30] However, one is less likely to get teachers to respond positively to an absolute than to a more realistic nonabsolute.

Never mind that the CCSS website promotes the absolute.[31]

In the explanation accompanying this "benefit most students" graphic, one can read more information regarding SFC's prior declaration of teacher support for "the standards themselves":

In other words, there is support among teachers for the standards themselves but concern about how students will respond to the standards. About one quarter of teachers surveyed are also worried that the standards will not "fit" for students who are behind grade level or otherwise have different educational needs. Despite this, over 78% of teachers believe that their understanding of effective practices to teach the CCSS will help them to differentiate instruction for students based on students' needs.[32]

Frankly, "differentiating instruction" will not matter if the repeatedly stated intention of ultimately preserving the connection between CCSS and assessments is retained (see Chapters 5 and 10). No matter how many years such a connection might be "delayed," in the end, both teacher and student will be graded by the CCSS assessments if U.S. Secretary of Education Arne Duncan, the National Governors Association, and billionaire Bill Gates have their way completely regarding CCSS "utility."

In sum, the SFC CCSS survey has accomplished what SFC intended: It provided a vehicle for publicly proclaiming that teachers regard CCSS positively. SFC presented its "findings" in an attractive, illustrated online brochure that lacks clarity (and researcher integrity) on a number of fronts but will likely be absorbed as unquestioned truth by an unassuming public. For more detail on the SFC survey instability and small sample, see my blog post of December 5, 2013, entitled, "Stand for Children Louisiana: Teachers 'Like' Common Core."[33]

GATES/SCHOLASTIC CCSS SURVEY "EARLY RELEASE"

No research purporting teacher support for CCSS would be complete without a survey sponsored by the Gates Foundation. In order to promote the image of CCSS as being embraced by teachers, Gates partnered with Scholastic to produce the 2013 version of the Gates education survey, Primary Sources. Even though the survey wasn't yet ready for release, Gates/Scholastic decided in October 2013 to publish an "early release,"[34] a report based on the part of the survey that focused on teachers' views of CCSS.[35] The information in this section on the Gates/Scholastic survey is primarily cited directly from my October 2013 blog post on the issue.[36]

Of course, the Gates/Scholastic survey's early release presents positive results: Teachers support CCSS. Never mind that Gates's partner in this survey project, Scholastic, has taken $4.5 million from Gates to "support teachers' implementation of the Common Core State Standards in mathematics."[37] If CCSS goes bust, Scholastic loses money.

In releasing a partial survey result, Gates is clearly attempting to rally support for CCSS. Indeed, it sure does sound good to say, *We surveyed 20,000 teachers nationwide, and they know about and want CCSS.*

I do not normally write reviews based on partial survey results. Releasing a partial result bespeaks an agenda to speedily influence an issue. I prefer to examine the entire result and then write. Nevertheless, because I know via his astounding CCSS financial support that Gates wants to sway public opinion in favor of CCSS (see Chapter 9), in October 2013, I offered the following observations to assist readers of my blog in critically digesting this slice of Gates-CCSS propaganda. My commentary refers to the 15-page report released by Gates and Scholastic on October 4, 2013.[38]

Concern One: Category Collapsing

On page 2 of the report, Gates and Scholastic note that "teachers are enthusiastic about implementation." However, if one considers the more detailed result presented on page 7, one sees that the "strongly agree" category is small (26% for teachers overall). The largest category is "somewhat agree"—an issue I wrote about previously in this chapter concerning the results of both the AFT CCSS survey[39] and the NEA CCSS survey.[40]

Teachers do not "enthusiastically support" CCSS. Most have reservations.

Concern Two: Question Wording

On page 5 of the report, the problem is with the question:

> Do you think the CCSS will be positive *for most students*, will they not make much of a difference *for most students*, or will they be negative *for most students*?[41] [Emphasis added]

This reducing CCSS suitability from that of the widely promoted "all students" to "most students" is a ploy also used in the SFC CCSS survey. It seems that we are now "leaving children behind." Recall that the broadcasted CCSS goal was to make *all* students college and career ready.[42] Substituting the word *most* in place of the CCSS-promoter-declared *all* is a public admission that CCSS is not suited for all students.

In addition, teachers are a lot less likely to answer positively to this question if they are asked about "all students" as opposed to "most."

As it is, with the term *most* as a qualifier, just over half (57%) of teachers responded that CCSS would be positive for "most" students. I wonder how many teachers who answered positively envisioned certain students falling through the CCSS cracks.

Concern Three: Unclear Question and Limited Response Choice

Another issue concerns the limited response choices. Some questions include the choice "somewhat." However, other questions omit the "somewhat" category. This omission means that a respondent who does not wish to choose the neutral category—"neither negative nor positive" in place of a "somewhat positive" option —can feel forced to choose "positive"—even if the respondent has some reservations. Certainly, a forced choice question might be used to shape a survey outcome.

Concern Four: Selling Curriculum and Assessment

One final observation, from page 9 of the report. Here is the opening statement:

> Seventy-four percent (74%) of teachers in Common Core states say implementation will require them to make changes in their teaching practice.[43]

The end of the page reads like a sales pitch for CCSS materials. Given that CCSS implementation "requires" them to "make changes," teachers need more time to find materials and plan lessons. Teachers need professional development. Enter Scholastic and other education companies. CCSS curricula are fast becoming big business.

So are CCSS assessments. The statement above from page 9 of the report notes that 74% of teachers report that they will be "required" to change their teaching practice. No mention about pressure to teach to the CCSS tests. This looming issue certainly does "change teaching practice"—for the worse.

The CCSS owners, NGA and CCSSO, realized that CCSS acceptance would require a nationwide public relations campaign. One sure way to convince the public of CCSS goodness is to broadcast that "teachers approve." Whether or not such is true can easily become lost in the frequency of the broadcast.

NATIONAL ASSOCIATION OF ELEMENTARY SCHOOL PRINCIPALS (NAESP) CCSS SURVEY(S)

Now that the two national teachers' unions, SFC, and Gates himself have created the hologram of teacher support for CCSS, it is time to publicize the idea that administrators are also enthusiastic about The Core. In December 2013, I received an email from the National Association of Elementary School Principals (NAESP) proclaiming that (you guessed it) "principals overwhelmingly support the CCSS initiative."[44] NAESP apparently discovered as much in the course of two surveys. In December 2013, I wrote a blog post about the NAESP survey(s); in this section, I draw from that posting.[45]

According to the NAESP email press release, the NAESP surveys show:

> Principals *overwhelmingly support the CCSS initiative* and have a strong willingness to continue to engage deeply in instructional leadership activities as states move forward with the new standards.
>
> Overall, the NAESP surveys show that the majority of the nation's elementary and middle-level principals strongly agree that CCSS will provide more meaningful assessments of student learning, increase students' skill mastery across subjects, and provide a curriculum frame leading to deeper understanding of conceptual thinking. Most principals in the states surveyed are familiar with the standards and the curricular changes that must accompany them, and most had received some level of professional development to lead teachers, families, and students through the transition to the new standards.[46] [Emphasis added]

The two surveys are actually a single survey of 1,100 principals in which a subset of 463 urban principals' responses are also reported separately.[47,48]

Note which organizations were involved with this survey "collaboration":

> NAESP conducted the Leadership for the Common Core survey in collaboration with an advisory committee composed of *representatives from the NGA, CCSSO,* American Association of School Administrators, National Association of Secondary School Principals, Teachers College at Columbia University, and the Wallace Foundation.[49] [Emphasis added]

The two CCSS copyright holders were involved with this NAESP survey. This is problematic for their vested interest in CCSS proliferation.

On to the survey content.

The first diagram (on page 4 of the included survey draft[50]) emphasizes that principals have made CCSS "a priority."[51] Of course they have. They are required to do so by law if their state boards and/or legislatures have adopted CCSS. Stating the obvious also serves another purpose: to solidify in the public mind that CCSS is here to stay and to dissuade those in power who might have second thoughts about CCSS to "stay the course."

The heart of the sell is found on page 9 of the full survey: "Principal Relative Agreement with Statements of Common Core Goals."[52] Percentages of principal "agreement" are reported for five statements regarding what CCSS will accomplish:

Provide a curricular framework for deeper learning.
Increase students' skill mastery.
Provide for more meaningful assessments.
Ensure student expectations are the same across the United States.
Raise United States student international test scores.[53]

The NAESP press release leads readers to believe that "strongly agree" was selected by "the majority of principals" for the first three statements listed above. Not true. The reported "strongly agree" percentages for each of the five statements above are 38%, 27%, 20%, 34% and 14%, respectively.[54]

Actually, "majority" means at least 51%.

The corresponding "strongly agree" percentages for the subset of 463 urban principals are 41%, 28%, 22%, 36%, and 16%.[55] (Note: Both statement wording and reporting order differ for the urban principals survey but are aligned in statement list reported here.)

Only 14% of the 1,100 principals and 16% of the urban principal subset "strongly agree" that CCSS will raise those reformer-coveted international test scores.

The real deception in this NAESP survey involves the choices principals were offered (and not offered) in registering their opinions regarding CCSS utility. The NAESP survey offers no "somewhat agree" choice.

The categories are reported at the bottom of page 9 (of the included survey draft):

Strongly disagree
Somewhat disagree
Agree
Strongly agree.[56]

Here is how the category set should have appeared:

Strongly disagree
Somewhat disagree
Somewhat agree
Strongly agree

If those conducting the survey really wanted to know what principals think about CCSS, this would have been an even better set of possible responses:

Strongly disagree
Somewhat disagree
Neither agree nor disagree
Somewhat agree
Strongly agree

As it stands, the NAESP survey has shaped the outcome by limiting the choices it offered to the principals taking the survey.

Though a neutral category would have been useful, the major issue is that principals had no option to "somewhat agree." This shaping of the survey outcome by omitting a "somewhat agree" category renders the "agree" category useless.

It is possible that the principals were given the "somewhat agree" option and that the term *somewhat* was removed from the survey report. Either way, the survey result is biased toward "agreement," and what is absent is any discussion of the reservation inherent in respondents' choosing "somewhat agree."

Given its overt category shaping, the NAESP survey is arguably a propaganda tool intended to influence public opinion in favor of CCSS.

CCSS: SIGNED, SEALED, AND DELIVERED

The CCSS MOU outlined the process for CCSS from start to finish—including its need for a public relations campaign undertaken by national-level, education-related organizations. One powerful means of fostering public acceptance for CCSS is to promote the idea that teachers (and administrators) embrace CCSS. And there is no tool quite so useful and blindly respected as a well-publicized survey. That a number of pro-CCSS surveys were produced by national organizations somehow connected to public education could only serve to make CCSS' place in American public education that much more certain. Never mind whether the surveys were skewed and the public manipulated. CCSS survival is all that matters. The determined end justifies the twisted means.

CHAPTER 8

NGA and CCSSO

Legal Owners of Common Core

In 2007, then-president George W. Bush's test-driven reform package, No Child Left Behind (NCLB), was due for reauthorization as the then-current version of the Elementary and Secondary Education Act of 1965 (ESEA). However, by 2007, the momentum behind NCLB was waning; Congress and the president were not as chummy, and Congress did not reauthorize NCLB.

Politically savvy individuals realized in 2007 that NCLB, with its lofty declaration of 100 percent proficiency in reading and math by 2014, was not faring well. Of course, in the test-driven-reformer mind, the failure of NCLB was that it allowed states to determine their own goals and use their own assessments to measure those goals.

National-level standardization was needed.

So, in November 2007, the Council of Chief State School Officers (CCSSO) promoted the idea of "voluntarily" developing a set of national standards in an effort to do so "before the federal government makes us do it," so to speak.[1] Now, this was not CCSSO's publicized stance on the issue; CCSSO was still advancing the idea of states leading their own separate standards and assessment efforts in their official reports.[2]

Another interesting development in 2007 was that politically connected edupreneur David Coleman and his SAP cofounder Jason Zimba decided to "assemble educators and researchers to design actions [to] . . . substantially improve student achievement."[3] They manifested this "assembling" in the form of a company serendipitously poised to "assist" with composing these "common" standards, Student Achievement Partners (SAP).

Not long after both CCSSO and SAP began prepping for and promoting the national standards idea, Achieve released its July 2008 *Out of Many, One* report, overtly a review of its American Diploma Project (ADP), which included hints of a "common core of standards" being realized by "a critical mass of states."[4] This report still included language that supported state standards and assessment autonomy—language that was molded into wording that served the single set of "state-led" standards and corresponding assessments in the Common Core State Standards (CCSS) memorandum of understanding (MOU) (see Chapter 5). For example, recall that the July 2008 Achieve report notes, "common does not mean identical"; the CCSS MOU addresses this by allowing states to add 15% to CCSS—thus, *technically* allowing for state English language arts (ELA) and math standards to be "unique." [5, 6]

Connecting the 2008 Achieve report and the CCSS MOU is all in the game. Yet organizing, realizing, and promoting the game required major funding—funding that those in charge could not ask of the federal government for fear of public backlash.

The answer lay in test-driven-reform-minded philanthropy.

Around the time that Achieve released its *Out of Many, One* report, in summer 2008, Coleman and CCSSO President Gene Wilhoit approached billionaire Bill Gates about the possibility of funding the CCSS effort. (More on this in Chapter 9.) Gates agreed; then it was "all systems go" for CCSSO and the National Governors Association (NGA) to advance the CCSS effort, which the NGA formally promoted in spring 2009, complete with a CCSS MOU for governors and state superintendents to sign. The CCSS MOU outlined the CCSS development process, which centered upon three groups: Achieve, ACT, and the College Board. Coleman and Zimba and their SAP were also in the center of this CCSS development, though as silent partners mysteriously behind the process, "assembling," so to speak—until the NGA released the names of its original 24-member work group as a result of public pressure.

The CCSS MOU was developed by the NGA and CCSSO, the two organizations credited in the CCSS MOU as leading the CCSS development process. (See Chapter 5.)

Though CCSSO might have attempted to "volunteer" for national standards before the federal government forced the issue, the effort was irrelevant as CCSS became grafted into President Obama's and U.S. Secretary of Education Arne Duncan's Race to the Top (RTTT) Program. (More to come on federal involvement in Chapter 10.)

As one might expect, Duncan insists that CCSS is not federally created, which technically is true. However, in the section of the CCSS MOU on the federal role, one can see that federal money was expected to permeate CCSS implementation and the creation of the CCSS-associated assessments (see Chapter 5). And where federal money is, there is federal control.

Both the Gates Foundation and the U.S. Department of Education paid millions toward CCSS and its associated assessments, respectively.

And yet, NGA, CCSSO, Achieve, and SAP all played principal roles in CCSS creation.

Now comes the question: Who owns CCSS?

The CCSS result is a product, and as such, someone needs to "own" it in order to preserve the set of standards *as a distinct entity*. Otherwise, states might get the idea that CCSS might be modified to better fit each state, and then where would we be? That would kill the "common standards" idea. Only a certain percentage of variation is allowed, and according to the CCSS MOU, this state-level freedom is restricted to not removing or replacing CCSS content, but only adding a modest percentage to it.

In a question-and-answer session with *MSNBC.com* in May 2014, American Federation of Teachers (AFT) President Randi Weingarten— an unwavering supporter of CCSS even in the face of opposition by her constituency[7, 8]—stated that she did not understand why the NGA and CCSSO needed to copyright CCSS:

> Standards are only meaningful once you see them in real practice. That's why so many of us question why the National Governors Association and the Council of Chief State School Officers—the very people who oversaw the writing of the standards—copyrighted them, rather than encouraging change and adjustment as educators saw the standards work in practice.[9]

Here is an answer for Weingarten: *CCSS must be rigid;* it must be fixed if education corporations are to market it to scale (nationwide). That is where the real profits are—in producing this *national-scale* CCSS, with its need for curriculum, professional development materials and seminars, test prep materials, the assessments, score reports, remediation materials—all of which could be produced both on paper and electronically. (Technology really expands the possibility for profits, with both hardware and software created to make consumers company-dependent.)

Interestingly, Weingarten's words spoken in May 2014 to *MSNBC.com* against CCSS copyright were sandwiched between other CCSS-supportive statements. For example, Weingarten said she supports CCSS because "we need a set of high standards in order to make sure our kids have the critical-thinking and problem-solving skills they need to prepare for life and citizenship, college and career"; then, after her questioning the CCSS copyright, she also added that CCSS "inspire[s] creativity." And still, Weingarten then mixed in the contradiction, "The K–2 standards seem developmentally inappropriate for our youngest children. . . . Without doubt . . . we need course correction."[10]

Such contradictions. But as to that CCSS rigidity, it must be there for ease of marketing.

Indeed, if states were to alter CCSS into that which is state-specific, that would really interfere with the plans of mega-education corporations such as Pearson. (More on Pearson and CCSS in Chapter 11.)

The Core must remain The Core, and for that, CCSS must legally belong to someone. As a matter of fact, it does. Legally, CCSS belongs to the NGA and CCSSO. In examining the CCSS license, I primarily draw on (and often cite directly from) evidence I gathered and originally published in a couple of blog posts I wrote in October 2013[11] and April 2014.[12] The CCSS license betrays the business of CCSS—one where profit potential abounds as those with power excuse themselves from responsibility for any and all consequences. Garnering profits and forsaking responsibility: cornerstones of corporate reform.

DEFINING KEY TERMS

Copyright law is complex. I am not a lawyer; I am a teacher and researcher. As such, I approach this chapter from the perspective of a researcher attempting to better educate herself (and by extension, my readers) on what exactly this CCSS license includes. In order to foster a clear understanding of this chapter, I offer the following definitions of key terminology:

> **Copyright:** the exclusive legal right, *given to an originator or an assignee* to print, publish, perform, film, or record literary, artistic, or musical material, and to authorize others to do the same.[13] [Emphasis added]
>
> **Public license:** another term for public copyright license.[14]
>
> **Terms of use:** [That] which one must agree to abide by in order to use a service. Terms of service *can also be merely a disclaimer, especially regarding the use of websites.*[15] [Emphasis added]
>
> **Fair use:** (in U.S. copyright law) the doctrine that brief excerpts of copyright material may, under certain circumstances, be quoted verbatim for purposes such as criticism, news reporting, teaching, and research, without the need for permission from or payment to the copyright holder.[16]

I will discuss more terminology in reference to the CCSS licensing document. However, time for some national standards copyright/terms of use background.

NCTM AND NCTE

In preparing to closely examine the CCSS license, I investigated the copyright situations of two other organizations that offer national standards: the National Council of Teachers of Mathematics (NCTM) and the National Council of Teachers of English (NCTE).

It is not unusual for national organizations to copyright their materials, including sets of standards. However, both the NCTM and NCTE standards are completely voluntary: Neither is connected to federal funding, neither must be adopted on a "by state" basis, and neither must be adopted in whole. Moreover—and this is huge—neither the NCTM nor the NCTE standards are connected to high-stakes tests. For these reasons, even though NCTM and NCTE have some form of copyright/terms of use, the CCSS copyright immediately holds more power for its inflexibility coupled with high-stakes consequences.

First, the NCTM copyright information.

NCTM Copyright/Terms of Use

Below, I have reproduced in full the information included on the NCTM website regarding its copyright and associated terms of use.[17] What I immediately notice is that NCTM is not using other companies to write materials (and potentially assessments) for its standards:

> All publications of the National Council of Teachers of Mathematics (NCTM), including print, electronic, and Web formats (including, but not limited to, images, text, illustrations, and audio clips) are protected by Copyright laws of the United States and are owned or controlled by NCTM, unless expressly noted. *The materials are provided solely for the personal, noncommercial use* of purchasers of publications, members, or visitors to NCTM sites.
>
> For ALL uses, except for translation requests, NCTM has authorized the Copyright Clearance Center[18] to process permissions for the following: photocopying, reprinting, or republication of any NCTM copyrighted material, including *Curriculum Focal Points for Prekindergarten through Grade 8* and *Principles and Standards for School Mathematics* (2000), for print, CD, or online; and distribution of NCTM journal articles or book chapters in electronic course packs for use in association with online courses on password-protected systems.
>
> To request permission for approved uses and pay the associated fees, please access Copyright Clearance Center at this link: www.copyright.com/ccc/search.do?operation=show&page=simple or contact the Copyright Clearance Center, Inc., 222 Rosewood Drive, Danvers, MA 01923, (978) 750-8400.

Copyright Clearance Center is a not-for-profit organization that provides licenses and registration for a variety of users.

For translation permission requests only:

To translate any NCTM copyrighted material, please send your request to permissions@nctm.org.

Note: Reproduction is limited to up to five articles or chapters in total from an NCTM source, or 25 percent of a complete journal or book, whichever is less. A source is defined as a book, or one of our four journals: *Journal for Research in Mathematics Education, Mathematics Teacher, Mathematics Teaching in the Middle School,* or *Teaching Children Mathematics.* Other restrictions may apply. Please see Copyright Clearance Center [19] for all conditions. [20]

In addition to the copyright information cited above, NCTM also includes disclaimer information regarding materials being "as is" on their site (known as *terms of use*). Keep in mind that this standard disclaimer refers to completely voluntary usage (or nonusage) of NCTM materials.

NCTM: Truly voluntary standards. Negotiable terms. Nothing coerced; nothing high-stakes. No promoted profit potential for education corporations.

And now, for NCTE.

NCTE Copyright/Terms of Use

Like NCTM, NCTE offers its own standards. [21] However, even though the NCTE website still includes the NCTE standards, [22] NCTE now showcases CCSS. [23]

NCTE does not readily offer information on its public license. The site does include the note at the bottom of its webpage, "All rights reserved in all media." [24] NCTE also offers a position statement entitled "Code of Best Practices in Fair Use for Media Literacy in Education." As does the NCTM site, the NCTE site includes the standard "as is" terms of use. [25]

As for the CCSS endorsement on the NCTE site, NCTE must abide by the CCSS public license, which I examine now.

CCSS PUBLIC LICENSE

The 2014 version of the CCSS public license opens with an introduction that notes that the standards "are protected by copyright and/or applicable law." [26] The intro also maintains that use of CCSS constitutes agreement to abide by the terms of the license.

Next comes the License Grant:

> The NGA Center for Best Practices (NGA Center) and the Council of Chief State School Officers (CCSSO) hereby grant a *limited, non-exclusive, royalty-free license* to copy, publish, distribute, and display the Common Core State Standards for purposes that support the Common Core State Standards Initiative. These uses may involve the Common Core State Standards as a whole or selected excerpts or portions.[27] [Emphasis added]

In other words, all of those who "support" CCSS are allowed to copy and use any or all of it without paying money to do so.

The section that follows is the Attribution; Copyright Notice:

> *NGA Center/CCSSO shall be acknowledged as the sole owners and developers of the Common Core State Standards, and no claims to the contrary shall be made.*
>
> Any publication or public display shall include the following notice: "© Copyright 2010. National Governors Association Center for Best Practices and Council of Chief State School Officers. All rights reserved."
>
> States and territories of the United States as well as the District of Columbia that have adopted the Common Core State Standards in whole are exempt from this provision of the License. [Emphasis added][28]

Based on the above excerpt, one can see that CCSS belongs to the National Governors Association (NGA) and the Council of Chief State School Officers (CCSSO). Keep in mind the definition of *copyright* at the outset of this section: A copyright *can* belong to one who is not responsible for creating the copyrighted document.

As per the remainder of the Attribution; Copyright section, states that adopt CCSS don't have to identify the NGA and CCSSO as the owners of CCSS—although many sites promoting CCSS do so ad nauseam.

The next section, Material Beyond the Scope of the Public License, underscores the fact that the license belongs only to the standards, not to the examples used to illustrate the standards. Many examples belong to the "public domain," meaning anyone is able to use them without needing to obtain permission. However, it seems that the NGA and CCSSO entered into agreement with both the Penguin Group (a subsidiary of Pearson[29]) and McGraw-Hill to use material copyrighted by Penguin and McGraw-Hill to illustrate CCSS:

> This License extends to the Common Core State Standards only and not to the examples. A number of the examples are comprised of materials that are not

subject to copyright, such as due to being in the public domain, and others required NGA Center and CCSSO to obtain permission for their use from a third party copyright holder.

With respect to copyrighted works provided by the Penguin Group (USA) Inc., duplication, distribution, emailing, copying, or printing is allowed only of the work as a whole.

McGraw-Hill makes no representations or warranties as to the accuracy of any information contained in the McGraw-Hill Material, including any warranties of merchantability or fitness for a particular purpose. *In no event shall McGraw-Hill have any liability* to any party for special, incidental, tort, or consequential damages arising out of or in connection with the McGraw-Hill Material, *even if McGraw-Hill has been advised of the possibility of such damages.*[30] [Emphasis added]

Such so-called education reform emphasis on the need to "hold public education accountable"—yet McGraw-Hill accepts no responsibility for the "accuracy of information" in the CCSS examples it provides. Most important, what the above acknowledgment of Penguin and McGraw-Hill inadvertently shows is that these two have a foot in the door, so to speak, to the profit potential available via CCSS. As already noted, CCSS "lead writer" David Coleman has a history with McGraw-Hill. (See Chapter 6 on Student Achievement Partners.) Indeed, CCSS is a layered business deal; Pearson is a major player in the CCSS game and is positioned to run all aspects of CCSS, from curriculum to assessment. (More to come in Chapter 11 on Pearson.)

The next two sections are the warranties/disclaimers and limits on liability. Below is the complete language of these sections:

The Common Core State Standards are provided as-is *and with all faults, and NGA center/CCSSO make no representations or warranties of any kind,* express, implied, statutory or otherwise, including, without limitation, warranties of title, merchantibility, *fitness for a particular purpose,* noninfringement, *accuracy,* or the presence or absence of errors, whether or not discoverable.

Under no circumstances shall NGA center or CCSSO, individually or jointly, be liable for any direct, indirect, incidental, special, exemplary, consequential, or punitive damages however caused and on any legal theory of liability, whether for contract, tort, strict liability, or a combination thereof *(including negligence or otherwise) arising in any way out of the use of the common core state standards, even if advised of the possibility of such risk and potential damage.* Without limiting the foregoing, *licensee waives the right to seek legal redress against,* and releases from all liability and covenants not to sue, NGA center and CCSSO.[31] [Emphasis added]

The CCSS license is pretty clear about protecting the NGA and CCSSO from any and all repercussions associated with CCSS to the degree that it even states that those signing on for CCSS sign away any right to sue. Compare this to the sales pitch from the CCSS website, one that promotes a message that CCSS most certainly will work:

> The Common Core State Standards provide a *consistent, clear understanding of what students are expected to learn,* so teachers and parents know what they need to do to help them. The standards are designed to be robust and relevant to the real world, reflecting the knowledge and skills that our young people need for success in college and careers. *With American students fully prepared for the future,* our communities will be *best positioned to compete successfully* in the global economy.[32] [Emphasis added]

So which is it? Is CCSS "warrantied" or not? When does the "as is" escape clause kick in?

The disclaimers/limits of liability take on new shades of meaning given the mandatory 100% acceptance of CCSS in order to receive federal RTTT funds. The CCSS MOU that states submit to the U.S. Department of Education to vie for RTTT funding binds all public school districts in a state to use CCSS "as is" based upon only two signatures: those of the governor and the state education superintendent. (More on RTTT in Chapter 10.)

The very people who sign for CCSS are the same ones whose respective national organizations (NGA and CCSSO) take credit for CCSS creation while excusing themselves from any and all responsibility for the heretofore-untested CCSS possibly not working.

In the CCSS license section on termination, NGA and CCSSO go beyond excusing themselves from responsibility; they note that *at any time* they can alter the terms of the license:

> *NGA Center and CCSSO reserve the right to release the Common Core State Standards under different license terms or to stop distributing the Common Core State Standards at any time;* provided, however, that any such election will not serve to withdraw this License with respect to any person utilizing the Common Core State Standards pursuant to this License.[33] [Emphasis added]

The termination section makes NGA's and CCSSO's ownership of CCSS much more powerful because they are able to alter the rules in any way they wish. Where this power becomes evident is in the conditions the

NGA and CCSSO wrote into a previous version of the CCSS license, dated November 24, 2010:

> Impermissible Uses:
>   The following are prohibited uses of the Common Core State Standards: (a) revising, including editing; (b) recasting, such as in the form of abridged or condensed versions, in a manner that, in the view of NGA Center and CCSSO, changes the meaning or intent of the Common Core State Standards or any part thereof; (c) sublicensing; (d) sale; (e) claiming of ownership, including copyright; (f) any use that may be prejudicial to the Common Core State Standards, NGA Center, or CCSSO; and (g) any use contrary to the express terms of this License. Notwithstanding the foregoing, the Common Core State Standards may be included in larger works published by the Licensee, even if such larger works are sold or copyrighted by the Licensee.[34]

I recall discussions about CCSS in which colleagues were alarmed that no content could be removed from CCSS—that teachers nationwide were locked into a rigid set of standards. There was talk of what is detailed above in this section of the license. People had seen the information about not removing CCSS content; then, such wording disappeared.

The last verifiable date in which the Impermissible Uses section above was part of the CCSS license is September 13, 2011.[35] By April 15, 2012, the CCSS license site, including this section, had been shut down.[36] The removal of the Impermissible Uses section does not mean that teachers, districts, and states were free to use their professional judgment in altering a set of standards that had not been tested. It only meant that the NGA and CCSSO were not being as obvious in attempting to enforce the standardization that CCSS was designed to bring. In truth, the CCSS MOU already included language to the effect that CCSS could not be altered, and state governors and state education superintendents had already signed the MOU—which carries the weight of a legally binding document, if for no other reason than its inclusion as part of a state's RTTT application.

What can be gleaned from this bit of CCSS license revision history is that the NGA and CCSSO can (and already have) revised the license on the CCSS that they own. However, there is another possibility unleashed by NGA and CCSSO's "reserved right" to alter the CCSS license: curriculum regulation.

The official word on the CCSS website is that CCSS is not a curriculum.[37] Whereas one might argue such a stance depending upon one's definition of curriculum (which I do in my book *A Chronicle of Echoes*),[38] the CCSS license opens up the possibility of the CCSS license "owners'" becoming the arbiters of the curricula that they "allow" to be associated with "their" CCSS. In fact, in March 2014, members of the Brookings Institution suggested the following:

> The Common Core [meaning NGA and CCSSO] should *vigorously enforce their licensing agreement*. In the past textbook writers and others have inappropriately claimed that they aligned course content. Supporters of standards based reform should recognize that low quality content could sink the standards *and enforce their copyright* accordingly.[39] [Emphasis added]

Note the CCSS website defense that CCSS is not a curriculum:

> The Common Core is not a curriculum. It is a clear set of shared goals and expectations for what knowledge and skills will help our students succeed. Local teachers, principals, superintendents, and others will decide how the standards are to be met. Teachers will continue to devise lesson plans and tailor instruction to the individual needs of the students in their classrooms.[40]

Technically, it seems that CCSS officials would still be able to say that CCSS is "not a curriculum" and that curriculum is "locally selected," even if the NGA and CCSSO expand their dictatorial reach and require that curriculum be submitted for their review prior to earning some CCSS seal of approval. In such a case, as arbiter, NGA and CCSSO could possibly promote "approved curricular options" from which districts might "choose." In short, NGA and CCSSO could possibly alter "their" CCSS copyright to require their approval of curricular materials used in school districts across the nation—thereby driving curriculum in the direction of their choosing.

After all, NGA and CCSSO *are* the owners of CCSS.

NGA AND CCSSO:
SERVING THEMSELVES AND PROFIT-DRIVEN COMPANIES

The CCSS license might resemble copyright/terms of use documents of other organizations that offer national standards; however, the coercive, high-stakes nature of CCSS makes the details of its license a mirror into both the profit motives and the utter lack of accountability that the NGA and CCSSO escape via their exclusive control over CCSS. Though technically CCSS is not a curriculum, as owners of CCSS, the NGA and CCSSO are in a position to alter the license and add language that requires NGA/CCSSO approval to connect curriculum with "their" CCSS. In addition, companies like Pearson and McGraw-Hill—which are already written into the license as those providing CCSS-related examples—stand to make a fortune from producing CCSS-focused materials. Moreover, in agreeing to CCSS as a component of RTTT (more to come on this issue in Chapter 10), governors and state superintendents are in essence agreeing to subject states to a product in which they (the superintendents and governors) hold partial ownership—an arguable conflict of interest. Finally, sadly, those facing the greatest consequences of this transaction— school districts, schools, teachers, and students—are nothing more than pawns in a game designed to boost the careers and fatten the bank accounts of those who are completely exempt from responsibility for their CCSS actions.

What a costly charade.

CHAPTER 9

Bill Gates Likes the Idea

In the summer of 2008, Council of Chief State School Officers (CCSSO) president Gene Wilhoit and Student Achievement Partners (SAP) founder David Coleman asked billionaire Bill Gates and his wife, Melinda, to provide millions in backing for the "common standards" they hoped would become nationally adopted—state by state, of course. Wilhoit and Coleman were positioned for this moment, with CCSSO making a "voluntary" pitch for national standards the focus of their November 2007 annual policy forum, and Coleman founding his Student Achievement Partners that same year. And by summer 2008, Achieve had produced its *Out of Many, One* report in which it promoted the idea of a "common core of standards" that a "critical mass" had "discovered" in their work on the American Diploma Project (ADP).

The "common core" concept was indeed coming together.

Now if someone would only finance the effort. . . . Hence Wilhoit's and Coleman's meeting with Gates and his wife.

The public did not know this meeting occurred until 6 years later.

In June 2014, *Washington Post* reporter Lyndsey Layton released a remarkable article* in which she includes information on Wilhoit's making the "Gates CCSS bankrolling" admission.[1] However, Gates is much more subtle in speaking about his funding of the Common Core State Standards (CCSS).

Included with her article is a 28-minute video of an interview Layton conducted with Gates following his keynote to one of the groups he financed to promote CCSS, the National Board for Professional Teaching Standards (NBPTS) Teaching and Learning Conference. Throughout much of the interview, Layton asks Gates pointed questions about his involvement in funding CCSS, and especially about public perceptions of his ubiquitous funding of American education "reform."

I will feature excerpts from that interview in this chapter—interspersed with my own commentary and supplemental facts, of course. My goal is to weigh Gates's words to Layton by comparing excerpts from the Gates–Layton interview with other Gates speeches and Gates Foundation grant priorities. In the March 2014 interview, Layton gets right to the point.

For her first question, she asks Gates about the March 2014 decision of the American Federation of Teachers (AFT) to cease accepting Gates funding. The decision to which Layton refers occurred as AFT president Randi Weingarten was participating as a CCSS panel member at the first Network for Public Education (NPE) conference in Austin, Texas, on March 2, 2014. I served on the panel with her. (She was pro-CCSS, and I was one of several members who were anti-CCSS.) The audience began speaking directly to Weingarten and expressing the desire that AFT cease receiving Gates funding. They believed AFT had compromised its commitment to teachers in favor of executing the will of a billionaire. Weingarten agreed to stop accepting Gates money for the AFT Innovation Fund.

In his interview with Layton, Gates is obviously shaken by Layton's question:

> Layton (L): The AFT (American Federation of Teachers) last week announced that they weren't going to take any more Gates money when it came to the Common Core. The assumption is there that they're somehow being bought, by, by [the] Gates [Foundation], that they're not voicing their own honest opinions of the Core, that there's something compromising about it. So I wondered, are you concerned at all that, that you're becoming a liability here, or how do you, how do you answer those concerns? People think that you're the unelected school superintendent of the country.

> [Gates waited nine seconds before answering.]

> Gates (G): Well, certainly . . . you've combined too many things there. There's no connection between the AFT, AFT Innovation Fund, it's a, it was more about teacher evaluation where locals would apply for various things. Anyway, it's not, ahh. . . . [2]

Clearly taken aback, Gates tries to say that the AFT Innovation Fund was separate from CCSS. Initially, it was. Gates had been funding the AFT Innovation Fund since July 2010. The first of two grants was for $4 million and included no mention of CCSS in its statement of purpose: "to support the American Federation of Teachers Innovation Fund and the union's teacher development and evaluation programs."[3] However, according to Gates's own grants search engine, CCSS had been grafted into the Innovation Fund by June 2012:

> American Federation of Teachers Educational Foundation
>
> **Date:** June 2012
>
> **Purpose:** to support the AFT Innovation Fund and work on teacher development and Common Core State Standards
>
> **Amount:** $4,400,000[4]

The history of AFT's receiving Gates Foundation money goes back to January 2009[5] and is unique to Weingarten's tenure as AFT president. (She was elected to the position in July 2008.[6]) Between 2009 and 2014, AFT accepted $11.3 million in Gates funding.[7] In June 2010, Gates paid $217,200 in "conference support" toward the AFT Convention in Seattle (Gates's hometown). One month later, in July 2010, he gave the keynote address.[8]

At the 2010 AFT Convention, George Schmidt of *Substance News* reported from inside the convention hall that Weingarten instructed AFT delegates to be nice to Gates—a man who openly advocates for larger class sizes, charter schools over traditional public schools, teacher evaluation based on student test scores, the ending of teacher pay based upon seniority, and CCSS:

> AFT President Randi Weingarten, who was reelected on July 10, told the convention that she had been going from delegation to delegation asking that delegates not be rude to Gates. Her forceful message, given the structure of the AFT, was not lost on most of the delegates. (Most of the local leaders of the AFT have to have regular relations with the AFT national office.)[9]

Schmidt further notes that some AFT delegates walked out of the convention, but most remained and were obedient to Weingarten's wishes; they were polite as Gates spoke, and many stood to give his speech a standing ovation. However, it was clear that Gates was protected in his appearance at the AFT convention. He was insulated from both the press and AFT members who disagreed with his agenda:

> *There were probably few places in the USA where you could find more people that day who knew, chapter and verse, every lie that Gates told in his speech.* From college

and university professors who had written extensively against the use of so-called standardized testing to classroom teachers who know the limitations of the claim (made by Gates repeatedly) that every classroom should have a "great" teacher (sort of like claiming that every spot in a baseball team's batting order should have a "great" slugging hitter), *the room was filled with people who could have debated Gates and who should have been allowed to ask him questions. Yet for all the talk about "democracy" at the AFT convention, the Gates event was strictly controlled.*[10] [Emphasis added]

Schmidt notes that only a single blogger from *Education Week* was allowed to ask Gates questions. This knowledge makes Layton's pointed 2014 interview all the more valuable.

Following her question about AFT's dropping Gates funding for its Innovation Fund, Layton next asks about the perception that Gates's funding so many education initiatives (CCSS, charter schools, teacher evaluation) is somehow "undemocratic":

> How about the simple notion that because you're funding so much of the . . . Common Core, and charter schools, and, and the teacher evaluation that your promoting it as, advocating for it, that you have become, kind of a, you're a very powerful figure in K–12 education right now, but you're unelected. Some people say that's undemocratic.[11]

Gates's response is that he may fund them, but he does not make the final decisions:

> We are not a factor in giving in those races or speaking out in those races. They'll pick . . . what they choose to do. The role the Foundation has come in is, okay, the number of new approaches where teachers are having an idea, are they getting funding? Try out that idea. So, if the pool of choices . . . are out there, for these political decisions to pick from, is larger. . . . The funding in education of what works good in general . . . is tiny. . . . Our voice is not there when the final choice is made of what to scale up; that's a governor, a superintendent, a school board, who decides all of that.[12]

Gates said this to Layton the day after he dined with 80 senators and other legislators.[13] It seems that he believes his dinnertime interactions with elected officials could not possibly influence their decisions on state and national education issues.

As concerns CCSS, Gates's response to Layton's "undemocratic" query is disconnected from a couple of realities. First, in Wilhoit's admission to asking Gates to fund CCSS, Gates's "voice" certainly was there when the decision to "scale up" CCSS was made. Wilhoit and Coleman asked Gates for the financial backing for CCSS in the summer of 2008, and by spring 2009, 46 states and 3 U.S. territories had signed a CCSS MOU. Indeed, in July 2009, as co-chair of the National Council of State Legislatures (what is Gates doing co-chairing a legislative group?), Gates was selling a number of reforms—including lifting charter school caps, increasing "measurement," developing longitudinal data systems, and, of course, promoting CCSS. Here are some of Gates's "no voice at decision time" words to legislators in 2009:

> *You [legislators] are the authorizers and appropriators of school reform in America.* The president and the Congress can make recommendations—and they have passed a stimulus package with billions of dollars you can spend to advance school reform—*but ultimately, you decide.* . . .
>
> I hope you decide to accelerate reform. . . .
>
> Without measurement, there is no pressure for improvement. . . .
>
> We need to take two enabling steps: we need longitudinal data systems that track student performance and are linked to the teacher; and we need fewer, clearer, higher standards that are common from state to state. The standards will tell the teachers what their students are supposed to learn, and the data will tell them whether they're learning it. . . .
>
> Fortunately, the state-led Common Core State Standards Initiative is developing clear, rigorous common standards that match the best in the world. . . .
>
> This is encouraging—but identifying common standards is not enough. *We'll know we've succeeded when the curriculum and the tests are aligned to these standards.*[14] [Emphasis added]

In the above speech excerpt, Gates is speaking in 2009 to legislators about a CCSS that has yet to be created. However, already CCSS is going to "match the best in the world" in Gates's mind—and he is earnestly persuading legislators that CCSS should exist, that legislatures should embrace it, and that curriculum and assessments should be aligned to it because "without measurement, there is no pressure for improvement."

But the test-driven pressure for improvement is not on *him*. In fact, a number of times in his March 2014 interview with Layton, Gates refers to the millions of dollars (and, according to Georgia State professor emeritus Jack Hassard, over $2.3 billion[15]) as a "rounding error" in comparison to the over $600 billion that U.S. K–12 education costs annually.

And for any consequences brought to bear via that "rounding error," the comparison Gates makes is specious because he is comparing his back room influence dollars to the total dollars spent in the United States to actually educate children. Gates believes that the "paltry" millions (likely a couple of billion) that he has paid to put America on the sure road to CCSS couldn't possibly matter in the face of the total cost of American K–12 education for 1 year. One wonders if he sees any possible negative outcomes from his actions as inconsequential. But of course, Gates's forking over millions (possibly billions) at the request of two men (Wilhoit and Coleman) in order to finance an education effort that has the potential to impact (standardize) schools nationwide is far from inconsequential.

Let us consider Gates grant monies paid to the two CCSS copyright owners, NGA and CCSSO.

In May 2008, the Gates Foundation gave the NGA $2.1 million "to help governors improve college and career ready rates and make state education systems internationally competitive."[16] In November 2009, Gates added another $500,000 "to build capacity and awareness among governors around postsecondary goals."[17] In February 2011, Gates paid the NGA yet another $1.3 million, this time directly naming CCSS in the grant explanation: "to work with state policymakers on the implementation of the Common Core State Standards, with special attention to effective resource allocation to ensure complete execution, as well as rethinking state policies on teacher effectiveness."[18]

Note that in the 2014 interview with Layton, Gates *just* told Layton that he doesn't get involved "in those races." However, he *is* willing to pay the National Governors Association (via its nonprofit) to "work with policymakers" on CCSS "implementation—*and* to "rethink state policies" on teacher evaluation.

Between May 2002 and June 2014, Gates paid the NGA a total of $25.8 million in the form of 12 grants.[19] And his involvement with the NGA does not end with his checkbook.

Gates formally speaks to the NGA.

In 1997, in his capacity as CEO of Microsoft, Gates delivered a speech about technology in government to the NGA in Las Vegas. (In that speech, Gates stated that the only other job he had in his life outside of Microsoft was as a page for state and federal government.[20]) This 1997 Gates speech predates Gates's involvements in education affairs (and his active efforts in shaping American education).[21]

After Gates began funding the NGA for education, he started talking to the group about his ideas for education. In February 2005, Gates delivered a keynote address to "governors from the 55 U.S. states and territories along with top business executives and prominent K–12 and higher education leaders" at the National Education Summit on High Schools, hosted by Achieve and the NGA.[22] In March 2011, Gates delivered yet another speech to the NGA. He advised them to increase class sizes, offer teachers merit pay, stop teacher pay based upon seniority, invest in charter schools (which he said have higher college enrollments yet cost less than traditional public schools), and trust his endorsement of CCSS. As the Washington Policy Center reports in a blog post entitled "Bill Gates Provides Guideposts for Nation's Governors on Education: Effective Teachers, Larger Class Sizes, Charter Public Schools and No Furlough Days":

> *Mr. Gates told the governors he has closely analyzed their Common Core standards initiative and is a strong supporter of them. The standards, he said, are a more focused, less repetitive approach than many states now have.* And by adopting the Common Core standards, teachers will be able to access sharable training materials online to improve their instruction.[23] [Emphasis added]

Based upon his own "analysis," Gates actively, deliberately, and intentionally promoted CCSS among the nation's governors, just as he did among the nation's legislators in 2009—and in 2014—just 1 day prior to telling Layton that at the time of decision, his "voice" was not in the room.

Now for CCSSO:

In July 2009, the Gates Foundation paid CCSSO $10 million to support a spectrum of reforms resembling NCLB and the subsequent nouveau NCLB, RTTT—namely, "to increase the leadership capacity of chiefs (state education superintendents) by focusing on standards and assessments, data systems, educator development and determining a new system of supports for student learning."[24]

"Focusing on standards and assessments" somehow equates to "increased leadership capacity." However, Gates does not view this defining of state superintendent roles in terms of standardized testing as promoting his own narrow view of what American mass education should look like.

In November 2009, Gates paid CCSSO another $3.2 million "to partner with federal, state, public, and private interests to develop common, open, longitudinal data standards."[25]

In June 2011, Gates paid CCSSO $9.4 million "to support the Common Core standards work."[26] In July 2013, Gates added another $4 million "to develop high quality assessments to measure the Common Core State Standards."[27]

Be apprised that I am just sampling from the millions in Gates pay-
outs to CCSSO. Since May 2002, the Gates Foundation has paid CCSSO
$84.6 million in the form of 20 grants.[28]

And now for the speaking that accompanies the money. As was true in
the case of the National Council of State Legislatures, Gates was also a co-
chair (and, in this case, trustee) of CCSSO. In that capacity, Gates spoke to
CCSSO in November 2010. He advanced his ideas on teacher pay, length
of school day/year (furloughs), increasing class sizes—and CCSS:

> I especially want to recognize your work in establishing Common Core State
> Standards. . . . The Common Core builds a foundation for defining and measur-
> ing excellence—and that will give traction to many reforms that follow.
>
> Others have asserted standards before, but yours are better. They are more
> relevant—because they're based on the knowledge and skills people need.
> They're clearer—so you can test whether a student knows them. And they're
> consistent across the states that adopt them, so educators can work together to
> improve our schools. . . .
>
> Aligning teaching with the common core—and building common data stan-
> dards—will help us define excellence, measure progress, test new methods, and
> compare results. Finally, we will apply the tools of science to school reform. . . .
>
> It's implementing common core standards that will let us measure student
> achievement, identify great teaching, and rebuild the budget based on excel-
> lence. You can lead this change, but you can't be expected to do it alone. *You'll
> need friends in business and philanthropy to stand with you. You can count on me.*[29]
> [Emphasis added]

The Gates voice: There for CCSSO and for the resulting CCSS standards
that *will* work.

It is not hard to imagine that Gates's voice is very much there when
"final decisions of what to scale up" are being made. His voice comes
across not only in his millions of dollars in funding but also in the description of how his millions are designated to be spent.

Gates believes he is not influencing final decisions on CCSS. That is
his first disconnect in his interview with Layton.

Gates's second disconnect in response to Layton's "undemocratic
financing" query comes from his apparent belief that the corporate reformer ideas that he funds—including CCSS—originated with teachers.
He seems to claim that teachers have the ideas; that he is the benevolent
yet neutral fiscal provider for teacher ideas; and that governors, superintendents, and school boards are deciding which of the teacher ideas to
"scale up."

CCSS was certainly no "teacher idea." It was first publicized by Achieve in its July 2008 *Out of Many, One* report—which the Gates Foundation paid $12.6 million to fund in February 2008, supposedly "to support Achieve's American Diploma Project."[30] As has been expounded particularly in Chapters 5 and 6 on the CCSS MOU and Student Achievement Partners, respectively, teachers were left on the fringes of CCSS development. They were reviewers and advisors, at best. Those involved in the second work group, the members who might be called "teachers," hailed chiefly from departments of education—which means that they provided a convenient group to be placed among the CCSS developers (and an easily controlled group given their direct employ in departments of education). These department of education participants are not current classroom teachers. As such, they will not have to implement CCSS in classrooms of their own.

Since CCSS directly affects current classroom teachers, shouldn't they have had a decisionmaking voice in the development of standards?

No, no. CCSS had to come from the minds of those for whom classroom teaching was either removed or virtually unknown.

In her 2014 interview with Gates, Layton next poses an idea to which I alluded previously: that Gates's pervasive presence in education funding allows him to "set the agenda." Layton also refers to Gates's having funded groups from across the political spectrum in support of CCSS:

> Well, let me tell you what, what I'm hearing when I talk to people in education policy. The running joke is *sooner or later, everybody works for Gates* because, when you look at how the breadth of, of your funding, and in terms of the advocacy work for the Common Core, you funded on the left of the spectrum, on the right of the spectrum: think tanks, you know, districts, unions, business groups. It's a wide variety. . . . It's harder to name groups, um, that are in education that haven't received funding that, from Gates, than it is to name all the groups that have. So, the suggestion is that because of that pervasive presence that you set the agenda, that it's harder to get, to get contrasting views and to get real, honest debate because you are funding such a wide variety of actors in this field.[31]

It's a pointed observation—to which Gates responds, "Boy, I guess we're not going to get to any substance."[32] Gates is obviously uncomfortable and notes that he does not know exactly which "right wing, left wing groups" Layton alludes to—so, she names several. Here is the exchange:

L: The American Enterprise Institute . . .

G: We don't fund political groups. We're not . . .

L: Think tanks . . .

G: . . . we don't, like Heritage, CATO, people like that. Uhh. . . .

L: The American Enterprise Institute . . .

G: That's some experts on educational policy.

L: Fordham . . .

G: Say . . .

L: Fordham, the Fordham Institute, to do their writing. . . .

G: These, these are not political things.[33]

Recall that the Fordham Institute promotes CCSS as "superior" even in states with standards that it has graded as equal to or better than CCSS. (See Chapter 4.) Fordham most certainly has a CCSS-promoting political agenda.

Gates has been giving the Fordham Institute grant money since 2003.[34] One million dollars was specifically earmarked in October 2009 to go toward "reviewing the common core standards and developing supporting materials."[35] Another million was paid "to track state progress towards implementation of standards and to understand how what students read changes in response to the standards."[36] Yet another million was paid "for general operating support."[37]

Yet Gates maintains that this funding is somehow divorced from politics. Indeed, he presents his political influence as being somehow neutralized. Recapping with Layton's last statement about Gates's funding the Fordham Institute:

L: Fordham, the Fordham Institute, to do their writing . . . .

G: These, these are not political things. . . . *We pay people to look into things. We don't fund people to say, okay, you like the Common Core. I've never done anything like that.* We do evaluations . . . and yes, we are guilty of funding things where *experts* look into things and say if they're good or not, and they may not get adopted, or the *experts* may decide that they don't like them. . . . Yes, we've engaged a lot of people. *It's a rounding error.* You know, education is a gigantic thing, and it deserves to have people of all political persuasions studying excellence. . . . *And it's not advocacy in the sense that, we have people study Common Core and tell us* . . . it's analysis to see what works.[38] [Emphasis added]

Gates uses the term *experts* to describe the likes of the Fordham Institute. It is unclear how he qualifies who is an "expert." If an "expert" is someone whose experience with the classroom is largely absent (and certainly not current), an abstraction viewed from the soft, think tank chair, then yes, the Fordham Institute and other "think tanks" are experts. They run on millions in philanthropic dollars and produce reports that shape the opinion of a public who trusts them because they appear official.

Gates also says that he doesn't pay people because they like what he likes. However, on its website, the Gates Foundation is clear that it directly contacts organizations with agendas in line with its "funding priorities":

> Q. How do I apply for a grant from the foundation?
> A. We do not make grants outside our funding priorities. In general, we directly invite proposals by directly contacting organizations. We do occasionally award grants though published Requests for Proposals (RFPs) or letters of inquiry.[39]

So, for Gates to tell Layton that he doesn't check out potential funding recipients to see if their agendas are in line with his foundation's "funding priorities" simply isn't true.

And one of Gates's funding priorities surely is implementation of CCSS. The Gates Foundation website has a search engine to allow the public (in keeping with federal law) to examine the grants it funds. A June 20, 2014, search of the keywords *common core implement* yielded 90 results of grants totaling approximately $122 million.[40]

Back to the Gates-Layton interview: When Layton asks about Weingarten's decision to not take Gates money any more for the Innovation Fund because AFT members view the money as "tainted," Gates responds, "That's politics":

> L: Well, are you concerned *at all* about, let's go to the AFT. So, uh, a week ago, Randi Weingarten said, even though she's a big supporter of the Common Core, she doesn't want to take this Gates money any more for the Common Core, you know, for the Innovation work they've been doing around the Common Core because her members have been complaining. They say, "It's tainted, or it . . . shifts the conversation, or it . . . somehow . . . tainted the picture or tainted the discussion."
> G: That's politics.

"That's politics"—yet Gates somehow sees himself outside of the politics of shelling out millions for CCSS and earmarking much of it for CCSS "implementation."

Gates does not consider AFT membership concerns about his funding as potentially driving AFT's agenda to be "substance." Layton does not let him off of the hook:

> I think that they're both intertwined right now with the Common Core. There's a lot of political pushback.

Gates adjusts himself in his seat and says,

> So, what is the substance? What is the thing that is being proposed as an alternative to the Common Core?

Gates is playing the game of "you can't disqualify CCSS if you offer no (national?) alternative."

He then shows just how out of touch he is:

> Now, when you poll the teachers, it's still a very popular thing. . . . Usually the status quo wins and the new idea loses. *This is a new idea that actually gets a majority of the teachers saying that they think it's good. And if you look at which teachers have been the most exposed to the idea, they're the ones who are the most positive about it.*[41] [Emphasis added]

Following Gates's disconnected assertion that teachers "like" CCSS, Layton also shifts to his mistaken idea that teachers are fine with CCSS—it's just the faulty implementation that's the problem.

This message—that CCSS is fine and that the problem is faulty implementation—is one that has been erroneously promoted in the media. It is a message that has found root in a number of public surveys on both CCSS in particular and education in general, as discussed in Chapter 7. If, indeed, teachers supported CCSS, then that would show itself in public venues on education, including the first annual Network for Public Education (NPE) conference, where the panel discussion on CCSS was heavily attended (several hundred people turned out on a Sunday morning in March 2014 in Austin, Texas). I was a member of that five-person panel, the same one mentioned previously in this chapter. Four of us (Paul Horton, Geralyn McLaughln, Jose Luis Vilson, and I) were currently working with children and dealing with the rigid, punitive nature of CCSS—and then there was Weingarten, whose limited classroom experience ended 17 years earlier, in 1997. Weingarten tried to shift the focus of the debate to implementation, whereas those of us dealing directly with CCSS wanted to talk about CCSS' ill fit, age- and situation-inappropriateness, and its purpose as a mechanism for test-driven reform.

During his initial 7 minutes at the microphone, Paul Horton raised the issue of Gates's funding of CCSS and the undue influence Gates has in education because of his money. In response, Weingarten reluctantly (as noted in her voice, her body language, and her hesitation) began to defend Gates and his funding of education. At this point, the audience began speaking directly to Weingarten in disagreement over the AFT's acceptance of Gates funding, evoking the (again) reluctant response from Weingarten that AFT would cease taking Gates funding for the AFT Innovation Fund.

The audience was not supportive of Weingarten's defense of Gates funding and her push for CCSS implementation. She could offer nothing fact-based to support her allegiance to CCSS. In her closing remarks, Weingarten stated that she "likes" CCSS and that her liking it "is personal" and goes back to her time in the classroom—a classroom she left almost 2 decades prior after only a single semester of full-time experience.[42]

In March 2014, in a CCSSO meeting attended also by former National Education Association president Dennis Van Roekel, Achieve president Michael Cohen, and Education Trust president Kati Haycock, Weingarten stated that she would continue to support CCSS even in the face of resistance from AFT membership. As reported by Andrew Ujifusa of *Education Week*:

> Weingarten added that she expects many of her members would call for outright opposition to the standards during the AFT's summer convention (July 2014), even though both the AFT and NEA support the standards and Weingarten said she wouldn't back away from the Common Core.[43]

Weingarten was willing to support CCSS even if the AFT membership did not.

In May 2014, the Chicago Teacher Union (CTU) drafted and approved a resolution opposing CCSS.[44] CTU presented its resolution at the July 2014 AFT convention for a vote by AFT delegates. On Sunday, July 13, 2014, the CTU resolution to reject CCSS lost by a vote of two-thirds of delegates in favor of a watery, pro-CCSS resolution endorsed by the AFT Executive Council. An apparent effort to pacify convention attendees disenchanted with CCSS, the AFT Executive Council resolution regarding CCSS *admits that CCSS was "corrupted"*—but let's keep it anyway. Also, the AFT plans to offer grants—funded via the Innovation Fund—that would be available to teachers and others wishing to "rewrite" CCSS—even though the AFT does not control CCSS.[45]

Weingarten told CCSSO that she would defend CCSS at the AFT convention, and she did exactly that by admitting CCSS had problems and offering money to teachers to "fix" it.

In response to the AFT decision to continue to endorse a "corrupted" CCSS, on July 14, 2014, the 50,000-member Badass Teachers Association issued a press release registering the organization's disapproval of continued AFT support.[46]

Teachers are not "fine" with CCSS "except for implementation."

The push for CCSS implementation does not end with Weingarten. In September 2013, NEA published its own survey parroting the AFT survey "finding" that 75% of teachers support CCSS.[47] Furthermore, at the March 2014 CCSSO meeting, Van Roekel indicated that the NEA "remained squarely behind the standards themselves [but] also expressed concern that teachers were not getting enough time to learn [CCSS]" (Ujifusa's words).[48]

Between the AFT and NEA, the publicized narrative shifts from teacher rejection of CCSS to teacher "dissatisfaction with implementation." It is an artificial albeit strategic shift in order for union leadership to continue to promote CCSS.

In the March 2014 interview with Layton, Gates becomes increasingly more comfortable (and obviously more pleased) about this turn in Layton's questioning to the *implementation* of CCSS. After all, he spent at least $112 million for CCSS implementation. Layton asks, "Are you concerned that with all this effort and, to get these standards in place in 45 states and DC, that it's going to collapse under, under poor implementation?"

Gates responds,

> When we talk about implementation, if we want to switch to substance land and not political land, then we should talk about particulars, we should talk about a district in a state, we should talk about going to the teachers and saying, "Did this go too fast? Did you need more training? What should happen here?" Uh, and, you bet, this is complicated stuff. Uh, you know, look, go into a few states and get into particulars, and I think that you'll find that those summaries,

uh, don't match up to the substance, but you will find things that, hey, should be changed, will change. . . . It takes time to roll something like this out. . . . This is serious stuff. And so, over-simplistic statements about, about it, aren't really advancing the idea that, hey, *this will have kids learning math at a far better progression. We should really get into why is this progression so much better? Why didn't this happen earlier? That is the substance of a kid who goes to college and gets put into remedial math, uh, you know, you should, we should be talking about those examples.* We should be talking about those kids.[49] [Emphasis added]

Once again, Gates attempts to shift discussion of highly politically charged CCSS away from politics. He states that it is important to consider CCSS—an attempt to standardize classrooms nationwide—on the micro level of "a district in a state." However, CCSS is not a tailored venture. It is designed to be brought "to scale" across the nation. In March 2014, Gates was interviewed by the American Enterprise Institute (AEI) (yet another Gates CCSS grant recipient: $1 million in June 2012 for "Exploring the Challenges of Common Core," among other issues);[50] in a 6-minute video clip from that interview, Gates tells AEI that if given the choice to choose "quality," states "ought to probably pick something in common." His reasoning?

You get more free market competition. *Scale is good for free market competition. Individual state regulatory capture is not good for competition.*[51] [Emphasis added]

Though it seems that Gates cannot help but return to the merits of CCSS in market-focused discussion, he also assumes that CCSS works (period) and that this will show in lowered remedial college course rates. No way to know this because as Gates speaks, CCSS is only just being instituted in states nationwide, and not as a pilot but in real time in real classrooms.

Layton asks Gates's opinion about CCSS implementation:

Right. So this is the solution. This is the best method that you think, going forward to cut down the remediation rate and prepare those kids for college—higher standards—these standards in particular?[52]

Despite the marked absence of widespread, inclusive, stakeholder-empowered involvement, Gates wholeheartedly approves of it:

There's a lot of work that's gone into making these [standards] good. I wish there were a lot of competition in terms of people had put tens of millions of dollars into how reading and writing could be improved, how math could be improved. *The more R and D* (research and development) *dollars, the more choices* where people are getting into the substance of, "Did the kids learn? *Did these kids have to go to remedial classes?" The Massachusetts kids do it less.* Why? Is it, is it because of the water? Maybe not.[53] [Emphasis added]

Gates defends CCSS based upon "R and D" (research and development) that supposedly occurred in CCSS development. However, my exploration into the development of CCSS shows it as a politically directed, manipulated, rushed process absent the participation (and often, the awareness) of those directly affected by CCSS—namely, teachers, local administrators, parents, and students. Indeed, in signing the CCSS MOU, most state governors and superintendents agreed to stand by a product that had yet to be produced. Furthermore, more than once in his interview with Layton, Gates uses Massachusetts as an example of a state with a fine education system. However, even Massachusetts was brought into the CCSS fold. Sameness. Standardization nationwide. At one point in the interview, Layton refers to CCSS as "national standards," and Gates corrects her, saying, "These are not national standards," to which Layton repeats the publicized tagline for CCSS: "Okay, they're common standards adopted by 45 states and the District of Columbia."[54]

Layton's interview with Gates only confirms what was already made obvious in Gates Foundation educational spending and Gates's own public words: Bill Gates has a definite agenda that he actively endeavors to impose upon public education, and that agenda includes CCSS.

Now, in what is arguably the tensest moment in her March 2014 interview with Gates, Layton presses Gates on his motives behind supporting CCSS. He rolls his eyes when Layton questions whether his interest in CCSS is prompted by self-interest.

L: There are people who hear that and think, "That's what he's doing. He really wants this because he wants to encourage the technology industry because he's the cofounder of Microsoft. It's, it's, he's being driven by business interests here." What, how would you respond to that? . . . That's kind of a pertinent question that a lot of people who, uh, who don't know you, are (asking), are wondering., . . .

G: *I'm saying, and I've, I hope I can make this clear, I believe in the Common Core because of its substance and what it will do to improve education, and that's the only reason I believe in the Common Core.* And I have no, you know, this is giving money away. This is philanthropy. *This is trying to make sure students have the kind of opportunity I had. . . .*[55] [Emphasis added]

Gates's response illustrates the fantastic disconnect between his entire education agenda (larger class sizes, teacher evaluation based upon student test scores, longer school day/year, and, of course, CCSS with its appendaged assessments) and his own education experience. Indeed, from grades 7 through 12, Gates attended the elite, selective-admission Lakeside School in Seattle—one that he notes in a 2005 speech at Lakeside School he valued for reasons one might expect to value a privileged education. For example, Gates valued Lakeside School for its smaller class sizes. Furthermore, he makes no mention of his having been subjected to standardized testing or his teachers having been "held accountable" when he was not applying himself as best he could. Gates even admits that he considered deliberately failing the entrance exam (showing that students have their own wills and can use those wills to manipulate testing outcomes) and said that he was allowed to pursue his interest in computers outside of any mandated standards. Gates even recalls being pleased that he had no classes on Fridays.[56]

In short, everything he said in that 2005 speech regarding what he values about Lakeside directly contradicts the spectrum of so-called education "reforms" into which he pours millions (billions?)—not the least of which is CCSS.[57]

Gates's children also attended private schools,[58] including Lakeside.[59]

At one point in his 2014 interview with Layton, she asks Gates if he would want CCSS for his own children:

Is this something that you would want for your *own* kids to, to, these standards, that you would want for your own kids to learn, too?

His response:

We all want our, our own kids to exceed . . . remember what this is. This is six, what you should know in sixth grade, what you should know in seventh grade, eighth grade. It's not how it's taught or anything like that. Yes. I expect my kids to know a superset of the Common Core standards at every single grade involved. *I expect them to have the reading skills, uhh, uh, above what the reading and writing skills are in the Common Core standards.* So, absolutely. I don't see who, who would not want that.[60] [Emphasis added]

Gates wants his children to have reading and writing skills "above" those of CCSS.

For the $28,000 per year per student that Gates is paying for his three children to attend Lakeside School, surely they will be exposed to reading and writing "above" CCSS.

And yet, this is the man who is bankrolling CCSS for (as Gates terms it at one point in his interview with Layton) "mass" education, which is certainly education away from the manicured lawns of Lakeside School.

In August and September 2013, I examined all the organizations that received money from the Gates Foundation for developing and implementing CCSS. Since that time, the number has grown. As of June 22, 2014, the Gates Foundation search engine identified 165 grants under the key word *common core*.[61]

The most recent as of this 2014 writing involves the Gates Foundation paying $1.2 million to the United Way Worldwide "to build support for the Common Core State Standards by engaging stakeholders and community leaders nationally and locally." [62]

Gates will not refer to CCSS as a "national" set of standards, but his foundation will pay a worldwide organization to promote CCSS "nationally."

Aside from the organizations already noted as accepting Gates CCSS funding in this chapter, here is a sampling of 11 additional organizations that the Gates Foundation paid in order to advance CCSS:

U.S. Chamber of Commerce Foundation

Date: November 2013
Purpose: To lead the effort to engage and educate state and local chambers to support Common Core State Standards
Amount: $1,383,041[63]

James B. Hunt, Jr. Institute for Educational Leadership and Policy Foundation, Inc.

Date: October 2013
Purpose: To support states in their continued implementation of the Common Core State Standards
Amount: $1,749,070[64]

Harvard University

Date: July 2013
Purpose: To support Education Next's work in four critical areas: Common Core standards and assessments, digital learning teacher effectiveness, and charter schools
Amount: $557,168[65]

National Association of State Boards of Education

Date: June 2013
Purpose: To support a development plan for the organization and its efforts to provide training and information to implement the Common Core State Standards
Amount: $800,000[66]

The Aspen Institute Inc.

Date: January 2013
Purpose: To support the Aspen Institute's Urban Superintendents Network, develop resources to integrate Common Core State Standards and educator effectiveness policies and practices, and use lessons from the field to inform national policy
Amount: $3,615,655[67]

Fund for Public Schools Inc.

Date: November 2012
Purpose: To support the New York City Department of Education's integration of Common Core implementation strategies with new forms of teacher professional development to align with emerging functionalities and capacity of Shared Learning Infrastructure
Amount: $1,815,810[68]

Student Achievement Partners Inc.

Date: June 2012
Purpose: To support teachers nationwide in understanding and implementing the Common Core State Standards
Amount: $4,042,920[69]

Scholastic Inc.

Date: November 2011

Purpose: To support teachers' implementation of the Common Core State Standards in Mathematics
Amount: $4,463,541[70]

Stanford University

Date: August 2011
Purpose: To support implementation of the Common Core State Standards
Amount: $1,400,000[71]

Association for Supervision and Curriculum Development

Date: February 2011
Purpose: To provide teachers and school leaders with supports to implement the Common Core State Standards at the district, school, and classroom levels
Amount: $3,024,695[72]

The Education Trust

Date: September 2009
Purpose: To develop a set of open-source literacy courses that align with the Common Core State Standards
Amount: $2,039,526[73]

In 2008, two individuals, CCSSO president Gene Wilhoit and Student Achievement Partners founder David Coleman, asked billionaire Bill Gates if he would pay for the standardization of American public school classrooms nationwide.

He said yes.

Perched above the democratic process by way of his billions, he continues to strategically keep his word.

CHAPTER 10

Arne Wants In
Common Core and Race to the Top

One of the great questions concerning CCSS is the degree of federal involvement in this set of "common" standards present in states across the nation. Indeed, Americans are skittish about the idea of national standards because of the potential for national standards to be controlled "nationally"—that is, by the federal government. In August 2013, the National Conference of State Legislatures (NCSL) registered its concerns about federal overreach in controlling American public education through CCSS:

> Legislators applaud the efforts and results thus far of these state-led consortia. However, federal actions have contributed to our concerns that this effort may have as its ultimate result a nationalized K–12 system that will not remain voluntary and may have already been compromised by actions of both the state-led consortia and the federal government.[1]

Though reflected in NCSL's 2013 statement, concerns about federal overreach into state-level public education were not new to 2013. Lynne Cheney's 1994 public rejection of the National History Standards struck a federal control nerve; the controversy was so great that the Clinton administration attempted to publicly distance itself from connection to the tainted national history standards by attributing them to the previous, G. H. Bush, administration.[2] At the 1996 National Education Summit, Clinton acknowledged the propensity for federal involvement in education reform to kill the reform (see Chapter 2).

In advancing the idea of "a common core of standards" as part of its July 2008 *Out of Many, One* report, Achieve was careful to note that this "common core" could be both "voluntary" and "state-led." The report focuses on the states involved in the American Diploma Project (ADP) as coming together without the involvement of the federal government:

In the past, there has been remarkably little state-to-state consistency in curriculum standards. However, today nearly a third of the states, which collectively
educate nearly 40 percent of the U.S. public school population, have embraced
[ADP] college- and career-ready standards. *These states have demonstrated the
feasibility of ensuring that there is a common core of expectations in English and
mathematics among states while preserving the ability of each state to set its own
standards without federal involvement.*[3] [Emphasis added]

Even though in this report, Achieve was not advocating (yet) for what
would become the rigid, licensed, inflexible CCSS, it was careful to note
that the "common core of standards" to which it referred had no connection to Uncle Sam.

Eight months before Achieve published its *Out of Many, One* report,
the Council of Chief State School Officers (CCSSO) promoted in its November 2007 meeting the idea of states "volunteering" to come together
before the federal government pushed states in such a direction. (See
Chapter 3.)

Recall also that CCSSO president Gene Wilhoit and Student Achievement Partners founder David Coleman did not approach the U.S. Department of Education (USDOE) to fund CCSS; they approached a billionaire, Bill Gates. (See Chapter 9.) However, that does not mean that
the federal government would not have its place at the CCSS table.

In asking Gates for millions to bankroll CCSS, Wilhoit recalls Gates's
asking for an assurance that states would agree to this state-led CCSS.
As the *Washington Post*'s Lyndsey Layton reports, the meeting involving
Wilhoit, CCSS "lead writer" David Coleman, and Gates and his wife, Melinda, occurred in the summer of 2008 in Seattle. Wilhoit and Coleman
had come to ask Gates to pay for CCSS. Gates asked Wilhoit for some assurance, and Wilhoit said that CCSS reality was not certain but that they
would try their best.[4]

Giving CCSS their best effort involved CCSSO's and the National
Governors Association's (NGA) creating a memorandum of understanding (MOU) for governors and state superintendents to sign. This CCSS
MOU obligated states to agree to a "state-led" process for creating and
adopting CCSS and agreeing to consortia-created assessments for CCSS.[5]

The CCSS MOU also outlined the federal role in CCSS.

Now, some signatories might not have been expecting a "federal role" as part of the CCSS agreement. However, in the momentum
created by being part of what Fordham Institute second president Michael Petrilli promotes as "a wave of innovation,"[6] governors and state

superintendents were arguably enticed to belong to this "in crowd of innovators." Moreover, the manner in which the federal role was worded in the CCSS MOU made it sound as though USDOE was willing to offer cash to states to "assist" with the "state-led" process being orchestrated by the NGA, CCSSO, Achieve, Student Achievement Partners, and Gates, among others.

Though discussed in Chapter 5, let us once again examine the CCSS MOU section on the federal role:

> **Federal Role.** The parties support a state-led effort and not a federal effort to develop a common core of state standards; there is, however, an appropriate federal role in supporting this state-led effort. In particular, *the federal government can provide key financial support* for this effort in developing a common core of state standards *and in moving toward common assessments, such as through the Race to the Top Fund authorized in the American Recovery and Reinvestment Act of 2009.* Further, the federal government can incentivize this effort through a range of tiered incentives, such as providing states with greater flexibility in the use of existing federal funds, supporting a revised state accountability structure, and offering financial support for states to effectively implement the standards. *Additionally, the federal government can provide additional financial support for the development of common assessments,* teacher and principal professional development, and other related common core standards supports, and a research agenda that can help continually improve the common core over time. Finally, the federal government can revise and align existing federal education laws with the lessons learned from states' international benchmarking efforts and from federal research.[7] [Emphasis added]

In signing this MOU, governors and state superintendents agreed that the federal government was to have a role in this yet-to-be-developed CCSS—and that role was to be one of extensive involvement in everything except the actual development of CCSS.

Most governors and state superintendents signed the CCSS MOU in the spring of 2009—in time for the June 2009 Hunt Institute–sponsored NGA Symposium announcement that "46 states and three U.S. territories" were already signed on for the CCSS effort.[8] Indeed, the Hunt Institute had already had a hand in actively promoting the "common standards" idea. In May 2008, the Gates Foundation paid the Hunt Institute $2.2 million "to promote the broad adoption of rigorous, internationally benchmarked education standards by states."[9] In June 2008, the Hunt Institute and NGA were promoting the CCSS spectrum of reform, including standards, curriculum, assessments, and more. Consider the words of key NGA member, North Carolina governor Jim Hunt:

> "How U.S. student achievement compares internationally is alarming," said former North Carolina Gov. Jim Hunt of the Hunt Institute. "If we are going to change our international standing and improve the quality of education, *it has to start with high, rigorous standards.*" . . .
>
> High, rigorous standards are the foundation of a strong education system. Content standards specify the knowledge and skills that students need at each grade level. *These standards must be supported by an aligned and clearly articulated system of curriculum, assessments, teacher preparation and professional development, textbook selection and appropriate supports for students.*[10] [Emphasis added]

With that statement, the NGA and the Hunt Institute outlined the expectation for CCSS to be more than a set of standards; CCSS was to be the foundation for a spectrum of reform. CCSS was to lead to the standardization of the entire public classroom, including "aligned" curriculum, teaching materials, teacher preparation, and assessments.

And according to the more formal CCSS MOU, the NGA and CCSSO declared the federal government to be "appropriately" involved in offering financial backing for everything except CCSS development.

The first evidence of USDOE connection with CCSS is the CCSS MOU reference to the "Race to the Top fund authorized in the American Recovery and Reinvestment Act [ARRA] of 2009." Keep in mind that the CCSS MOU predates by months the official announcement of a federally sponsored "Race to the Top." However, in order for this language to be included in the "state-led" CCSS MOU, the federal government must have communicated as much to the NGA and CCSSO. Race to the Top (RTTT) was coming, and federal ARRA money would somehow be available through RTTT to those states that signed this CCSS MOU.

ARRA is otherwise known as the "stimulus package" that the 111th Congress signed into law in February 2009.[11] Though ARRA was supposedly designed to "stimulate" the American economy, the Congressional Budget Office (CBO) and Joint Committee on Taxation projected that between 2009 and 2019, ARRA would increase budget deficits by $831 billion.[12] It appears counterintuitive to "stimulate the economy" by increasing the U.S. budget deficit. Nevertheless, billions were made available via an ARRA that was to be administered by the heads of federal agencies.[13] In the case of ARRA funding earmarked for public education, U.S. Secretary of Education Arne Duncan is the overseer of the education-allotted billions. The ARRA document subsection on the USDOE includes numerous funding designations: $13 billion toward "education of the disadvantaged"; $100 million designated as "impact aid"; $720 million toward "school improvement programs"; $200 million earmarked for "innovation and improvement"; $12.2 billion designated for "special education"; $680 million for "rehabilitation services and disability research"; $15.84 billion toward "student financial assistance"; $60 million for "student aid administration"; $100 million designated for "higher education"; $250 million earmarked for the "institution of education sciences," and $2.1 billion for Head Start and Early Head Start programs. The total of these 11 designations equals $45.3 billion, with marginal funding designated for administrative purposes in a number of categories.[14]

All funds above are clearly tied to the Elementary and Secondary Education Act (ESEA), except for the $2.1 billion for Head Start and Early Head Start.[15] The degree to which ARRA is tied to ESEA is important in answering the question of whether or not Duncan violated his federal role in his promoting of CCSS.

ARRA also appropriated $53.6 billion toward the State Fiscal Stabilization Fund (SFSF).[16] Although SFSF funds can be used toward programs established and maintained under ESEA, the SFSF funds are not awarded under the heading of ESEA—a crucial point for Duncan's overt CCSS push.[17] To monies from the SFSF fund Duncan has attached what he terms the "Four Assurances of the ARRA" that he and the NGA publicized at the Hunt/NGA Governors Symposium in June 2009:

1. Adopt internationally benchmarked standards and assessments that prepare students for success in college and the workplace.
2. Recruit, develop, retain, and reward effective teachers and principals.
3. Turn around low-performing schools.
4. Build data systems that measure student success and inform teachers and principals how they can improve their practices.[18]

Each of Duncan's "assurances" centers on the "standards" and requires standards-aligned assessments in order to determine what he considers "success." In order to qualify for a slice of the ARRA $53.6 billion at Duncan's discretion (in other words, SFSF funds), states were required to abide by the "assurances" noted above, which are related to the "assurances" listed in the "state applications" section of the SFSF document.[19]

Notice that these "assurances" do not mention common standards (and certainly not a "common core of standards"). There has been a bit of tag-teaming going on in order to sell the "common core" idea to governors and state superintendents, and Duncan (and the federal government) has stayed strategically on the fringes. As noted in Chapter 6, David Coleman admitted "convincing governors and others" to sign on for CCSS. Duncan has a longstanding history with Coleman, one that goes back to 2001 and Duncan's time as Chicago Schools CEO (see Chapter 6). Coleman was also involved in the assessment business and capitalized on the mandates of No Child Left Behind (NCLB) (see Chapter 6). It was Coleman who accompanied CCSSO president Gene Wilhoit on the hours-long meeting to ask Gates to bankroll CCSS. Duncan could not use federal money to directly bankroll CCSS, even if it were "state-led" and not "national" standards.

In creating the CCSS MOU, the NGA and CCSSO worked in a section on the "federal role," and they made it sound enticing—USDOE was there to give money to all aspects of CCSS except its creation. So, technically, USDOE did not have a hand in CCSS development.

Nevertheless, in referring in the CCSS MOU to ARRA funds and even to the not-yet-created RTTT, the NGA and CCSSO betray the intention for CCSS to become tied to RTTT. And here comes more subtlety: In the June 2009 Hunt/NGA Governors Symposium report, the NGA proudly proclaims that aside from the 21 governors in attendance, other governors representing 46 states and three U.S. territories have already "committed to the Common Core State Standards Initiative."[20] Though Duncan was present at the 2009 symposium, and though he did promote the idea of standards "that prepare students for success in college and the workplace"—the now-common CCSS descriptor[21]—he did not directly connect CCSS to the ARRA via the language of his "four assurances." The June 2009 symposium report did mention the RTTT to come, as noted in Duncan's address to the 21 governors in attendance:

> In his keynote address, Secretary Duncan spoke of the ARRA, which was passed by Congress in February 2009 and provides an unprecedented $100 billion in federal funding for education. *This funding is tied to four assurances . . .* , and the secretary emphasized the importance of working in concert toward all four of the goals. *More than $4 billion of this money has been reserved for the competitive Race to the Top grants,* which present the nation's governors with an extraordinary opportunity to make bold reforms in education. In a budget year when most states are struggling just to keep education funding stable, the Race to the Top funds provide governors who are ready to push for innovative education reform with much-needed funding.[22] [Emphasis added]

As the June 2009 NGA report aptly notes, states are desperate for money to fund education. This makes any money—whether it is tied to "four assurances" or to not-yet-released stipulations of RTTT—quite the lure for susceptible governors and state superintendents.

Governor and state superintendent susceptibility aside, Duncan was careful not to directly connect CCSS to RTTT in his June 2009 speech. In order to tie CCSS to ARRA (and specifically, SFSF) money instead, Duncan would use RTTT—the initiative mentioned in the CCSS MOU but that did not formally exist at the time that the NGA and CCSSO composed the CCSS MOU (at some point between February and May 2009, the months that ARRA was announced and that Louisiana signed the MOU,[23] respectively). Of course, the degree of separation was necessary so that it would appear that Duncan was not mandating state adoption of CCSS as a requirement to "compete" for RTTT money.

On July 24, 2009, President Obama and Duncan formally announced the RTTT competition, with $4.35 billion in ARRA funds specifically from SFSF earmarked for RTTT.[24] According to the USDOE press release, the RTTT "winners" would be states and districts that are "leading the way on school reform" or (in the same paragraph) "driving reform."[25]

It should come as no surprise that the criteria for winning the competition for RTTT funds were Duncan's previously announced "four assurances"—the same four that serve as the criteria for SFSF state funding decisions.[26] In the RTTT press release, Obama declared that these four criteria are "what works":

> "This competition will not be based on politics, ideology, or the preferences of a particular interest group. Instead, it will be based on a simple principle—whether a state is ready to do *what works.* We will use the best data available to determine whether a state can meet a few key benchmarks for reform—*and states that outperform the rest will be rewarded with a grant. Not every state will win and not every school district will be happy with the results.* But America's children, America's economy, and America itself will be better for it," President Obama said in a speech at the U.S. Department of Education headquarters in Washington.
>
> *The centerpiece of the Obama administration's education reform efforts is the $4.35 billion Race to the Top Fund*, a national competition which will highlight and replicate effective education reform strategies in four significant areas:
>
> *Adopting internationally benchmarked standards and assessments that prepare students for success in college and the workplace;* Recruiting, developing, rewarding, and retaining effective teachers and principals; Building data systems that measure student success and inform teachers and principals how they can improve their practices; and Turning around our lowest-performing schools.[27]
> [Emphasis added]

This press release was the official herald for the RTTT competition. States could submit lengthy applications to vie for a slice of the $4.35 billion dedicated to this "race." In "phase one" of the RTTT competition, 40 states and DC "competed"[28] in a "race" that ended with two winners— Delaware and Tennessee. Delaware received $100 million and Tennessee $500 million to implement Duncan's "four assurances."[29]

Not to worry, says USDOE. Plenty of money left. There will be a second round for those states that did not "win" by promising to follow Duncan's "four assurances" initially publicized at the June 2009 Hunt/NGA Governors Symposium. For "phase two," 35 states and DC vied for the remaining $3.4 billion advertised in March 2010.[30] In August 2010, USDOE announced that there were an additional 10 "winners": DC, Florida, Georgia, Hawaii, Maryland, Massachusetts, New York, North Carolina, Ohio, and Rhode Island. The awards ranged from $75 million to $700 million. The total awarded amount for phase two was $3.325 billion. The allotted $3.4 billion in ARRA funds for phase two of RTTT was effectively spent.

But Duncan hoped to budget $1.35 billion in 2011 for a phase three.

As it turns out, USDOE did have a phase three for RTTT; seven states entered[31] and, amazingly, all seven won. However, the total available was substantially less than in the previous two phases: $200 million. The awards to the seven "winners" ranged between $17 million and $43 million.

What this "race" did was financially obligate the 18 "winners" to follow a set of test-driven reforms prescribed by USDOE—including that one about "benchmarked standards" to make students "college and career ready."

So. Did USDOE require RTTT applicants to sign on for CCSS?

Technically, no. In constructing the CCSS MOU, the NGA and CCSSO used language to entice states to sign on and be "state led" with the promise of potential funding to underwrite the CCSS bandwagon— with the federal role described as "appropriately" funding all except CCSS development. The CCSS MOU mentions RTTT and ARRA, information that originated with the federal government and somehow found its way into the MOU.

Technically, Duncan did not directly put his hands on states' standards.

That does not mean he did not participate in manipulating components of the CCSS process.

In spring 2009, prior to any official announcement of RTTT, 46 states and three U.S. territories had already signed that MOU—which conveniently made sure the CCSS MOU was in place by the time RTTT was announced and the RTTT application made ready for states to complete.

The RTTT application rubric shows what USDOE requires of RTTT applicants. It includes a section entitled "Standards and Assessments," which is worth a possible 70 points, or 14% of the total application points. Under this heading, it is clear that USDOE expects states to "participate in consortium developing high-quality standards" and to "adopt" such standards.

USDOE is dancing right on the line called "federal overreach."

In requiring states to have "common," "consortium-developed" standards, USDOE is imposing its will upon the states. In other words, RTTT leaves no room (and offers no point-value credit toward securing RTTT funds) for states that do not wish to participate in a "common standards consortium."

Some may say that USDOE did not force states to compete for RTTT; therefore, USDOE did not force states to participate in a "standards-developing consortium." And yet, not signing up was a pretty sure way to lose the race for cash.

If the ARRA funds for RTTT had fallen under the jurisdiction of ESEA, then USDOE would have clearly overstepped in requiring states to participate in a "common standards consortium" in order to qualify for RTTT funding. However, the $4.35 billion earmarked for RTTT was not under ESEA. The RTTT funding was only under SFSF.[32] This might appear to be unnecessary dissection; however, it is important. The $100 billion in ARRA assistance can be divided into two allotments: the $53.6 in SFSF funding[33] and the remaining (roughly) $46 billion primarily designated "to carry out" ESEA programs.[34]

The fact that Duncan is using SFSF money for RTTT (and not ARRA money that was put under ESEA jurisdiction) contributes to his skirting the popularly held assumption that the federal government could not tie federal funding to federal judgments about the suitability of state standards. According to ESEA Subpart Two, section 9527, USDOE is not to tie ESEA funding to federal government judgments about state standards:

(C) Prohibition on requiring federal approval or certification of standards-

(1) IN GENERAL—Notwithstanding any other provision of Federal law, no State shall be required to have academic content or student academic achievement standards approved or certified by the Federal Government, *in order to receive assistance under this Act*.[35] [Emphasis added]

Duncan and USDOE dodge this ESEA restriction of "standards approval" by funding RTTT through SFSF monies.

What Duncan and USDOE do manage to accomplish with the "consortium-developed common standards" language in the RTTT application is to cement state participation in CCSS by offering states the "opportunity" to submit their CCSS MOUs as evidence of "consortium-developed common standards" participation.[36]

The RTTT application even includes language from the CCSS MOU—without identifying the CCSS MOU as the source. Consider this description of "common standards" from the RTTT *Application for Initial Funding*:

> Common set of K–12 standards means a set of content standards that define what students must know and be able to do and that are substantially identical across all States in a consortium. A State may supplement the common standards with additional standards, provided that the additional standards do not exceed 15 percent of the State's total standards for that content area.[37]

This stipulation—that "common standards" "not exceed 15 percent of the state's total standards for that content area"—is taken straight from the CCSS MOU (see Chapter 5).

The RTTT application does not mention CCSS by name. However, the intent for RTTT to promote CCSS is unmistakable. In June 2009—1 month prior to the official RTTT press release—46 states and three U.S. territories just happened to sign on for CCSS—a "consortium" for developing "common standards," to be followed by "common assessments." And Duncan just happened to devote $350 million to "support the development of high-quality assessments" as announced at the June 2009 Hunt/NGA symposium.[38] As another matter of coincidence, in order to garner RTTT points for assessments, USDOE also required states to be involved in "developing and implementing high-quality assessments"—via consortium[39]—which they could verify with their signed MOU.

Thus far, Duncan and USDOE have come as close as is possible to violating the ESEA stipulation that the federal government not direct state standards without crossing over.

The money to fund RTTT is not ESEA money.

The inclusion of "common, consortium-developed" standards as a requirement of RTTT does not violate federal law because RTTT is not funded under ESEA.

Duncan has successfully skirted overstepping any legal restriction on his authority. That does not mean the public is pleased, and it does not mean his participation in maneuvering states into CCSS adoption is ethical. Most of all, it does not mean that his slick actions have not contributed to the general belief that the federal government cannot be trusted in regard to its involvements in state education affairs.

Through a complex weaving, U.S. Secretary of Education Arne Duncan promoted CCSS as a welcomed component of RTTT. Thus, the federal government was undeniably connected to CCSS before there even was a CCSS.

The wording of the RTTT application form does not include direct mention of CCSS. However, it does describe what CCSS is—consortium-developed standards to which states have bound themselves via a MOU that, in turn, USDOE accepted as RTTT-necessitated proof of the state commitment to the only "consortium-developed standards" game in town. Furthermore, USDOE expects these "common" standards to be accompanied via "common" assessments—also mentioned as an inseparable component of CCSS in the CCSS MOU—and USDOE just so happens to have used SFSF money to provide the initial funding for two CCSS assessment consortia.

Let us briefly consider the two assessment consortia that received ARRA funding from USDOE: the Partnership for Assessment of College and Careers (PARCC)[40] and the Smarter Balanced Assessment Consortium (SBAC).[41] As of June 26, 2014, PARCC included 13 states (Arizona, Arkansas, Colorado, Illinois, Maryland, Massachusetts, Mississippi, New Jersey, New Mexico, New York, Ohio, Rhode Island, Pennsylvania) and DC, with Pennsylvania participating in both PARCC and SBAC.[42, 43] Maryland served as fiscal agent for the USDOE grant once Florida, the original fiscal agent, dropped PARCC in November 2013.[44, 45] In an effort to ensure its survival in the long term, PARCC became a nonprofit in March 2014. In the official announcement on the PARCC website, "PARCC the Nonprofit" announces that it "will continue to be state led."[46] The website does not mention federal oversight.

As of April 1, 2014, SBAC, more commonly known as Smarter Balanced, included 23 states (California, Connecticut, Delaware, Hawaii, Idaho, Iowa, Maine, Michigan, Missouri, Montana, Nevada, New Hampshire, North Carolina, North Dakota, Oregon, Pennsylvania, South Carolina, South Dakota, Vermont, Washington, West Virginia, Wisconsin, and Wyoming) and the U.S. Virgin Islands. Washington State was the fiscal agent for the USDOE grant.[47] SBAC also describes itself as "state led"[48] and does not mention USDOE oversight.[49–51]

And now, about that federal oversight into both testing consortia:

PARCC received a $170 million federal startup grant, and SBAC a $160 million federal startup grant. Furthermore, both consortia received an additional $16 million to help consortia states "transition" to the resulting assessments. (Transitioning to common assessments happens to be one of the RTTT criteria.[52]) Both consortia received a grant notification letter dated September 28, 2010, which included the clear intent that USDOE would be actively involved in assessment development:

> This award is subject to the attached grant conditions related to administering the grant, monitoring sub-recipients, reporting, maintaining adequate financial controls and procedures regarding the selection, award, and administration of contracts or agreements. *Further, in accordance with 34 CFR 75.234(b), this award is classified as a cooperative agreement and will include substantial involvement on the part of the Department of Education program contact.* As noted in the grant award documents, *we expect that PARCC and the Department will successfully negotiate and complete a final cooperative agreement* the recipient signs and returns no later than January 7, 2011. [Emphasis added] [53,54]

If there were any doubt that USDOE intended to insert itself into the work of the two "state-led" testing consortia, the "cooperative agreement" referenced above makes USDOE involvement as clear as a freshly cleaned window:

> In accordance with 34 CFR 75.200(b)(4), this award is a cooperative agreement because the Secretary of Education (Secretary) has determined that substantial communication, coordination, and involvement between the U.S. Department of Education (Department or ED) and the recipient is necessary to carry out a successful project.[55]

Here are some of the expectations outlined in the cooperative agreement:

> These assessments are intended to play a critical role in educational systems; provide administrators, educators, parents, and students with the data and information needed to continuously improve teaching and learning; *and help meet the President's goal of restoring, by 2020, the nation's position as the world leader in college graduates.*[56] [Emphasis added]

Remember, America has decided to "race to the top" globally based upon the superficial measure of the number of college graduates. This way, we can once again become a world power.

Moving on.

More cooperative agreement language:

Specifically, the recipient will develop an assessment system that measures student knowledge and skills against a common set of college and career-ready standards in mathematics and English language arts in a way that covers the full range of those standards. . . . The recipient's assessment systems developed with the RTTA (Race to the Top Assessments) grants will assess all students, including English learners and students with disabilities . . . . Finally, the assessment systems will produce data (including student achievement data and student growth data) that can be used to inform (a) determinations of school effectiveness; (b) determinations of individual principal and teacher effectiveness for purposes of evaluation; (c) determinations of principal and teacher professional development and support needs; and (d) teaching, learning, and program improvement.[57, 58]

In "offering" to fund the CCSS assessments, USDOE invited itself to oversee the assessments and to make sure that the two "state-led" assessment consortia were complying with the test-driven intention of RTTT. The cooperative agreement continues with the details of USDOE oversight of its financial investment in the two CCSS-tied testing consortia.

In accepting USDOE funding, the two testing consortia agreed to a definite federal presence in CCSS assessment development. As for Duncan: He achieved more with the $350 million in USDOE grants for the two CCSS testing consortia than he did with RTTT alone. Via RTTT, Duncan managed to tie 18 states and DC to CCSS and its "consortia-developed common assessments." However, in funding SBAC and PARCC, Duncan not only reined in many more states; he reined them into so-called "state-led" assessments that the federal government actively controlled, at least in part.

Some might wonder why Duncan funded two CCSS assessment consortia rather than one.

I think doing so offered states (and the public) the illusion of choice: USDOE-financed-and-monitored PARCC, or USDOE-financed-and-monitored SBAC.

As a means to a "common assessment" end, CCSS was intended to provide the foundation for the USDOE, test score–dependent "four assurances" hovering over ARRA education funding and especially over the SFSF component of ARRA education funding. For the most part, with his carefully planned, technically correct distance from CCSS, Duncan did well in stopping just short of federal overreach into state education affairs.

Nevertheless, despite all of this care, Duncan *could* cross over a clear line in attempting to connect state waivers from the languishing NCLB (due for a 2007 reauthorization that did not happen; see Chapter 1) via the condition that states adopt "college and career ready" academic standards—*if* his enforcement involved limits on ESEA-related funding. Such a condition precludes CCSS and would qualify as a clear violation of ESEA Subpart Two, section 9527. NCLB was a 2001 reauthorization of ESEA, and because it was, Duncan could not make himself the judge over state standards suitability and tie the consequences of states' not adopting CCSS to any ESEA-related fiscal sanctions. In May 2014, Duncan threatened to withdraw Indiana's NCLB waiver when Indiana dropped CCSS in favor of developing its own new state standards. Duncan's office asserted that Indiana needed to offer proof that the new standards (and associated assessments) fit the condition of "college and career ready." Otherwise, Indiana could face sanctions related to not adhering to NCLB. Duncan did not specifically state that he would alter any NCLB-related funding.[59]

Once again, he is perched on the edge of federal overreach. Moreover, Duncan lacks finesse with the American public, especially on the occasion of his shifting the blame for CCSS resistance from the Tea Party to American mothers. As education writer Valerie Strauss records in the *Washington Post*:

> On Friday [November 15, 2013], Duncan spoke in Richmond, Va., about the growing opposition to Common Core and their implementation in states around the country before a meeting of the Council of Chief State Schools Officers Organization. Education Department communications chief Massie Ritsch said in an e-mail that he does not believe that there is a full transcript of Duncan's remarks, but he referred to the following write-up from *Politico*'s Libby Nelson, who was at the event:
>
> > Education Secretary Arne Duncan told an audience of state superintendents this afternoon that the Education Department and other Common Core supporters didn't fully anticipate the effect the standards would have once implemented.
> >
> > *"It's fascinating to me that some of the pushback is coming from, sort of, white suburban moms who—all of a sudden—their child isn't as brilliant as they thought they were* and their school isn't quite as good as they thought they were, and that's pretty scary," Duncan said. "You've bet your house and where you live and everything on, 'My child's going to be prepared.' That can be a punch in the gut."[60] [Emphasis added]

Concealed in his insult to "White suburban moms" is the admission that his "four assurances"—of which "common standards" is the hub—are not the guarantees he is trying hard to manipulate "state-led" America into believing that they are.

Has Duncan overstepped his authority?

Possibly.

In August 2014, it seemed that Duncan had crossed the line in revoking Oklahoma's NCLB waiver[61] following Oklahoma's rejection of CCSS in favor of its former state standards on June 5, 2014.[62] Nevertheless, even here Duncan is perched on a technicality. USDOE revoked Oklahoma's waiver so close to the beginning of the 2014–2015 school year that USDOE-directed sanctions over Oklahoma's ESEA Title I funding would not take effect until the 2015–2016 school year.[63]

Thus, Duncan *technically* has not yet taken control of Oklahoma's Title I money as a result of the state's rejecting CCSS.

In October 2014, Oklahoma superintendent Janet Baresi announced Oklahoma's plan to reapply for the waiver.[64] In order for Oklahoma to receive a NCLB waiver renewal, Duncan required that Oklahoma higher education institutions grant the former Oklahoma state standards their approval. However, in the press, Duncan was relatively quiet about the issue. His well-known public push for a CCSS that he was supposedly not involved with might have cued him in that he was too close to federal overreach for his own CCSS- and CCSS-assessments-promoting good.

Duncan surely must be aware that public opinion is not rooted in technicality.

CHAPTER 11

Those "Powerful Market Forces"

Pearson Wins

In March 2014, billionaire Bill Gates participated in an interview with the American Enterprise Institute (AEI), one of the many organizations he financially supports in his effort to promote the Common Core State Standards (CCSS) (see Chapter 9). In a 6-minute video clip from the AEI interview, Gates purports to explain various aspects of CCSS, including the reason for the "common" component. His explanation has nothing to do with educational quality:

> If [states] have two [sets of standards] they're comparing, they ought to probably pick something in common because, to some degree, this is an area where, if you do have commonality, it's like an electrical plug, You get more free market competition. *Scale is good for free market competition. Individual state regulatory capture is not good for competition.*[1] [Emphasis added]

His mechanical analogy of education as an object to "plug in" aside, Gates says that the "commonality" of CCSS "is good for free market competition"; however, he immediately notes that he prefers market competition on a level beyond that of the state. In other words, education companies that are smaller—and are more likely to be vested in their locales—are not the market Gates wishes to promote.

Gates is thinking bigger. Much bigger.

In her March 2014 interview with Gates, *Washington Post* reporter Lyndsey Layton asks Gates about Gates's Microsoft and the business relationship it has with international education corporation Pearson—and the possibility that Gates is promoting CCSS because of the potential for Microsoft to benefit financially from CCSS-related business arrangements.

Gates is not pleased with the question, and he states that Microsoft's business arrangement with Pearson is not connected to CCSS.[2]

Still, Gates clearly promotes CCSS so that American education can be brought "to scale"—and to a level that only national and international education corporations could manage. Microsoft is a major corporation, and as such, it could benefit from CCSS. Layton's question is appropriate and appears to hit a nerve with the billionaire founder of Microsoft.

As Layton points out, Pearson is also a major corporation that could benefit from CCSS.

As to Gates's stated benefit of CCSS as promoting free market competition: Small education businesses, step aside. CCSS is for the big boys.

So much for "free market competition."

Ever since the outset of CCSS, Pearson's profit-hungry radar has been on alert. The intent of this chapter is to examine Pearson's profitability hopes regarding CCSS. First, a brief word about the history of Pearson Education.[3, 4]

A CENTURY AND A HALF OF PEARSON

Pearson was not always a company in the education market. Far from it. In 1844, Samuel Pearson founded a construction company, S. Pearson and Son, in Yorkshire (England). In 1879, Samuel retired and gave his share of the firm to his grandson, Weetman, who then became partner to his own father, George Pearson. In 1884, Pearson relocated its headquarters from Yorkshire to London. Under Weetman's direction, Pearson prospered. Weetman turned Pearson into one of the largest building contractors in England. The Pearson business good fortune continued when, in its work in Mexico in 1910, Pearson struck oil and later sold its oil shares to Shell-Royal Dutch. Beginning around 1910, aside from construction, Pearson became involved in oil, coal mines, electricity, and aviation. Add to these expanded business involvements the fact that in 1921, Pearson acquired a number of United Kingdom local newspapers, from which it created Westminster Press. Around 1935, Pearson turned its attention away from building, and its oil, coal mines, electricity, and aviation interests became nationalized (i.e., the government took them over).[5] Also around 1935, Weetman's son, Clive, became chairman of the company. In the early 1950s, Pearson gained a controlling interest in the *Financial Times*.

Once Clive's nephew, Weetman John Churchill Pearson, entered the business in the mid-1950s, Pearson gradually became an "industrial group" via a business strategy called *acquisition*. As *Investopedia* notes,

> Acquisitions are often made as part of a company's growth strategy whereby it is more beneficial to take over an existing firm's operations and niche compared to expanding on its own.[6]

Here is a summary of Weetman John's "acquisition" contribution:

> Clive's nephew, Weetman John Churchill Pearson, became increasingly involved
> in the affairs of the family company, taking over as chairman when his uncle re-
> tired in 1954. The company had a controlling interest in Lazards, the merchant
> bank, and a variety of other financial and industrial investments, including West-
> minster Press, a chain of provincial newspapers. Over the next twenty-three years,
> the company was transformed by acquisition into a broadly based and highly
> profitable industrial group by buying well-managed firms which had a strong
> position in niche markets and which were capable of being developed over the
> long term.[7]

Since the 1950s, Pearson acquisitions have centered on publishing,
including education publishing. Here are some of Pearson's acquisitions
since the mid-1950s: *Financial Times* (1957), Longman Publishing
(1968), Penguin Publishing (1970) (Penguin expanded into the Penguin
Group in 1983), Addison-Wesley (1988), HarperCollins Educational
Publishing (1996) (also in 1996, Pearson's Penguin Group acquired the
Putnam Berkley Group), Simon and Schuster (1998), Dorling Kindersley
and NCS (2000), Rough Guides (2002), Edexcel (2003), AGS Publishing (2005), Harcourt Assessment and Harcourt Education International
(2007), Wall Street English (2009), Medley Global Advisors (2010),
Connections Education, Schoolnet, TutorVista (2011), EmbanetCom-
pass (2012), and Grupo Multi (2013).[8]

There's more.

In 1985, Pearson's *Financial Times* expanded to New York, then to
Germany in 1999 as *Financial Times Deutschland*. Pearson moved its *Financial Times* into Asia in 2003 and Australia in 2004. In 2012, Penguin
combined with Random House to become the world's largest trade pub-
lisher. And Pearson continues to purchase stakes in other companies—
presumably with an eye to eventually own them if doing so might prove
profitable (e.g., Pearson holds a 61% stake in Interactive Data and a 75%
stake in CTI Education Group).[9]

Pearson is *huge*, and it continues to grow. Here is the Reuters description of Pearson in 2014:

> Pearson plc (Pearson), incorporated on August 12, 1897, is an international
> media and education company with its principal operations in the education,
> business information and consumer publishing markets. The Company deliv-
> ers the content in a range of forms and through a variety of channels, including
> books, newspapers and online services. It offers services, as well as content, from
> test creation, administration and processing to teacher development and school

software. It operates in more than 70 countries worldwide, its major markets are the United States (55% of sales) and Europe (22% of sales). Pearson consists of three worldwide businesses: Pearson Education, The FT Group and The Penguin Group. Effective August 27, 2013, Pearson acquired BioBehavioral Diagnostics Co.[10]

CCSS fits a company as huge and as financially aggressive as Pearson like a multimillion- (billion-?) dollar glove on an ever-expanding hand. (Notice that the acquisition mentioned last is that of a company to "diagnose behavior"—as in student behavior. But that is another topic for another book.)

I'm sure that for Pearson executives, CCSS was love at first dollar sign.

THE PEARSON-COMMON CORE ENGAGEMENT

Pearson appeared on the CCSS scene in 2009, at which time its nonprofit, the Pearson Charitable Foundation (PCF), paid the Council of Chief State School Officers (CCSSO) a $100,000 "grant."[11] PCF paid CCSSO two additional "grants" in 2010 ($340,000)[12] and 2011 ($100,000).[13] Thus, by way of its nonprofit (which Pearson "the For-profit" happens to primarily fund[14] and which Gates also funds),[15] Pearson paid over half a million dollars to one of the two organizations that holds the license for CCSS.

An engagement ring in its CCSS love affair.

Indeed, the CCSS license includes language that identifies two education companies as supplying CCSS examples: McGraw-Hill and Penguin Group.[16]

McGraw-Hill is the company that purchased CCSS "lead writer" David Coleman's Grow Network in 2004 and for which Coleman worked until 2007, the year that he founded his nebulously defined education company, Student Achievement Partners (see Chapter 6).

Penguin Group is a Pearson acquisition—the same Pearson that owns the nonprofit PCF that donated over half a million to CCSS license holder, CCSSO.

Cozy, isn't it?

Interestingly, on November 18, 2014, Pearson announced that its nonprofit arm, PLC, would close at the end of 2014. The explanation was that Pearson plans "to integrate all of its corporate responsibility activities and functions into its business as a way to maximise social impact."[17]

PLC or no, along the lines of "maximizing" its "impact," Pearson Education is definitely depending on CCSS to turn handsome profits. And to a company the size of Pearson, with its 2013 sales at GBP 5.2 billion (approximately $8.8 billion),[18] CCSS holds promise for profits in a variety of products and services.

PEARSON: "WE'RE BIG, SO QUALITY BECOMES IRRELEVANT"

"Bigger" does not necessarily mean "better," as evidenced in Pearson Education's history of test scoring errors, delays, and other issues in which the Pearson product disrupts education flow around the country. As I note in a blog post from May 2014:

> In September 2013, FairTest Public Education Director Bob Schaeffer compiled a list of Pearson's testing errors, questionable practices, and subsequent fines/lawsuits dating back to 1998.
>
> Schaeffer documented 38 incidents—24 of which have happened since 2011.
>
> High-stakes testing failures have high-stakes consequences. Here are several highlights from Schaeffer's list. Each incident is noted by year and state in which the Pearson error incident occurred:
>
> 2000 Minnesota—45,739 *misgraded* graduation tests leads to lawsuit with $11 million settlement—judge found "years of quality control problems" and a "culture emphasizing profitability and cost-cutting."
>
> 2005 Virginia—computerized test *misgraded*—five students awarded $5,000 scholarships [based on misgraded test results]
>
> 2009–2010 Wyoming—Pearson's new computer adaptive PAWS [Proficiency Assessments for Wyoming Students] *flops*; state declares company in "*complete default* of the contract;" $5.1 million fine accepted after negotiations but not pursued by state governor
>
> 2012 New York—More than 7,000 New York City elementary and middle school students *wrongly blocked from graduation* by inaccurate "preliminary scores" on Pearson tests
>
> 2012 New York—More than two dozen *additional errors* found in New York State tests developed by Pearson
>
> 2012 Mississippi—Pearson pays $623,000 for *scoring error repeated over four years that blocked graduation* for five students and wrongly lowered scores for 121 others
>
> 2013 New York—Pearson makes three test scoring mistakes *blocking nearly 5,000 students* from gifted-and-talented program eligibility

2013 Virginia—4,000 *parents receive inaccurate test scorecards* due to Pearson error in converting scores to proficiency levels.[19]

Despite Pearson's established history of testing errors that have profoundly impacted the education systems in a number of states, in May 2014, one of the two CCSS testing consortia, the Partnership for Assessment of Readiness for College and Careers (PARCC), awarded Pearson the contract to develop the PARCC test. As reported by *Education Week*'s Sean Cavanagh and also included in my May 2014 Pearson blog post:

> The global education company Pearson has landed a major contract to administer tests aligned to the common core standards, a project described as being of "unprecedented scale" in the U.S. testing arena by one official who helped negotiate it.
>
> The decision to award the contract, announced Friday [April 30, 2014], was made by a group of states developing tests linked to the common core for the Partnership for Assessment of Readiness for College and Careers, one of two main consortia of states creating exams to match the standards.
>
> *Pearson is expected to perform a broad range of duties under the contract, including development of test items, delivery of paper-and-pencil and computerized test forms, reporting of results, analysis of scores,* and working with states to develop "cut scores," or performance standards for the exams. [20, 21] [Emphasis added]

That "Pearson is expected to perform a broad range of duties" fits with Gates's assertion that CCSS will bring education in states nationwide "to scale." A nationally expansive education endeavor such as CCSS requires a mammoth company to "scale" it nationwide. However, it seems that Pearson's past performance becomes irrelevant because "market competition" is slim as a result of a lack of mammoth-education competition.

Or is it?

One curious fact is that former CCSSO president Gene Wilhoit—who was president of CCSSO during the time that Pearson's nonprofit, PCF, donated half a million dollars to CCSSO—became one of three board members for the PARCC nonprofit, launched in February 2014.[22] (The other two PARCC board members are Laura Slover, formerly with Achieve and serving on the CCSS development groups,[23] and Paul Pastorek, former Louisiana superintendent who cosigned the CCSS MOU for Louisiana.)[24] A second curious fact, this one noted in press related to Pearson's winning the PARCC contract, was that Pearson was the only bidder. Within days of reporting Pearson's PARCC contract win, *Education Weekly* carried the story of the American Institutes for Research (AIR) lawsuit against PARCC for allegedly shaping the bidding process to favor Pearson:

> A decision to give the education provider Pearson a major, potentially lucra-
> tive contract for common core testing is being challenged by a competitor who
> claims the award was made through a process that was unfair and biased in favor
> of the eventual winner.
>
> The American Institutes for Research, a Washington-based organization
> that has a substantial place in the testing field, has filed a legal action in New
> Mexico state court *that argues the contract was awarded in a process that was il-
> legal, and structured in a way that wrongly benefited one company—Pearson.* . . .
>
> A Mississippi state official, part of the negotiating team on the contract,
> could not put a dollar value on the contract, but described its size to *EdWeek* as
> "unprecedented" by the standards of the U.S. testing industry. . . . [25]

In June 2014, Fox News reported the estimated value of the PARCC
contract to be $240 million per year.[26] As the *Education Week* report con-
tinues:

> In court documents, AIR officials say they would have submitted an official pro-
> posal to do the testing work, if they thought the bidding process was fair. But
> they ultimately did not believe they had a legitimate chance to win, and so they
> decided not to turn in a proposal.
>
> In the end, Pearson ended up being the only bidder, a PARCC state official
> told *EdWeek*. . . .[27]

On the surface, it might appear that AIR just missed its chance by
choosing not to submit a proposal. However, it appears that the Request
for Proposals (RFPs) favored a company that already had a platform in
place for—well—Pearson alone:

> In December, AIR filed a protest with the state, citing several objections to the
> RFP put forward for the testing project. For instance, AIR argued that the so-
> licitation improperly tied assessment services to be provided in the first year of
> the tests with work in subsequent years, essentially creating a "bundling of work"
> that unfairly restricts competition. *That bundling of work favors Pearson, because
> it would rely on a content/delivery platform already developed by Pearson for the
> PARCC tests,* AIR said in a Dec. 11, 2013 letter to New Mexico's education
> department.[28] [Emphasis added]

As of June 11, 2014, New Mexico judge Sarah Singleton suspended
Pearson's arrangement with PARCC pending a speedy review of the RFP
process

When asked by counsel for the State if the [PARCC-Pearson] contract could go forward in the meantime, Singleton denied the request.

"I don't want you to go forward until you've heard their protest," she said adding that they must hear AIR's protest and decide if the request for proposal needs to be reconsidered.

"So how long will it take you? I would like to try to do it as soon as possible," Singleton added during the hearing, "because I don't want those poor school children sitting around next year not knowing what they're going to be tested on."

Officials for all parties involved, the PARCC, Pearson, and AIR, declined to comment sighting [*sic*] that the case was still open.[29]

Judge Singleton's words show that she does not understand that the "poor school children" are tied to CCSS as the "what" that they will "be tested on." Nevertheless, her judgment is mistrustful of PARCC's attempt to dismiss AIR's request on a technicality. New Mexico state purchasing agent Lawrence Maxwell gathered and reviewed written documentation on the contract protest. However, Maxwell's decision is not necessarily the final word on the multimillion-dollar matter:

In his letter, Maxwell said that officials at Pearson and New Mexico's department of education, would be given the right to respond to the AIR's protest by June 18. AIR would then have one week after that to respond to what the other two entities have to say.

There won't be a public hearing on the case, Maxwell said. Instead, "the decision of the state purchasing agent will be based entirely on the written record."

New Mexico state law says that once a decision is made by the state procurement agent or office, a party can appeal that decision in the courts. *So the battle over the PARCC contract could be a fairly protracted one, if all the parties in play pursue all of their options.*[30] [Emphasis added]

In situations in which the "free market" appears to be rigged, the courts are brought in, and "college and career readiness" is shown to be worth loads of cash—enough for one entity to sue another over the right to run the power-wielding assessment arm of contemporary American public education.

Whichever education mega-company or other organization develops and executes PARCC, one truth is certain: That organization will have incredible power over the futures of millions of Americans—individual students, teachers graded using student test scores, and schools and districts whose existence depends on standardized test scores. Notice that one of the tasks accorded to Pearson in its PARCC contract is "helping" states "to develop cut scores." A cut score is the determined threshold for what the one setting it considers "acceptable performance."

As was proven in New York in 2013—where Education Commissioner John King "set" the cut scores for a Pearson-CCSS test in such a way that he was able to tell the public that he "expected" a 30–37% passing rate[31]—he who sets the cut score rules the education system.

PEARSON AND COMMON CORE: INDISPENSABILITY IS THE KEY

In case there is any doubt that Pearson is well aware of the incredible profit value of CCSS, one should consider what Pearson executives discuss in their business meetings. In May 2014, I wrote a post about Pearson's February 28, 2014, earnings call, a meeting in which Pearson discussed its 2013 results with attention to the future—a future dependent upon CCSS-driven profitability. I used a meeting transcript produced by the company Seeking Alpha.[32] Although the transcript is almost 14,000 words long, Seeking Alpha allows me to directly quote only 400 words—quite the challenge. Much of what I include in this section comes directly from my blog post.[33]

Interestingly, in all of those approximately 14,000 words, there is no discussion of the millions Pearson has paid in numerous fines over the years—fines related to its test-item and scoring blunders. Surely such ineptitude affects profits.

Not addressed.

This much is true: Pearson is in education for the money. Of course it is. The company exists to make a profit—a long-term, sustainable profit.

In this meeting, Pearson CEO John Fallon and chief financial officer Robin Freestone are addressing several market analysts: Sami Kassab (Exane BNP Paribas, Research Division); Mark Braley (Deutsche Bank AG, Research Division); Rakesh Patel (Goldman Sachs Group Inc., Research Division); Matthew Walker (Nomura Securities Co. Ltd., Research Division); Ian Whittaker (Liberum Capital Limited, Research Division); Claudio Aspesi (Sanford C. Bernstein & Co., LLC., Research Division); Patrick Wellington (Morgan Stanley, Research Division); and Nick Michael Edward Dempsey (Barclays Capital, Research Division).[34]

The presence of eight market analysts makes it easy to remember that, above all, Pearson is a for-profit with business interests in education. To Pearson, education is business.

Fallon opens the meeting by explaining why profits were not as fine as they might have been for Pearson in 2013. He assures the participating financial analysts not to worry, that "we are determined to return Pearson to sustained earnings growth as quickly as [possible]."[35]

Of course, Pearson expects CCSS to deliver:

> The [schools business] sector is awaiting a major curriculum change brought about by Common Core. As we expected, it has been implemented slowly as budgets and policy align state by state.[36]

Fallon assumes that CCSS will drive state policy. This is an interesting assertion, given that CCSS is supposedly "state-led." According to Fallon, it is CCSS that "leads" the states—and specifically, the *curriculum* in those states.

Yes, the assessment component of CCSS is quite the golden goose, but not only for the estimated $240 million per year that the PARCC assessment is worth. There are also the auxiliary benefits. For example, in 2012, Pearson contracted with both of the CCSS assessment consortia (PARCC and Smarter Balanced) to develop a "technology readiness tool" to assist states in transitioning to CCSS assessments.[37] However, even this assessment prep tool is not the real coup.

Whichever company (or companies) develops the CCSS assessments automatically has credibility with school districts for providing curriculum aligned with those assessments.

Think about it: Why would a district whose existence depends on handsome test scores purchase curriculum from an education company with no connection to the high-stakes assessments when such curricular helps are available from the company that created the test itself? Furthermore, the more desperate the district is for high test scores, the more likely that district will "find" the money to purchase Pearson curriculum to accompany Pearson-developed tests.

And remember, Pearson is even willing to "help" states determine how to set cut scores. In doing so, Pearson holds much power in determining state passing rates—or failure rates. Moreover, in its "helping," Pearson also steps into the world of professional development. Another market. "Assisting" states in reducing the number of "failing" students creates *yet another market* for Pearson to exploit.

So what if Pearson has an established record for botching the assessment process and negatively impacting the lives of thousands of students?

Just pay the fine and move on. Sloppiness becomes irrelevant.

Ahh, the potential for unprecedented profits in the world of education that is centered upon high-stakes testing!

Just be patient, Fallon assures those who are concerned about profitability. Those supposedly "state-led" CCSS states will need that "aligned" curriculum—just the way that the National Governors Association (NGA) said in 2008 that CCSS, curriculum, and assessments would align[38] and Gates said in 2009 that they should align.[39]

Fallon also notes that the "curriculum change" is also affecting Pearson's profits in the United Kingdom (UK), where there is also a version of CCSS:

> As with Common Core in the U.S., we are investing now in . . . this [UK] curriculum change that starts in 2015.

That's right: The United Kingdom has its own version of CCSS, loosely called the "reformed GCSEs" (General Certificate of Secondary Education[40]) and "reformed A levels" (advanced-level high school coursework, usually considered the standard for university admission[41]). To enhance understanding, I will offer a brief aside on the UK version of CCSS. For the sake of space, I will focus on the "reformed GCSEs."

Notice how eerily similar the UK promotion of its "slimmed-down national curriculum" sounds to CCSS:

> Employers, universities and colleges are often dissatisfied with school leavers' literacy and numeracy even though the proportion of young people achieving good grades has gone up in recent years. Around 42% of employers need to organise additional training for young people joining them from school or college.
>
> We believe making GCSEs and A levels more rigorous will prepare students properly for life after school. It is also necessary to introduce a curriculum that gives individual schools and teachers greater freedom to teach in the way they know works and that ensures that all pupils acquire a core of essential knowledge in English, mathematics and sciences. . . .
>
> To give teachers more freedom over their teaching, we are introducing a *slimmed-down national curriculum* for 5- to 16-year-olds to be taught in maintained schools from 2014. . . .
>
> The new curriculum for all subjects contains the essential knowledge that all children should learn, but will not dictate how teachers should teach.[42]

Though the general sales pitch sounds similar to CCSS, the UK "reformed GCSEs" differ from CCSS on a few key points. First of all, the United Kingdom already has a national curriculum; in the United States, the federal government is forbidden to produce a national curriculum.[43] Second, the UK version of CCSS began with published content in November 2013 in English and math in 2015; however, it goes beyond those two subjects. In April 2014, the United Kingdom published "reformed GCSEs" for subjects in areas including sciences, languages, and social sciences. Furthermore, the nation plans to conclude with revisions in the area of fine arts in September 2016.

An important way in which the UK "reform" differs from that in America is that the UK "reformed GCSEs" are not tied to high-stakes tests outside of teacher or school control. The United Kingdom will use some national tests, but these appear to be limited in number and not automatically associated with teacher evaluation:

> To give schools greater freedom, we will:
> remove the current system of national curriculum levels *so that schools have the freedom to design their own assessments against the new national curriculum.* . . .
> In 2010, the Secretary of State commissioned Lord Bew to undertake an independent review of testing, assessment and accountability at key stage 2. Lord Bew published the final report of his review in June 2011.
> *Following Lord Bew's recommendation, from 2013 there will be no externally marked test of English writing. Pupils' ability in the composition element of writing will be subject to teacher assessment only.* The new grammar, punctuation and spelling test will assess pupils' ability in these skills.[44] [Emphasis added]

Thus, as they stand in June 2014, the UK "reformed GCSEs" are not a central component to high-stakes testing outcomes; they do not lead to any "necessary" consortia-developed testing designed to impact individual students and "grade" teachers and schools, and they include teacher judgment as a component of assessment.

Big differences.

I find it ironic that the United Kingdom has a national curriculum, a concept forbidden in the United States[45] for fear that the federal government would use it to override state and local autonomy, and yet, the UK government is showing no interest in using its national curriculum as a means to panicking the UK public into some international competition dependent upon high-stakes testing outcomes. The United Kingdom is not trying to "become" a 21st-century world power. Meanwhile, the United States *is* a 21st-century world power, and its USDOE is micromanaging state education "autonomy" in the name of "racing to the top."

Still, Pearson is depending upon the profits to be garnered by the United Kingdom's national curriculum reforms. National-level reforms cater to mammoth corporate structures such as Pearson.

Returning to the February 2014 Pearson earnings call: Fallon assures his analysts that all will be well by 2015:

These [cyclical and policy-related] factors will be a drag on us again in 2014, but after that, these headwinds start to ease. And in time, as the curriculum change comes through, as the enrollments recover, they start to blow at our backs again rather than in our faces.[46]

Fallon sees 2014 as an opportunity to prepare Pearson to become infused in America's inevitable, CCSS-determined education market:

We are choosing exactly this moment to push ahead with the largest restructuring in the history of Pearson . . . if we can [and as we] successfully embed ourselves with our customers. . . . [W]hat that work does is shift us much more quickly and much more irreversibly to where the biggest sources of future demand are. . . . [W]e're . . . stepping-up our investment in North America, with an extra GBP 60 million ($102 million) in 2013 alone. . . . We're doing so to get ahead of the forces reshaping our industry . . . and to reduce our exposure to the corresponding risks.[47]

Pearson is banking on definite CCSS implementation in these United States via "embedding" itself—making its products and services indispensable. "Irreversible" in the CCSS market. It reminds me of a drug dealer offering "free" hits as a means of ensuring future junkie dependence. Of course, following such a plan surely is more respectable if the dealers wear tailored suits and sit in plush leather chairs in board rooms while discussing the matter via conference call.

It is Freestone who refers to "invest[ing] to build scale" in higher education—building "to scale" being a term Bill Gates used to describe the supposed "free market" advantage of CCSS over "equally good," state-level standards. Freestone adds:

The important point is that once we get through that period of investment . . . incremental revenue per student then becomes very profitable. And these are long-term contracts with high renewal rates. . . . As we transition from print to digital, we move from a license to a subscription selling, with revenues spread over multiple years. This reduces revenue and margin short term, but it gives us a more visible business *and greater market opportunity in the long term. And as we reach scale, the benefits again are very significant indeed.*[48] [Emphasis added]

Though her reference in this case is to Pearson's higher education market, Freestone's statement puts me in mind of LA's iPad software license renewal fees. In that situation, Los Angeles Unified School District (LAUSD) chose Pearson's unfinished product over products already in use and receiving solid reviews from the users. The Pearson product came "bundled"; however, what was not readily apparent was the software renewal fee that would occur after 3 years.[49]

Embedding. Make the Pearson license renewal *indispensable* to education functioning.

Freestone refers to "scale" again when discussing Pearson's role in the K–12 education market:

> As in higher ed, no silver bullets to help . . . prepare . . . pupils. . . . *So we contribute by offering . . . curriculum; data-driven adaptive learning; enhanced teaching development; assessments* which test higher-order skills. But actually, *our most important role is actually helping to implement and scale the significant changes* that are required to adopt digital, or actually, blended learning. . . . Again, same model as in higher education, these new business models create much bigger revenue opportunities as we get into bigger addressable markets. . . .[50] [Emphasis added]

Freestone continues with Pearson's plan "to capitalize" on "that megatrend" of online learning. She discusses "building new partnerships" with Apple and Microsoft.

In his March 2014 interview with *Washington Post* reporter Lyndsey Layton, Gates denied that Microsoft was benefiting from CCSS. However, according to Freestone,[51] there is always the potential for future Microsoft profits related to CCSS via a Pearson-Microsoft partnership.

In Pearson's February 2014 earnings call, one of the analysts (Whittaker) raises the question of Pearson's dependence on 2015 CCSS implementation for future profits. Fallon uses editorials on CCSS as evidence that CCSS will move forward (such sophisticated research, eh?) and comments that before CCSS, "local, stand-alone operating companies" were an impediment to not being able to "scale at anything."

That is true. Those "stand-alone" companies upon which local economies depend are indeed a nuisance to corporate-nurturing "scale."

My 400 words are used up for directly quoting the Pearson earnings call. I must resort to paraphrasing.

Whittaker has asked once about an alternate plan of action if CCSS doesn't work as anticipated. Fallon responded initially that all of CCSS need not work in 2015, just some of it. Whittaker insists upon hearing about Fallon's alternate plan of action; Fallon offers no substantive alternate plan.

Mega-corporation Pearson is dependent on long-term CCSS implementation. Allow the implications of that realization to sink in.

Another analyst, Walker, asks about guarding profits against open access. Fallon is unfazed; he notes that dependence on Pearson products will be so embedded into American education that free downloads provided by other entities than Pearson offer no threat.

PEARSON:
TAILOR-MADE FOR THOSE POWERFUL MARKET FORCES

When Gates speaks of the importance of CCSS in bringing American public education "to scale," one cannot help but wonder whether his mind is specifically on the benefits of CCSS not only to his own Microsoft, but also to Pearson. As for Pearson's market strategy, it wants to either shut down competition or subsume and also make its bloated, corporate self indispensable to American public education. CCSS is tailor-made for the Pearson philosophy of embedding and acquisition, and like so many organizations involved in the CCSS venture, Pearson is positioned to benefit from its initial "investment" in CCSS license owner, CCSSO.

CCSS is the gift that Pearson counts on to keep giving.

Conclusion
So What Have We Learned Here?

For years following my first hearing of CCSS in early 2010, I held a relatively benign attitude toward the standards. The assistant principal who introduced the upcoming CCSS to me and my English-teaching colleagues also told us that math would be taught differently and attempted to conduct an exercise to show us how math instruction would be impacted. I did not understand the point of having the English department participate in what was supposed to be a CCSS math exercise, yet I still did not have information enough to form a solid opinion on CCSS. Throughout 2010 and 2011, CCSS and its associated assessments remained an abstract idea to me.

Once the Louisiana legislature surprised Louisiana teachers in March 2012 with so-called "accountability" legislation tying teacher livelihood to student test scores, I began to see how this now-nationwide CCSS and its "more rigorous" assessments could easily translate into hyper-focus on two core subjects at the expense of a well-rounded education experience, chiefly because the associated high-stakes assessments were intended to negatively label teachers and schools that did not achieve some arbitrarily set cut score.

I had not yet formally researched CCSS, but I was beginning to understand its greater purpose as a tool to lock education into a fixed position in order to better situate the endgame of consequence-leveling standardized testing. I began researching and writing about CCSS in earnest in May 2013, with my examination of the American Federation of Teachers (AFT) CCSS survey discussed in Chapter 7. In July 2013, I learned that our state superintendent had decided to move full CCSS implementation ahead 1 year, to 2013–2014 instead of 2014–2015. It was a strategic move: Get CCSS in place prior to the 2014 legislative session. This way, it proved less convenient for the legislature to extract CCSS from Louisiana classrooms.

Between 2010 and 2013, I learned enough to doubt the shiny good-ness of "state-led, college and career ready" CCSS. Since 2013, I have learned that through CCSS and its attendant assessments, a number of entities are vying for national-scale control over public education. The federal government apparently wants to drive public education via CCSS and its tests, as do a number of strategically positioned, powerful busi-nesses and businesspeople, philanthropists, politicians, and nonprofits. However, in the end, America's public schools belong to the American public. Thus, any orchestrated seizure of a basic democratic institution in the name of pseudo-democracy is bound to fail because democracy can-not be forced from the perch of power, wealth, and privilege.

Yet the entire CCSS process has been delivered from such a perch—a grand and fatal flaw in the CCSS scheme.

CCSS cannot work. It is destined for the education reform trash heap, just like the punitive, test-driven No Child Left Behind (NCLB) from which it emerged.

America, once and for all, we need to put an end to policies and programs that betray our vulnerability for worshiping standardized test scores. Test-centric education allows for incredible scapegoating and profiteering even as it bankrupts our children's education experience. Such a waste.

Therefore, let us learn some lessons from the overwhelming and inev-itable failure that is CCSS. The following list is not exhaustive; however, it does leave room for pause concerning CCSS' destined failure.

One lesson is that CCSS development was anything but the NGA-and CCSSO-advertised open process. Had it been so, a book on the origin, development, and promotion of CCSS would not have includ-ed nearly the amount of as-yet-unconsolidated information offered in these pages. On the contrary, in an open process, much of the informa-tion in this book would have been familiar to the general public 6 years following CCSS conception and 5 years following CCSS completion in June 2010.

A second lesson is that CCSS is principally the creation of those outside of the K–12 classroom. Many in CCSS-content-inclusion, decisionmaking roles have never been classroom teachers. A few were even accorded the status of "expert" based solely upon their edupreneur positioning. Some were once classroom teachers but have been away from the K–12 classroom for years. Many of these "inside" individuals were likely sincere in their ef-forts to design CCSS. However, what appears sound on paper might not readily translate into success in practice. Yet there was no piloting of CCSS, and this incredible oversight continues to be excused by CCSS promoters.

The dearth of current K–12 classroom teachers as key decisionmakers leads us to a third lesson: Current K–12 teachers would have known that they would be expected to apply CCSS in their own classrooms. As a result, they would have been ever-mindful of practical issues related to CCSS. Thus, they would have been less likely to buy into the idea of one set of inflexible, untested standards in the first place. As a result, the CCSS idea as promoted by Achieve, NGA, and CCSSO would likely have died a quick death under teacher practitioner scrutiny—especially given the 2008 NGA declared intention to tie CCSS to high-stakes assessments.

A fourth lesson is that the idea of CCSS being "state-led" on a national scale is manufactured. In order for the majority of U.S. "states" to agree to CCSS, the term *state* must refer to only a couple of state-level authorities who are deciding on behalf of entire state populations. This is known as "top-down" leadership—and the so-called "state" decision is prone to self-destruct once the public realizes it has had its voice silenced by the top.

This artificial "state-led" promotion of CCSS leads us to a fifth lesson: No level of American governance exists that might support the likes of CCSS. In proclaiming that it is not federal but instead represents individual states "coming together," CCSS purports to exist in a governance "no-man's-land" between the individual state level and the federal level. Not only does this create friction between federal involvement and state autonomy in state education affairs, it also requires that state sovereignty over education be surrendered to some intermediary entity—such as the NGA or CCSSO—or, in the case of CCSS assessments, assessment consortia such as PARCC or Smarter Balanced. The surrendering of sovereignty by state agencies can present conflicts with state constitutions.

Related to the fifth lesson, a sixth lesson concerning CCSS and governance is the repeatedly demonstrated federal tactic of hovering uncomfortably close to impeding state sovereignty in CCSS "oversight." Whereas the federal government is quick to point out that CCSS is "not a federal program," U.S. Secretary of Education Arne Duncan has made it clear that he wants states to remain in CCSS and is willing to both publicly campaign for his preference and exert his power to force states to remain. Thus, one might justifiably conclude that any national-standards-type effort indeed runs the already-proved risk of the attempted federal smothering of state education autonomy.

Not exclusive to CCSS but applicable nonetheless, a seventh lesson is that so-called philanthropic spending can exert undue influence over state education affairs. As a result, the democratic process is thwarted by the potential purchasing of multi-organization involvement in promoting the preferences of a few extremely wealthy individuals. Furthermore, the situation is exacerbated when the wealthy individual is deemed an "expert" in a field simply because he or she has money and is willing to "donate" in order to promote a personally preferred course of action.

An eighth lesson I would like to note is that CCSS was not even declared "superior" to all state English and math standards, yet it was pushed in all states in order to create an unprecedented U.S. "scale" education market. This ploy can only benefit education mega-corporations like Pearson. Promoting CCSS to scale does not benefit children. It does not contribute to efficiency in addressing state education issues. It does not even benefit local education markets. It serves only the profit margins of the Big Boys.

It reduces public education to a dollar sign.

But here is the final lesson: American public education does not have to resign itself to CCSS. Each of the chapters in this book elucidates CCSS' vulnerabilities—weaknesses that might be used as ammunition to bring down what originated from the top down. Like New Coke and subprime mortgages, CCSS is designed to fail. Let's help it along. It is time to counteract overused CCSS promotional slogans with the truth— in school board meetings, letters to the editor, emails to elected officials, television and radio interviews, faculty meetings, parent organizations, professional education organizations. Break CCSS from the bottom up.

To accomplish this task, friends of American public education, I offer my research in support.

Glossary of Key Individuals, Organizations, and Terms

Achieve, Inc.: A nonprofit organization created by the National Governors Association in 1996. The board of directors is comprised of both governors and business executives. Achieve, Inc. produced the American Diploma Project (ADP) in 2005. One of three chief organizations responsible for developing CCSS as declared in the CCSS MOU. The other two were ACT and the College Board.

Adequate Yearly Progress (AYP): State-determined, state-standards-based, standardized-test-measured goals under NCLB. Schools failing to meet such goals ran the risk of having faculty or principals fired or spending Title I funding to allow students to attend other schools, including charter schools.

American College Testing (ACT): Testing company that was one of three chief organizations responsible for developing CCSS as declared in the CCSS MOU. The other two were Achieve and the College Board.

American Diploma Project (ADP): A network created by Achieve in 2005 as an effort to encourage states to align their high school standards, assessments, and graduation requirements to determinations of college and career readiness. A precursor to K–12 CCSS.

American Federation of Teachers (AFT): The second largest teachers' union in America. Founded in Chicago in 1916, AFT's membership of approximately 1.6 million in 2014 includes nurses.

American Recovery and Reinvestment Act (ARRA): The federal stimulus package authorized in February 2009 by the 111th Congress. ARRA funding for education was directed in part to ESEA and in part to another fund, the State Fiscal Stabilization Fund (SFSF). The federally funded CCSS assessments were paid for using SFSF money.

A Nation at Risk: The 1983 report produced by the Reagan administration's National Committee on Excellence in Education. This report is often cited as evidence that American public education is not producing a globally competitive workforce.

Cheney, Lynne: Chair of the National Endowment for the Humanities who in 1994 publicly rejected the national history standards she had previously supported. Cheney's rejection tapped into concerns about national standards being "federal" standards.

Coleman, David: Education businessman. Founder of Grow Network and Student Achievement Partners and president of the College Board. One of five key individuals involved in writing CCSS.

Coleman Report of 1966: Challenged ESEA efficacy; considered standardized test scores a measure of educational success.

College and Career Readiness Standards (CCRS): Intended to be the "anchors" for CCSS, CCRS were supposed to be developed first (in the summer of 2009) as a frame for CCSS. However, the CCRS for math disappeared. Whereas the CCSS website includes CCRS ("anchor standards") for English language arts (ELA), it does not have CCRS "anchor standards" for math.

College Board: Company founded in 1900 and known for its Advanced Placement (AP) and Scholastic Aptitude Test (SAT). One of three chief organizations responsible for developing CCSS as declared in the CCSS MOU. The other two are Achieve and ACT. College Board CEO David Coleman was named CEO following his lead role in writing CCSS.

Common Core State Standards (CCSS): A controversial set of K–12 standards in English language arts (ELA) and math owned by the National Governors Association (NGA) and Council of Chief State School Officers (CCSSO).

Common Core State Standards Memorandum of Understanding (CCSS MOU): The NGA-CCSSO-drafted agreement signed by governors and state education superintendents in 2009. The CCSS MOU was the blueprint for the creation of CCSS. Furthermore, the CCSS MOU was accepted as proof of a state's commitment to common standards and common assessments for the Obama administration's Race to the Top program.

Council of Chief State School Officers (CCSSO): A nonprofit established in 1949 and comprised of state education department heads nationwide. CCSSO is one of the two copyright owners of CCSS.

Data Quality Campaign: A nonprofit focused on educational data collection; associated with Education Trust. DQC purports to guide states in educational data collection, including creating unique student identifiers and connecting student data to specific teachers for the purposes of teacher evaluation.

Duncan, Arne: U.S. Secretary of Education with the Obama administration. Advocate of test-driven reform, Duncan promoted Obama's Race to the Top (RTTT) Program, an extension of the test-driven reform created by No Child Left Behind (NCLB).

Education Summit, 1989: The first formal education summit; included governors and President George H. W. Bush. Yielded Bush's America 2000, precursor to President Clinton's Goals 2000.

Education Trust: Nonprofit education organization founded in 1996 and purportedly focused on closing educational achievement gaps among students of color. Ed Trust has been involved in both the American Diploma Project and CCSS. Ed Trust President Kati Haycock also advocated for No Child Left Behind as a means of closing achievement gaps.

Elementary and Secondary Education Act of 1965 (ESEA): Introduced federal, Title I funding for educating children in poverty. It was reauthorized by Congress in 1972, 1978, 1983, 1989, 1994, and 2001, with the 2001 reauthorization being No Child Left Behind (NCLB).

ESEA: Elementary and Secondary Education Act of 1965. Legislation introduced by the Johnson administration as part of its "War on Poverty." Usually reauthorized every several years but not reauthorized since 2001 when it was reauthorized as NCLB. Introduced Title I funding for schools in an effort to improve academic achievement of less financially advantaged students.

"Failing School": A school with standardized test scores or graduation rates determined to be too low when compared with a given score threshold set by a person or group imposing said standard.

Family Educational Rights and Privacy Act (FERPA): A federal law originally designed to protect student educational records. However, FERPA allows for identifiable information to be released to certain agencies unless parents specifically request that such identifiable information not be released.

Finn, Chester: Former assistant secretary of education and founding president of the Fordham Institute. Succeeded in 2014 by former Fordham Institute executive vice president Michael Petrilli.

Fordham Foundation/Institute: A nonprofit "conservative" education policy organization established in 1959 in Dayton, Ohio, as the Fordham Foundation; the Fordham Institute was joined to the Foundation in 2007. The Fordham Institute relocated to Washington, DC. In July 2010, the Fordham Institute released an influential report grading state standards and found in favor of CCSS even though it did not grade CCSS as superior to existing standards in all states.

Gerstner, Louis, Jr.: IBM CEO whose influence led to the establishment of Achieve, Inc. in 1996. Gerstner spoke to the NGA in 1995 and pushed for national standards and also hosted a 1996 educational summit at the IBM conference center. Achieve, Inc. was created at the 1996 educational summit.

Goals 2000: Enacted version of House Resolution 1804, passed by Congress in January 1994. Built on President George H. W. Bush's America 2000. Promoted the idea of national standards and included language that put American education in competition with other nations' education systems.

Guidera, Aimee: Former NGA policy person who created the Data Quality Campaign.

Haycock, Katherine "Kati": President of the Education Trust. Haycock's background is in education policy. She considers test-driven education reform a means of closing educational achievement gaps among students of color.

Howe, Harold: U.S. education commissioner who authorized the Coleman Report of 1966.

Improving America's Schools Act (IASA) of 1995: The 1994 reauthorization of ESEA. Directed state standards and state assessments to be applied to students benefiting from Title I funding.

James B. Hunt Institute (Hunt Institute): Established in 2001 and named for former North Carolina governor James B. Hunt (who sits on the board of the associated nonprofit, the Hunt Institute Foundation). With the National Governors Association, the Hunt Institute cohosted two symposia (2008 and 2009) that were influential in promoting CCSS and its federally funded, consortium assessments.

The June 2009 symposium report stated that 46 states and three territories had already committed to CCSS.

LEA: Local education agency.

National Assessment of Educational Progress (NAEP): A national exam established in 1996 as a result of a 1964, Carnegie-Foundation-funded exploratory study on education assessment. Beginning in 2002, NAEP has been administered in grades 4 and 8 in reading and math as a condition of NCLB.

National Association of Elementary School Principals (NAESP): Professional organization of elementary and middle school principals and other educational leaders. Founded in 1921.

National Conference of State Legislatures (NCSL): Bipartisan organization created in 1975 to support state legislatures and the legislative process. NCSL has a nonprofit arm, the NCSL Foundation for State Legislatures, created in 1982.

National Council of Teachers of English (NCTE): Professional organization of English teachers established in 1911 in reaction to dissatisfaction with the effects of college entrance requirements on the high school English classroom.

National Council of Teachers of Mathematics (NCTM): Established in 1920, NCTM is a professional organization of mathematics teachers.

National Education Association (NEA): Largest teachers' union in the United States. Founded in 1857; merged with the American Teachers Association in 1966.

National Education Standards and Improvements Council (NESIC): A panel proposed under Clinton's Goals 2000 that was supposed to certify national standards. This panel never materialized.

National Governors Association (NGA): An organization of the nation's governors, formed in 1908. In 1974, NGA started its own nonprofit, the NGA Center for Best Practices. NGA started another nonprofit, Achieve, Inc., in 1996. NGA is one of the two copyright owners of CCSS.

Network for Public Education (NPE): Organization created in 2013 through the efforts of education historian Diane Ravitch and other advocates of traditional public education. Members include education professionals, parents, and students.

No Child Left Behind Act of 2001 (NCLB): 2001 reauthorization of ESEA under President George W. Bush. It tied school existence to student standardized test scores, began the labeling of schools as "failing," and required that Title I funding be used to provide "choice" to attend other schools, including charter schools, to students in schools deemed to be failing. Emphasized the unrealistic (and unmet) goal of "100% proficiency in reading and math by 2014."

Partnership for Assessment of Readiness for College and Careers (PARCC): One of two federally funded testing consortia associated with CCSS. Established in 2011 with a 4-year federal grant of $170 million.

Payzant, Thomas: Former high school teacher who was assistant secretary of elementary and secondary education under President Bill Clinton.

Petrilli, Michael: Former executive vice president of the Fordham Institute and president of same, effective 2014.

Pimentel, Susan: Former Achieve associate who was grafted in as a "founder" of Student Achievement Partners (SAP) in 2011.

Race to the Top (RTTT): Test-driven education reform centerpiece of the Obama administration. A supposed competition among states to demonstrate educational via the adoption and implementation of common standards and common assessments.

Slover, Laura McGiffert: CEO of the PARCC assessment nonprofit and former senior vice president of Achieve, one of three organizations named in the CCSS MOU as central to CCSS development (the other two organizations were ACT and the College Board). Slover was one of only a few individuals on both the CCRS and CCSS development groups.

Smarter Balanced Assessment Consortium (SBAC): One of two federally funded testing consortia associated with CCSS. Established in 2011 with a 4-year federal grant of $160 million.

Stand for Children (SFC): Education nonprofit formed in 1996. By 2011, SFC was known for its union-busting tactics and its support for test-driven reforms. As of 2013, SFC operated offices in 10 states: Arizona, Colorado, Illinois, Indiana, Louisiana, Massachusetts, Oregon, Tennessee, Texas, and Washington.

State Fiscal Stabilization Fund (SFSF): A fund established in 2009 specifically for the disbursement of $53.6 billion earmarked for education in the 2009 American Recovery and Reinvestment Act (ARRA). Approximately $43 billion more from ARRA was earmarked to be spent under ESEA.

Student Achievement Partners: Education company founded in 2007 by David Coleman and Jason Zimba; registered as a nonprofit in 2011. An organization at the center of CCSS development but not declared as such in the CCSS MOU.

Teacher-Student Data Link Project (TSDL): A cross-state effort to connect student educational outcome data to specific teachers. Supported by the Data Quality Campaign.

TIMSS: Trends in International Math and Science Study. Created by the International Association for the Evaluation of Achievement. First conducted in 1995 and recurring in 4-year cycles. TIMSS has involved various grade levels but mostly grades 4 and 8.

Title I: Federal funding introduced in the Elementary and Secondary Education Act of 1965 (ESEA); paid to states to assist with educating students in poverty, and also to fund libraries, state departments of education, and research.

Wilhoit, Gene: Former president of the Council of Chief State School Officers. Wilhoit and Student Achievement Partners founder David Coleman asked billionaire Bill Gates and his wife Melinda to fund CCSS development.

Notes

Chapter 1

1. Public law 107-110. (2002, January 8). [Legislation]. Retrieved from www2.ed.gov/policy/elsec/leg/esea02/107-110.pdf

2. Bill summary and status: 107th Congress: H.R. 1: All congressional actions with amendments. (2001–2002). [Legislation summary]. Retrieved from thomas.loc.gov/cgi-bin/bdquery/z?d107:HR00001:@@@S

3. Social Welfare History Project. (2014). Elementary and Secondary Education Act of 1965 [Online article]. Retrieved from www.socialwelfarehistory.com/events/elementary-and-secondary-education-act-of-1965/

4. See Note 3.

5. Hanna, Julia. (2005, August). The Elementary and Secondary Education Act: 40 years later. Harvard Graduate School of Education [News release]. Retrieved from www.gse.harvard.edu/news_events/features/2005/08/esea0819.html

6.–7. See Note 3.

8.–9. Coleman, James S., et al. (1966). Equality of educational opportunity. National Center for Educational Statistics [Report]. Retrieved from mailer.fsu.edu/~ldsmith/garnet-ldsmith/Coleman%20Report.pdf

10.–12. See Note 5.

13.–14. Improving America's Schools Act of 1994: Reauthorization of the Elementary and Secondary Education Act. (1995, September). [Legislation]. Retrieved from www2.ed.gov/offices/OESE/archives/legislation/ESEA/brochure/iasa-bro.html

15. See Note 5.

16. H.R. 1804 Goals 2000: Educate America Act. (1994, January 25). [Legislation]. Retrieved from www2.ed.gov/legislation/GOALS2000/TheAct/index.html

17. Austin, Tammy L. (n.d.). Goals 2000: The Clinton administration education program [Unpublished paper]. Retrieved from www3.nd.edu/~rbarger/www7/goals200.html

18.–20. Section 102: National education goals. (1994, January 25). H.R. 1804 Goals 2000: Educate America Act [Legislation]. Retrieved from www2.ed.gov/legislation/GOALS2000/TheAct/sec102.html

21. U.S. Department of Education. (2008, October). How the final regulations for Title I hold schools, districts, and states accountable for improving graduation rates [Article]. Retrieved from www2.ed.gov/policy/elsec/reg/proposal/uniform-grad-rate.html

22. Ravitch, Diane. (2013). *Reign of error: The hoax of the privatization movement and the danger to America's public schools.* New York, NY: Alfred A. Knopf. Retrieved from books.google.com/books?id=GwF5oj29OBAC&pg=PT95&lpg=PT 95&dq=90+percent+graduation+rate+diane+ravitch&source=bl&ots=3mKaIGjcmX &sig=X0UErKHIl1YPEScRCZf2PFMMELo&hl=en&sa=X&ei=KWmHU7qVIunes ASSioF4&ved=0CGMQ6AEwBw#v=onepage&q=90%20percent%20graduation%20 rate%20diane%20ravitch&f=false

23. Section 203: Duties. (1994, January 25). H.R. 1804 Goals 2000: Educate America Act [Legislation]. Retrieved from www2.ed.gov/legislation/GOALS2000/ TheAct/sec203.html

24. Section 201: Purpose. (1994, January 25). H.R. 1804 Goals 2000: Educate America Act [Legislation]. Retrieved from www2.ed.gov/legislation/GOALS2000/ TheAct/sec201.html

25. diGrazia, Kerry. (1995, April 9). Push for US standards hurts Goals 2000 effort. *Baltimore Sun.* Retrieved from articles.baltimoresun.com/1995-04-09/ news/1995099099_1_standards-development-national-education-goals-national-standards

26. Ravitch, Diane. (1996, Summer). 50 states, 50 standards: The continuing need for national voluntary standards in education. *Brookings.* Retrieved from www. brookings.edu/research/articles/1996/06/summer-education-ravitch

27. Diegmueller, Karen. (1994, November 2). Panel unveils standards for U.S. history. *Education Week.* Retrieved from www.edweek.org/ew/ articles/1994/11/02/09hist.h14.html

28. UCLA Department of History. (n.d.). Gary B.Nash [Biography]. Retrieved June 15, 2014, from www.history.ucla.edu/people/emeriti-ae-1/emeriti?lid=953

29.–30. US Department of Education New York State Archives. (n.d.). Federal education policy and the states, 1945–2009: The George H. W. Bush years: America 2000 proposed. Retrieved June 15, 2014, from www.archives.nysed.gov/ edpolicy/research/res_essay_bush_ghw_amer2000.shtml

31. Associated Press. (1995, January 19). Multicultural history standards rejected by Senate in 99–1 vote. *Los Angeles Times.* Retrieved from articles.latimes. com/1995-01-19/news/mn-21834_1_history-standards

32. Goals 2000. (2013, November 2). *Wikipedia: The Free Encyclopedia.* Retrieved June 15, 2014, from en.wikipedia.org/wiki/Goals_2000#National_ Standards_for_Arts_Education

33.–34. Whitney, Sue. (c. 2004). Answering questions about support for NCLB [Web page]. Retrieved June 15, 2014, from www.wrightslaw.com/heath/nclb. support.htm

35. U.S. Department of Education. (2001, January). Archived: Executive summary of the No Child Left Behind Act of 2001. Retrieved June 15, 2014, from www2.ed.gov/nclb/overview/intro/execsumm.html

36. Ravitch, Diane. (2010). *Death and life of the great American school system.* New York, NY: Basic Books.

37.–38. See Note 35.

39. Wiggins, Grant. (2012, December 12). The odd correlation between SES and achievement: Why haven't more critical questions been asked? A call to action [Web log post]. Retrieved from grantwiggins.wordpress.com/2012/12/12/

the-odd-correlation-between-ses-and-achievement-why-havent-more-critical-questions-been-asked-a-call-to-action/

40. Popham, W. James. (1999, March). Why standardized tests don't measure educational quality. *Educational Leadership*. Retrieved from www.ascd.org/publications/educational-leadership/mar99/vol56/num06/Why-Standardized-Tests-Don't-Measure-Educational-Quality.aspx

41. Illinois State Board of Education. (2006, January 6). School restructuring: Federal No Child Left Behind Act of 2001: Guidance document 06-01 [Policy brief]. Retrieved from www.isbe.state.il.us/nclb/pdfs/restructuring_guidance_0106.pdf

42.–43. Cato Institute. (2007, November/December). School's out: The failure of No Child Left Behind. [Policy report]. Retrieved from www.cato.org/policy-report/novemberdecember-2007/schools-out-failure-no-child-left-behind

44. South Carolina Department of Education. (2003, December 8). New study confirms vast differences in state goals for academic 'proficiency' under NCLB [News archive]. Retrieved from ed.sc.gov/news/more.cfm?articleID=385

45. Peterson, Paul, & Hess, Frederick. (2008, Summer). Few states set world class standards: In fact, most render the notion of proficiency meaningless. *Education Next*. Retrieved from educationnext.org/few-states-set-worldclass-standards/

46. Pipkin, Cameron. (n.d.). Common Core and NCLB. *School Improvement Network* [Web log post]. Retrieved fromwww.schoolimprovement.com/common-core-360/blog/common-core-and-NCLB/

47. Schneider, Mercedes K. (2013, November 24). Common-Core-aligned curriculum and other Duncan/NGA-decided issues [Web log post]. Retrieved from deutsch29.wordpress.com/2013/11/24/common-core-aligned-curriculum-and-other-ngaduncan-decided-issues/

48. Dillon, Sam. (2007, November 6). For a key education law, reauthorization stalls. *New York Times*. Available at www.nytimes.com/2007/11/06/washington/06child.html?_r=0

49. Guisbond, Lisa, et al. (2012, January). NCLB's lost decade for educational progress: What can we learn from this policy failure? *FairTest*. Retrieved from fairtest.org/sites/default/files/NCLB_Report_Final_Layout.pdf

50. See Note 42.

Chapter 2

1. Applebome, Peter. (1996, March 27). Education summit calls for tough standards to be set by states and local districts. *New York Times*. Retrieved from www.nytimes.com/1996/03/27/us/education-summit-calls-for-tough-standards-be-set-states-andlocal-school.html

2. Eakin, Sybil. (1996, Summer). Forum: National education summit. *Technos Quarterly*. Retrieved from www.ait.net/technos/tq_05/2eakin.php

3. Ravitch, Diane. (1996, Summer). 50 states, 50 standards: The continuing need for national voluntary standards in education. *Brookings*. Retrieved from www.brookings.edu/research/articles/1996/06/summer-education-ravitch

4. Federal education policy and the states, 1945–2009: The George H. W. Bush years: Education summit. (n.d.). Retrieved June 15, 2014, from www.archives.nysed.gov/edpolicy/research/res_essay_bush_ghw_edsummit.shtml

5.–7. See Note 1.

8. 501c3 lookup. (2013). National Governors Association Center for Best Practices [Nonprofit organization search engine result]. Retrieved June 15, 2014, from 501c3lookup.org/national_governors_association_center_for_best_practices/

9. Achieve, Inc. (2014). Our history. Retrieved from www.achieve.org/history-achieve

10. 501c3 lookup. (2013). Achieve, Inc. A resource center for standards, assessment [Nonprofit organization search engine result]. Available at 501c3lookup.org/achieve_inc_a_resource_center_on_standards_asse/

11. Achieve, Inc. (2014). Our board of directors. Retrieved from www.achieve.org/our-board-directors

12.–16. Gerstner, Louis, Jr. (1995, July 30). Remarks of Louis V. Gerstner, Jr., chairman and CEO, IBM Corporation at the National Governors' Association Annual Meeting, Burlington, Vermont [Speech]. Retrieved August 2014 from www.clintonlibrary.gov/assets/storage/Research%20-%20Digital%20Library/cohen/Box%20013/2012-0160-S-lou-gerstner-speech-letter.pdf

17. See Note 2.

18. Applebome, Peter. (1996, March 26). Governors and business leaders gather to map route to elusive new era of education. *New York Times*. Retrieved from www.nytimes.com/1996/03/26/us/governors-business-leaders-gather-map-route-elusive-new-era-education.html

19. Achieve, Inc. (1996, March 27). 1996 National Education Summit. Retrieved from www.achieve.org/files/1996NationalEducationSummit.pdf

20. See Note 9.

21.–23. Achieve, Inc. (1998, December). Academic standards and assessments benchmarking evaluation for Michigan [Report]. Retrieved from www.achieve.org/files/Michigan-Benchmarking12-1998.pdf

24. See Note 11.

25.–27. See Note 21.

28. See Note 12.

29. See Note 21.

30. Thomas B. Fordham Institute. (2014). About us. Retrieved from edexcellence.net/about-us

31.–32. See Note 21.

33. Entrepreneur. (n.d.). *Benchmark* [Online encyclopedia definition]. Retrieved June 15, 2014, from www.entrepreneur.com/encyclopedia/benchmark

34. See Note 21.

35. Achieve, Inc. (2014). Achieving the Common Core. Retrieved from www.achieve.org/achieving-common-core

36. See Note 21.

37. Common Core State Standards Initiative. (2014). About the standards. Retrieved from www.corestandards.org/about-the-standards/

Chapter 3

1.–4. Achieve, Inc. (1999). 1999 national education summit [Report]. Retrieved from www.achieve.org/files/1999SummitOverview.pdf

5. James B. Hunt, Jr., Institute for Educational Leadership and Policy, & National Governors Association Center for Best Practices. (2009). Perfecting the formula: Effective strategies—educational success: A report from the 2009 governors education symposium. Retrieved from www.nga.org/files/live/sites/NGA/files/pdf/0910GESREPORT.pdf

6. See Note 1.

7.–8. Achieve, Inc. (2001). 2001 national education summit [Report]. Available at www.achieve.org/files/2001NationalEducationSummitBriefing%20Book.pdf

9.–10. Achieve, Inc. (2014). Our history. Retrieved from www.achieve.org/history-achieve

11. Achieve, Inc., Education Trust, & the Thomas B. Fordham Foundation. (2008). Ready or not: creating a high school diploma that counts [American Diploma Project report]. Retrieved from www.achieve.org/files/ReadyorNot.pdf

12. Gerstner, Louis, Jr. (1995, July 30). Remarks of Louis V. Gerstner, Jr., chairman and CEO, IBM Corporation at the National Governors' Association Annual Meeting, Burlington, Vermont [Speech]. Retrieved August 2014 from www.clintonlibrary.gov/assets/storage/Research%20-%20Digital%20Library/cohen/Box%20013/2012-0160-S-lou-gerstner-speech-letter.pdf

13.–15. Achieve, Inc., Education Trust, & the Thomas B. Fordham Foundation. (2008). Ready or not: creating a high school diploma that counts [American Diploma Project report]. Retrieved from www.achieve.org/files/ReadyorNot.pdf

16. Lewin, Tamar. (2014, March 5). A new SAT aims to realign with schoolwork. *New York Times*. Retrieved from mobile.nytimes.com/2014/03/06/education/major-changes-in-sat-announced-by-college-board.html?referrer&_r=0

17. See Note 11.

18.–19. Schlechty, Phillip C. (2004). Chapter 1: Introduction. *Shaking Up the Schoolhouse* [Book excerpt]. Retrieved from catdir.loc.gov/catdir/samples/wiley031/00009570.pdf

20. Wood, William C. (2010, June 28). Literacy and the entry-level workforce: The role of literacy and policy in labor market success. Employment Policies Institute [Report]. Retrieved from www.epionline.org/study/r127/

21. Peters, Gerhard. (n.d.). George W. Bush, XLIII President of the United States: 2001–2009: Commencement address at Yale University in New Haven, Connecticut, May 21, 2001. *American Presidency Project*. Available at www.presidency.ucsb.edu/ws/?pid=45895

22. Willingham, Daniel. (2013, February 18). What predicts college GPA? [Web log post]. Retrieved from www.danielwillingham.com/daniel-willingham-science-and-education-blog/what-predicts-college-gpa

23. Kinsley, Michael. (2003, January 20). How affirmative action helped George W. *CNN.com*. Retrieved from www.cnn.com/2003/ALLPOLITICS/01/20/timep.affirm.action.tm/

24. See Note 11.

25. Achieve, Inc. (2006). Closing the expectations gap 2006: An annual 50-state progress report on the alignment of high school policies with the demands of college and work [Report]. Retrieved from www.achieve.org/files/50-state-06-Final.pdf

26. Achieve, Inc. (2011). Closing the expectations gap 2011: Sixth-annual 50-state progress report on the alignment of high school policies with the

demands of college and careers [Report]. Retrieved from www.achieve.org/files/AchieveClosingtheExpectationsGap2011.pdf

27. See Note 12.

28.–31. Achieve, Inc. (2008, July). *Out of many, one: Toward rigorous common core standards from the ground up* [Report]. Retrieved from www.achieve.org/files/OutofManyOne.pdf

32. Illinois State Board of Education. (2007, November 14). [Meeting minutes]. Retrieved from www.isbe.net/board/meetings/2007/nov07/2007-11.pdf

33. State of Delaware Department of Education. (2007, November 12). Data Quality Campaign praises Delaware [Press release]. Retrieved from www.doe.state.de.us/news/2007/1112.shtml

34.–36. See Note 28.

Chapter 4

1. Achieve, Inc. (2008, July). *Out of many, one: Toward rigorous common core standards from the ground up* [Report]. Retrieved from www.achieve.org/files/OutofManyOne.pdf

2. Business and Money. (2013, May 7). National Alliance of Business. Retrieved from business-money.org/national-alliance-of-business-nab

3. See Note 1.

4. *Education Week*. (n.d.). Editorial projects in education research center: Influence: The Education Trust [Influence index entry]. Retrieved June 15, 2014, from www.edweek.org/media/edtrust.pdf

5. Canisius College. (n.d.). About Canisius. Retrieved June 1, 2014, from www.canisius.edu/about-canisius/mission/

6. U.S. Department of Education. (n.d.). Kati Haycock [Biography]. Retrieved June 1, 2014, from www2.ed.gov/about/bdscomm/list/hiedfuture/bios/haycock.pdf

7. National Assessment Governing Board. (2012). Kati Haycock [Biography]. Retrieved June 1, 2014, from www.nagb.org/newsroom/naep-releases/longterm-trend2012/bio-haycock.html

8. George Mason University. (n.d.). Brown event speakers: Kati Haycock [Biography]. Retrieved June 1, 2014, from library.gmu.edu/finley/finleybios.html

9. 501c3 lookup. (2013). Education Trust, Inc. [Nonprofit organization search engine result]. Retrieved from 501c3lookup.org/EDUCATION_TRUST_INC/

10. Canisius College. (n.d.). Education Trust [Biography]. Retrieved June 1, 2014, from www.canisius.edu/masters-counseling/education-trust/

11. Education Trust, Inc. (2009). About the Education Trust. Retrieved June 1, 2014, from www.edtrust.org/dc/about

12.–14. Haycock, Kati. (2013, February 7). Written testimony of Kati Haycock, president, the Education Trust: United States Senate Health, Education, Labor and Pensions Committee. Retrieved from www.help.senate.gov/imo/media/doc/Haycock1.pdf

15. Richardson, Joan. (2011, November 1). Emphasize the ambitious: Q&A with Kati Haycock. *Education Week* [Reprint from *Phi Delta Kappan*]. Retrieved from www.edweek.org/ew/articles/2011/11/01/kappan_haycock.html

16.–17. U.S. Department of Education. (2002, July 24). Key policy letters signed by the education secretary or deputy secretary. Retrieved fromwww2.ed.gov/policy/elsec/guid/secletter/020724.html

18. Schneider, Mercedes. (2013, November 24). Common Core, aligned curriculum, and other NGA/Duncan-decided issues [Web log post]. Retrieved from deutsch29.wordpress.com/2013/11/24/common-core-aligned-curriculum-and-other-ngaduncan-decided-issues/

19. See Note 15.

20. Common Core State Standards Initiative. (2014). Myths vs. facts. Retrieved from www.corestandards.org/about-the-standards/myths-vs-facts/

21. Schneider, Mercedes. (2014, April 27). My book: *A chronicle of echoes: Who's who in the implosion of American public education* [Web log post]. Retrieved from deutsch29.wordpress.com/my-book-a-chronicle-of-echoes-whos-who-in-the-implosion-of-american-public-education/

22. See Note 15.

23. National Governors Association. (2008, June 10). Governors explore strategies to make the United States a global leader in education [Press release]. Retrieved from www.nga.org/cms/home/news-room/news-releases/page_2008/col2-content/main-content-list/title_governors-explore-strategies-to-make-the-united-states-a-global-leader-in-education.html

24. Eakin, Sybil. (1996, Summer). Forum: National education summit. *Technos Quarterly*. Retrieved from www.ait.net/technos/tq_05/2eakin.php

25. LinkedIn. (n.d.). Kevin Carey [Resume]. Retrieved June 1, 2014, from www.linkedin.com/pub/kevin-carey/43/326/263

26. Carey, Kevin. (2012, July 13). Requiem for a failed education policy: The long slow death of No Child Left Behind. *New Republic*. Retrieved from www.newrepublic.com/article/politics/104960/requiem-failed-education-policy-the-long-slow-death-no-child-left-behind

27. See Note 18.

28. Achieve, Inc. (2014). Achieving the Common Core. Retrieved from www.achieve.org/achieving-common-core

29. Schneider, Mercedes. (2013, October 14). The Common Core memorandum of understanding: What a story [Web log post]. Retrieved from deutsch29.wordpress.com/2013/10/14/the-common-core-memorandum-of-understanding-what-a-story/

30. U.S. Education Delivery Institute. (2011). IRS Form 990. Retrieved from bulk.resource.org/irs.gov/eo/2013_03_EO/30-0041047_990_201206.pdf

31. Edinnovations. (2012). IRS Form 990. Retrieved from bulk.resource.org/irs.gov/eo/2013_03_EO/27-3195260_990EZ_201206.pdf

32. Data Quality Campaign. (2012). IRS Form 990. Retrieved from bulk.resource.org/irs.gov/eo/2013_02_EO/27-4566795_990_201206.pdf

33. Edinnovations. (2013). IRS Form 990. Retrieved from bulk.resource.org/irs.gov/eo/2014_03_EO/27-3195260_990EZ_201306.pdf

34. See Note 30.

35. Data Quality Campaign. (n.d.). Aimee Rogstad Guidera [Biography]. Retrieved from www.dataqualitycampaign.org/node/52/

36. Idealist. (c. 2012). Data Quality Campaign [Nonprofit organization search engine]. Retrieved June 1, 2014, from www.idealist.org/view/nonprofit/35mzH7wgXp9MD/

37. Data Quality Campaign. (n.d.). Board of directors. Retrieved June 1, 2014, from www.dataqualitycampaign.org/who-we-are/board-of-directors/

38. Data Quality Campaign. (n.d.). State analysis by essential element [Report].

Available at www.dataqualitycampaign.org/node/388/

39. Schneider, Mercedes. (2013, November 12). The Data Quality Campaign: Encouraging states to ramp up data collection [Web log post]. Available at deutsch29. wordpress.com/2013/11/12/the-data-quality-campaign-encouraging-states-to-ramp-up-data-collection/

40. National Archives and Records Administration. (2011, December 2). *Federal Register*, Part II: Department of Education. Retrieved from www.gpo.gov/fdsys/pkg/FR-2011-12-02/pdf/2011-30683.pdf

41. Data Quality Campaign. (n.d.). Data FAQs. Retrieved June 1, 2014, from www.dataqualitycampaign.org/why-education-data/data-faqs/

42. Data Quality Campaign. (2012, April 1). Strengthening the teacher-student data link to inform data quality efforts [Report]. Retrieved from www.dataquality-campaign.org/find-resources/strengthening-the-teacher-student-data-link-to-inform-teacher-quality-efforts/

43. Bill and Melinda Gates Foundation. (2009, November). CELT Corporation [Database search result]. Retrieved June 1, 2014, from www.gatesfoundation.org/How-We-Work/Quick-Links/Grants-Database/Grants/2009/11/OPP1005842

44. Education Trust, Inc. (2012). IRS Form 990. Available at bulk.resource.org/irs.gov/eo/2014_03_EO/52-1982223_990_201306.pdf

45. U.S. Education Delivery Institute. (2012). IRS Form 990. Retrieved from bulk.resource.org/irs.gov/eo/2014_03_EO/30-0041047_990_201306.pdf

46.–47. Finn, Chester E., Jr. (2008). *Troublemaker: A Personal History of School Reform Since Sputnik*. Princeton, NJ: Princeton University Press.

48. Thomas B. Fordham Institute. (2011). Chester E. Finn, Jr., president [Biography]. Retrieved from edexcellence.net/about-us/fordham-staff/chester-e-finn-jr

49. U.S. Department of State. (2013, February 12). Chester E. Finn, Jr. [Biography]. Retrieved from www.state.gov/p/io/unesco/members/49143.htm

50. Hoover Institution. (2014). Chester E. Finn, Jr., senior fellow [Biography]. Retrieved from www.hoover.org/fellows/10338

51. Lynde and Harry Bradley Foundation. (c. 2008). Chester E. Finn, Jr.: *Troublemaker* [Book review]. Retrieved June 2, 2014, from www.bradleyfdn.org/On-Lion-Letter/ID/239/Chester-E-Finn-Jr-emTroublemakerem

52. See Note 48.

53. Schneider, Mercedes K. (2014). *A chronicle of echoes: Who's who in the implosion of American public education*. Charlotte, NC: Information Age Publishing.

54. Thomas B. Fordham Institute. (n.d.). Standards-based reforms. Retrieved November 13, 2014 from edexcellence.net/policy-priorities/standards-based-reforms

55. Schneider, Mercedes. (2013, December 26). The Fordham strong arm of letter grades for state standards [Web log post]. Retrieved from deutsch29.wordpress.com/2013/12/26/the-fordham-strong-arm-of-letter-grades-for-state-standards/

56. See Note 48.

57. LinkedIn. (n.d.). Mike Petrilli [Resume]. Retrieved from June 2, 2014, from www.linkedin.com/pub/mike-petrilli/4/b12/40a

58. Thomas B. Fordham Institute. (2011). Michael J. Petrilli, Executive vice president [Biography]. Retrieved from edexcellence.net/about-us/fordham-staff/michael-j-petrilli

59. Stanford University. (2005, September 28). Michael J. Petrilli named Hoover Institution research fellow [Press release]. Retrieved from www.hoover.org/news/press-releases/29357

60. Ravitch, Diane. (2014, January 2). Mercedes Schneider eviscerates Fordham grading system [Web log post]. Retrieved from dianeravitch.net/2014/01/02/mercedes-schneider-eviscerates-fordham-grading-system/

61. Fordham Foundation. (2012). IRS Form 990. Retrieved from bulk.resource.org/irs.gov/eo/2013_12_EO/31-6032844_990_201212.pdf

62. Fordham Institute. (2012). IRS Form 990. Retrieved from bulk.resource.org/irs.gov/eo/2013_12_EO/31-1816446_990_201212.pdf

63. See Note 61.

64. U.S. Department of Education. (2010, June 2). Statement on National Governors Association and state education chiefs common core standards [Press release]. Retrieved from www.ed.gov/news/press-releases/statement-national-governors-association-and-state-education-chiefs-common-core-

65.–66. Carmichael, Sheila Byrd, et al. (2010, July). The state of state standards—and the Common Core—in 2010. Thomas B. Fordham Institute [Report]. Retrieved from www.math.jhu.edu/~wsw/FORD/SOSSandCC2010_FullReport-FINAL.pdf

67. Boulard, Garry. (2010, September). Interview with Chester Finn. National Council of State Legislatures. Retrieved from www.ncsl.org/research/education/interview-with-chester-finn.aspx

68. U.S. Department of Education. (2009). The nation's report card: Mathematics 2009: National Assessment of Educational Progress at grades 4 and 8 [Report]. Retrieved from nces.ed.gov/nationsreportcard/pdf/main2009/2010451.pdf

69. U.S. Department of Education. (2009). The nation's report card: Reading 2009: National Assessment of Educational Progress at grades 4 and 8 [Report]. Retrieved from nces.ed.gov/nationsreportcard/pdf/main2009/2010458.pdf

70. See Note 55.

71. Thomas B. Fordham Institute. (2014, November 17). Fordham Institute to evaluate Common Core assessments on quality and content alignment [Press release]. Retrieved from edexcellence.net/articles/fordham-institute-to-evaluate-common-core-assessments-on-quality-and-content-alignment

Chapter 5

1. Achieve, Inc. (2008, July). *Out of many, one: Toward rigorous common core standards from the ground up* [Report]. Retrieved from www.achieve.org/files/OutofManyOne.pdf

2. Council of Chief State School Officers. (2012, June 13). Gene Wilhoit, CCSSO executive director announces retirement [Press release]. Retrieved from www.ccsso.org/News_and_Events/Press_Releases/Gene_Wilhoit_CCSSO_Executive_Director_Announces_Retirement.html

3. Content in context. (2011). David Coleman, Student Achievement Partners, LLC [Program biography]. Retrieved from contentincontext.org/2011/index.php/program-speakers/151-david-coleman

4.–5. Layton. Lyndsey. (2014, June 7). How Bill Gates pulled off the swift Common Core revolution. *Washington Post.* Retrieved from www.washingtonpost.com/politics/how-bill-gates-pulled-off-the-swift-common-core-revolution/2014/06/07/a830e32e-ec34-11e3-9f5c-9075d5508f0a_story.html

6.–7. National Governors Association, Council of Chief State School Officers, & Achieve, Inc. (2008). Benchmarking for success: Ensuring U.S. students receive a world-class education [Report]. Retrieved from www.edweek.org/media/benchmakring%20for%20success%20dec%202008%20final.pdf

8. Cody, Anthony. (2014, June 7). Can California offer a new model for accountability? Or are we still chasing test scores? *Education Week.* Retrieved from blogs.edweek.org/teachers/living-in-dialogue/2014/06/can_california_offer_a_new_mod.html

9.–10. See Note 6.

11. Schneider, Mercedes. (2014, May 1). The Common Core sales job, part one [Web log post]. Retrieved from deutsch29.wordpress.com/2014/05/01/the-2008-common-core-sales-job-part-one/

12. Schneider, Mercedes. (2014, May 5). The Common Core sales job, part two [Web log post]. Retrieved from deutsch29.wordpress.com/2014/05/05/the-2008-common-core-sales-job-part-two/

13. Schneider, Mercedes. (2014, May 27). The Common Core sales job, part three [Web log post]. Retrieved from deutsch29.wordpress.com/2014/05/27/the-2008-common-core-sales-job-part-three/

14. Grossman, Tabitha, et al. (2011, October). Realizing the potential: How governors can lead effective implementation of the Common Core State Standards. National Governors Association [Report]. Retrieved from www.nga.org/files/live/sites/NGA/files/pdf/1110CCSSIIMPLEMENTATIONGUIDE.PDF

15. *Investopedia.* (n.d.). Memorandum of understanding: MOU [Definition]. Retrieved from www.investopedia.com/terms/m/mou.asp

16. Schneider, Mercedes. (2014, March 22). 46 states tied to Common Core in 2009? [Web log post]. Retrieved from deutsch29.wordpress.com/2014/03/22/46-states-tied-to-common-core-in-2009/

17. U.S. Department of Education. (2010). Race to the Top fund: States' applications, scores, and comments for Phase 1. [Document storage page.] Retrieved from www2.ed.gov/programs/racetothetop/phase1-applications/index.html?exp=0

18. Schneider, Mercedes. (2013, October 14). The Common Core memorandum of understanding: What a story [Web log post]. Retrieved from deutsch29.wordpress.com/2013/10/14/the-common-core-memorandum-of-understanding-what-a-story/

19.–20. State of Delaware. (2010, January 19). Race to the Top: Application for initial funding: Appendix [U.S. Department of Education archive]. Retrieved from www2.ed.gov/programs/racetothetop/phase1-applications/appendixes/delaware.pdf

21. Measured Progress. (n.d.). NECAP [New England Common Assessment Program]. Retrieved June 15, 2014, from www.measuredprogress.org/necap

22. Ravitch, Diane. (2013, May 20). Providence students challenge Commissioner Gist to debate issues [Web log post]. Retrieved from dianeravitch.net/2013/05/20/providence-students-challenge-commissioner-gist-to-debate-issues/

23.–24. See Note 19.

25. Common Core State Standards Initiative. (2014). What parents should know. Retrieved from www.corestandards.org/what-parents-should-know/

26.–27. See Note 19.

28. Schneider, Mercedes. (2013, October 13). The Common Core public license: Guess who wins? [Web log post]. Retrieved from deutsch29.wordpress. com/2013/10/13/the-common-core-public-license-guess-who-wins/

29. Schneider, Mercedes. (2014, April 2). The Common Core license: Open for NGA and CCSSO alteration [Web log post]. Retrieved from deutsch29.wordpress. com/2014/04/02/the-common-core-license-open-for-nga-and-ccsso-alteration/

30. See Note 19.

31. Haimson, Leonie. (2011, April 17). Sandra Stotsky on the mediocrity of the Common Core ELA standards [Web log post]. Retrieved from parentsacrossamerica. org/sandra-stotsky-on-the-mediocrity-of-the-common-core-ela-standards/

32. National Governors Association. (2009, September 24). Common Core State Standards Initiative validation committee announced [Press release]. Retrieved from www.nga.org/cms/home/news-room/news-releases/page_2009/col2-content/ main-content-list/title_common-core-state-standards-initiative-validation-commit-tee-announced.html

33. National Governors Association & Council of Chief State School Officers. (2010, June). Reaching higher: The Common Core State Standards Validation Committee [Report]. Retrieved from www.corestandards.org/assets/CommonCoreRe-port_6.10.pdf

34. See Note 19.

35. National Governors Association. (2009, July 1). Common Core State Standards development work group and feedback group announced [Press release]. Retrieved from www.nga.org/cms/home/news-room/news-releases/page_2009/ col2-content/main-content-list/title_common-core-state-standards-development-work-group-and-feedback-group-announced.html

36. See Note 31.

37.–38. See Note 35.

39. Schneider, Mercedes. (2014, April 23). Those 24 Common Core 2009 work group members [Web log post]. Retrieved from deutsch29.wordpress. com/2014/04/23/those-24-common-core-2009-work-group-members/

40. See Note 19.

41. See Note 35.

42. Schneider, Mercedes. (2014, April 25). A tale of two NGA press releases and then some [Web log post]. Retrieved from deutsch29.wordpress. com/2014/04/25/a-tale-of-two-nga-press-releases-and-then-some/

43. Pimentel, Susan. (2013). Education Nation opening remarks. *NBC News* [Video]. Retrieved from vimeo.com/76725406

44. Bertin, Mark. (2014, January 22). When will we ever learn: Dissecting the Common Core State Standards with Dr. Louisa Moats [Web log post]. Retrieved from www.huffingtonpost.com/mark-bertin-md/when-will-we-ever-learn_b_4588033.html

45. See Note 42.

46. See Note 35.

47. National Governors Association & Council of Chief State School Officers. (2010). Common Core State Standards Initiative: K12 standards development teams

[List]. Retrieved June 15, 2014, from Retrieved from www.nga.org/files/live/sites/
NGA/files/pdf/2010COMMONCOREK12TEAM.PDF

48. See Note 42.

49. Schneider, Mercedes. (2014, April 9). The three La. Common Core development teachers work for LDOE [Web log post]. Retrieved from deutsch29.wordpress.
com/2014/04/09/the-three-la-common-core-development-teachers-work-for-
ldoe/

50. LouisaMoats.com. (2010). About Dr. Moats: Education and bio. Available
at louisamoats.com/Education_&_Bio.php

51. See Note 44.

52.–53. See Note 1.

54.–55. See Note 19.

56. U.S. Department of Education. (2009, July 24). President Obama,
U.S. Secretary of Education Duncan announce national competition to advance school reform [Press release]. Retrieved from www2.ed.gov/news/
pressreleases/2009/07/07242009.html

57. See Note 19.

Chapter 6

1. State of Delaware. (2010, January 19). Race to the Top: Application for initial
funding: Appendix [U.S. Department of Education archive]. Retrieved from www2.
ed.gov/programs/racetothetop/phase1-applications/appendixes/delaware.pdf

2. National Governors Association. (2009, July 1). Common Core State Standards development work group and feedback group announced [Press release]. Retrieved from www.nga.org/cms/home/news-room/news-releases/page_2009/
col2-content/main-content-list/title_common-core-state-standards-development-
work-group-and-feedback-group-announced.html

3. Schneider, Mercedes. (2014, April 25). A tale of two NGA press releases and then
some [Web log post]. Retrieved from deutsch29.wordpress.com/2014/04/25/a-
tale-of-two-nga-press-releases-and-then-some/

4. Student Achievement Partners. (n.d.). About us. Retrieved June 18, 2014,
from achievethecore.org/about-us

5. Student Achievement Partners. (2013, January 29). Gene Wilhoit joins Student
Achievement Partners as partner [Press release]. Retrieved from achievethecore.org/
press-release/gene-wilhoit-joins-student-achievement-partners-partner

6. Schneider, Mercedes. (2014, September 11). The (NY, DC, LA and CA)
story of Eureka Math [web log post]. Retrieved from deutsch29.wordpress.
com/2014/09/11/the-ny-dc-la-and-ca-story-of-eureka-math/

7. McCallum, Bill. (2013, October 31). What I learned by testifying in Wisconsin [Web log post]. Retrieved from isupportthecommoncore.net/2013/10/31/
what-i-learned-by-testifying-in-wisconsin/

8. See Note 2.

9. Carr, Sarah. (2013, September 4). Teachers feel urgency of Common Core
standards. *Advocate* [Reprint from *Hechinger Report*]. Retrieved from theadvocate.
com/home/6914390-125/common-core

10. Schneider, Mercedes. (2014, April 23). Those 24 Common Core 2009
work group members [Web log post]. Retrieved from deutsch29.wordpress.
com/2014/04/23/those-24-common-core-2009-work-group-members/

11. Hess, Rick. (2013, February 11). Straight up conversation: Common Core guru Jason Zimba [Web log post]. Retrieved from blogs.edweek.org/edweek/rick_hess_straight_up/2013/02/rhsu_straight_up_conversation_sap_honcho_jason_zimba.html

12.–13. See Note 11.

14. Coleman, David, & Zimba, Jason. (2008). Math and science standards that are fewer, clearer, higher to raise student achievement at all levels. Opportunity Equation. Carnegie Corporation of New York Institute for Advanced Study [Report]. Retrieved from dev.opeq.blenderbox.com/standards-and-assessments/math-science-standards-are-fewer

15. Common Core State Standards Initiative. (n.d.). Standards-setting considerations. Retrieved June 18, 2014, from www.corestandards.org/assets/Considerations.pdf

16. See Note 14.

17. Sahlberg, Pasi. (2014, October 6). Why Finland's schools are top-notch [Editorial]. *CNN Opinion*. Retrieved from www.cnn.com/2014/10/06/opinion/sahlberg-finland-education/

18. See Note 14.

19. Chicago Public Schools. (2002, September). An educational plan for the Chicago public schools [Archived report]. Retrieved June 18, 2014, from web.archive.org/web/20070721122744/www.stratplan.cps.k12.il.us/pdfs/District_Strategies/ED_plan_PDF.pdf

20. Chicago Public Schools. (2003, November 19). Amend board report 03-0625-PR46: Approve exercising the first option to renew an agreement with Grow Network, Inc. for consulting services [Archived contract renewal agreement]. Retrieved from web.archive.org/web/20100528102120/www.cps.edu/About_CPS/The_Board_of_Education/Documents/BoardActions/2003_11/03-1119-PR36.pdf

21. U.S. Department of Education. (2012, November 19). Arne Duncan, U.S. Secretary of Education—Biography. Retrieved from www2.ed.gov/news/staff/bios/duncan.html

22. U.S. Department of Education. (2009, July). President Obama, Secretary Duncan announce Race to the Top [Web log post]. Retrieved from www.ed.gov/blog/2009/07/president-obama-secretary-duncan-announce-race-to-the-top/

23. See Note 2.

24. McGraw-Hill Financial. (2004, July 19). McGraw-Hill Education acquires Grow Network, Establishes leadership position in assessment reporting and customized content [Press release]. Retrieved from investor.mhfi.com/phoenix.zhtml?c=96562&p=irol-newsArticle&ID=592486&highlight

25. Center for Children and Technology. (2005, January 1). Linking data and learning: The Grow Network study [Promotional report]. Retrieved from cct.edc.org/publications/linking-data-and-learning-grow-network-study

26. Public Agenda. (2008, Spring). Board member news: David Coleman [Biography]. Retrieved from www.publicagenda.org/files/spring2008_newsletter.pdf

27. See Note 11.

28. See Note 2.

29. State of Indiana. (2010, August 3). Education Roundtable presenter bios: David Coleman. Retrieved from www.in.gov/edroundtable/files/2-Presenter_Bios_8-3-10.pdf

30. Association of Education Publishers. (2011, June 7). David Coleman. Content in context [Presenter schedule and biography]. Retrieved from contentincontext. org/2011/index.php/program-speakers/151-david-coleman

31. Global Education Leaders Program. (n.d.). Bill and Melinda Gates Foundation Host Day Speakers: David Coleman [Biography]. Retrieved June 18,2014, from www.innovationunit.org/sites/default/files/Host%20Day%20speakers.pdf

32. Coalition for Student Achievement. (2009, April). Smart options: Investing the recovery funds for student success. Retrieved from www.broadeducation.org/ asset/429-arrasmartoptions.pdf

33. See Note 26.

34. 501c3 lookup. (2013). Student Achievement Partners, Inc. [Nonprofit organization search engine result]. Retrieved from 501c3lookup.org/student_ achievement_partners_inc/

35. GE Foundation. (2011). IRS Form 990. Retrieved from bulk.resource.org/ irs.gov/eo/2012_12_PF/22-2621967_990PF_201112.pdf

36. Student Achievement Partners. (2011). IRS Form 990. Retrieved from bulk. resource.org/irs.gov/eo/2013_02_EO/27-4556045_990_201112.pdf

37. See Note 30.

38. Raspuzzi, Dawson. (2012, September 20). Coleman to retire as college president after this year. *Bennington Banner.* Retrieved from www.benningtonbanner. com/ci_21587212/elizabeth-coleman-retire-college-president-after-this-year

39. Goldstein, Dana. (2012, September 19). The schoolmaster. *Atlantic.* Retrieved from www.theatlantic.com/magazine/archive/2012/10/the-schoolmaster/ 309091/

40. Manta. (2013, June 3). Student Achievement Partners, LLC [Business profile search engine result]. Retrieved from www.manta.com/c/mxgkpd8/student-achievement-partners-llc

41. Membersgive. (2014). Student Achievement Partners, Inc. [Nonprofit donation search engine result]. Retrieved from www.guidestar.org/PartnerReport. aspx?ein=27-4556045&Partner=Amex

42. Illinois State Board of Education. (2007, November 14). [Meeting minutes]. Retrieved from www.isbe.net/board/meetings/2007/nov07/2007-11.pdf

43.–44. Council of Chief State School Officers. (2011, November). 2011 Annual policy forum [Program workbook]. Retrieved from programs.ccsso.org/projects/ Membership_Meetings/APF/documents/2011APF%20eWorkbook.pdf

45. stlgretchen. (2013, June 17). Straight from David Coleman's mouth about Common Core. He's making the educational decisions for all children [Web log post]. Retrieved from web.archive.org/web/20130622064249/www. missourieducationwatchdog.com/2013/06/straight-from-david-colemans-mouth. html

46. List of current United States governors. (2009, January 2). *Wikipedia: The Free Encyclopedia* [Archive]. Retrieved from web.archive.org/web/20090102214055/ en.wikipedia.org/wiki/List_of_current_United_States_Governors

47. Governors endorse "common core" of standards, leave debate for later. (2009, February 24). *Education Week.* Retrieved from blogs.edweek.org/edweek/ NCLB-ActII/2009/02/governors_endorse_common_core.html?qs=Common+Cor e+State+Standards

48. State of Delaware. (2007, November 12). Data Quality Campaign raises Delaware [Press release]. Retrieved from www.doe.state.de.us/news/2007/1112.shtml

49.–50. See Note 32.

51. See Note 15.

52. Discover the Networks. (n.d.). Joyce Foundation [Organization search engine result]. Retrieved June 18, 2014, from www.discoverthenetworks.org/funderprofile.asp?fndid=5310

53. See Note 19.

54. Pearson. (2014). Office of the chief education advisor: Sir Michael Barber [Biography]. Retrieved from www.pearson.com/michael-barber.html

55. See Note 32.

56. Schneider, Mercedes. (2014, June 9). Why would *WashPost* wait three months to release a Gates interview? [Web log post]. Retrieved from deutsch29. wordpress.com/2014/06/09/why-would-washpost-wait-three-months-to-release-a-gates-interview/

57. Council of Chief State School Officers. (2012, June 13). Gene Wilhoit, CCSSO executive director announces retirement [Press release]. Retrieved from www.ccsso.org/News_and_Events/Press_Releases/Gene_Wilhoit_CCSSO_Executive_Director_Announces_Retirement.html

58. See Note 4.

59. Thomas, Doug. (2014, May 9). What must be done in the next two years: David Coleman. 2011 Institute for Learning senior leadership meeting keynote address [Video]. Retrieved from www.youtube.com/watch?v=xHdV-wDQUR0

60. Institute for Learning. (2011, December). What must be done in the next two years. 2011 IFL Senior Leadership Meeting, David Coleman, Keynote speaker [Transcript]. Retrieved from file:///C:/Documents%20and%20Settings/User1/My%20Documents/Downloads/What_must_be_done.pdf

61. Lewin, Tamar. (2012, May 16). Backer of Common Core school curriculum is chosen to lead College Board. *New York Times.* Retrieved from www.nytimes. com/2012/05/16/education/david-coleman-to-lead-college-board.html?_r=0

62. See Note 2.

63. Arizona English Language Learners Task Force. (2007, December 13). Minutes of the meeting of the Arizona English Language Learners Task Force. Retrieved from www.azed.gov/wp-content/uploads/PDF/12-31-07MinutesELLTaskForce.pdf

64.–65. StandardsWork. (2010, November 25). Board of directors: Susan Pimentel, Co-founder, StandardsWork [Archived biography]. Retrieved from web.archive. org/web/20101125025837/www.standardswork.org/board.asp

66. StandardsWork. (n.d.). Board of directors: Susan Pimentel, Cofounder, StandardsWork [Biography]. Retrieved June 18, 2014, from www.standardswork. org/board.asp

67. Schneider, Mercedes. (2013, December 02). More on the Common Core, Achieve, Inc., and then some [Web log post]. Retrieved from deutsch29.wordpress. com/2013/12/02/more-on-the-common-core-achieve-inc-and-then-some/

68. Finn, Chester E., Petrilli, Michael J., & Stotsky, Sandra. (2000). *State of State Standards 2000: English, History, Geography, Mathematics, Science.* Washington, DC: Thomas B. Fordham Foundation. Retrieved from books.google.com/books?id=lnuxPkjSKHwC&pg=PT31&lpg=PT31&dq=fordham+standards+review+2000&source=bl&ots=wzAniSCKyE&sig=3fz0zIIRBT_s9cMU5ix12rw5K2k&hl=en&sa=X&ei=YPecU_nPOqLC8QGQiICoBg&ved=0CGUQ6AEwBw#v=onepage&q=fordham%20standards%20review%202000&f=false

69. See Note 68, p. 66.

70. Carmichael, Sheila Byrd, et al. (2010, July). The state of state standards—and the Common Core—in 2010. Thomas B. Fordham Institute [Report]. Retrieved from www.math.jhu.edu/~wsw/FORD/SOSSandCC2010_FullReportFINAL.pdf

71.–72. National Assessment Governing Board. (2011, September 6). Education consultant Sue Pimentel appointed to National Assessment Governing Board [Press release]. Retrieved from www.nagb.org/content/nagb/assets/documents/newsroom/press-releases/2011/2011-appointments/release-pimentel.pdf

73. See Note 4.

74. National Governors Association, & Council of Chief State School Officers. (n.d.). Common Core State Standards Initiative: Summary of public feedback on the draft college- and career-readiness standards for English-language arts and mathematics. Retrieved June 18, 2014, from www.corestandards.org/assets/CorePublicFeedback.pdf

75. National Governors Association. (2009, September 21). Common Core State Standards available for comment [Press release]. Retrieved from www.nga.org/cms/home/news-room/news-releases/page_2009/col2-content/main-content-list/title_common-core-state-standards-available-for-comment.html

76. See Note 74.

77. See Note 75.

78.–79. Pimentel, Susan. (2013). Education Nationopening remarks. *NBC News* [Video]. Retrieved from vimeo.com/76725406

80. Common Core State Standards Initiative. (2014). English language arts standards: Anchor standards: College and career readiness anchor standards for language. Retrieved from www.corestandards.org/ELA-Literacy/CCRA/L/

81. Common Core State Standards Initiative. (2014). Mathematics standards. Retrieved from www.corestandards.org/Math/

82. National Governors Association. (2010, March 10). Draft K–12 Common Core State Standards available for comment [Press release]. Retrieved from www.nga.org/cms/home/news-room/news-releases/page_2010/col2-content/main-content-list/title_draft-k-12-common-core-state-standards-available-for-comment.html

83. Partnership for Assessment of Readiness for College and Careers. (2013, September 26). PARCC governing board meets, appoints PARCC chief executive officer [Press release]. Retrieved from www.parcconline.org/parcc-governing-board-meets-appoints-parcc-chief-executive-officer

84. National Governors Association & Council of Chief State School Officers. (2010, June). Reaching higher: The Common Core State Standards Validation Committee [Report]. Retrieved from www.corestandards.org/assets/CommonCoreReport_6.10.pdf

85. See Note 40.

86. See Note 4.

Chapter 7

1. State of Delaware. (2010, January 19). Race to the Top: Application for initial funding: Appendix [U.S. Department of Education archive]. Retrieved from www2.ed.gov/programs/racetothetop/phase1-applications/appendixes/delaware.pdf

2. Achieve. (2011, October). Strong support, low awareness: Public perception of the Common Core State Standards [Report]. Retrieved from www.achieve.org/files/PublicPerception-CCSS-FinalReport.pdf

3. Ravitch, Diane. (2013, May 10). Randi Weingarten: Why I support the Common Core standards [Web log post]. Retrieved from dianeravitch.net/2013/05/10/randi-weingarten-why-i-support-the-common-core-standards/

4. Schneider, Mercedes. (2013, May 24). Hart, Weingarten, and polling about Common Core [Web log post]. Retrieved from deutsch29.wordpress.com/2013/05/24/hart-weingarten-and-polling-about-common-core/

5. Bidwell, Allie. (2014, August 20). Common Core support in free fall. *US News and World Report.* Retrieved from www.usnews.com/news/articles/2014/08/20/common-core-support-waning-most-now-oppose-standards-national-surveys

6. Gallup. (n.d.) How does Gallup polling work? Retrieved July 27, 2014, from www.gallup.com/poll/101872/how-does-gallup-polling-work.aspx

7. Ravitch, Diane. (2013, May 10). Hart Research responds to Schneider critique: Correction [Web log post]. Retrieved from dianeravitch.net/2013/05/10/hart-research-responds-to-schneider-critique-correction/

8. American Federation of Teachers. (2013, May 3). AFT poll of 800 teachers finds strong support for Common Core standards and a moratorium on stakes for new assessments until everything is aligned [Press release]. Retrieved from www.aft.org/newspubs/press/2013/050313.cfm

9. Leibbrand, Jane, & Seagren, Alice. (2014, May 6). Charting a common-sense course for the Common Core. *Education Week.* Retrieved from www.edweek.org/ew/articles/2014/05/07/30leibbrand.h33.html

10. Strauss, Valerie. (2013, April 30). AFT's Weingarten urges moratorium on high stakes linked to new standardized tests. *Washington Post* [Web log post]. Retrieved from www.washingtonpost.com/blogs/answer-sheet/wp/2013/04/30/afts-weingarten-urges-moratorium-on-high-stakes-linked-to-new-standardized-tests/

11. Schneider, Mercedes. (2013, September 12). NEA says its members "strongly support" Common Core? [Web log post]. Retrieved from deutsch29.wordpress.com/2013/09/12/nea-says-its-members-strongly-support-common-core/

12. Schneider, Mercedes. (2013, August 27). A brief audit of Bill Gates' Common Core spending [Web log post]. Retrieved from deutsch29.wordpress.com/2013/08/27/a-brief-audit-of-bill-gates-common-core-spending/

13. Walker, Tim. (2013, September 12). NEA poll: Majority of educators support the Common Core State Standards. *NEA Today.* Retrieved from neatoday.org/2013/09/12/nea-poll-majority-of-educators-support-the-common-core-state-standards/

14. See Note 11.

15. Grannan, Caroline. (2011, July 11). Jonah Edelman on outfoxing teachers' unions: Transcribed remarks [Web log post]. Retrieved from parentsacrossamerica.org/jonah-edelman-on-outfoxing-teachers-unions-transcribed-remarks/

16. Edelman, Jonah, & Crown, James Schine. (2011). If it can happen there, it can happen anywhere: Transformational education legislation in Illinois [Presentation]. Retrieved July 4, 2014, from www.aspenideas.org/session/if-it-can-happen-there-it-can-happen-anywhere-transformational-education-legislation

17. Ravitch, Diane. (2012, September 30). Can Stand for Children save its soul? [Web log post]. Retrieved from dianeravitch.net/2012/09/30/can-stand-for-children-save-its-soul/

18. Bill and Melinda Gates Foundation. (n.d.). Stand for Children [Database search result]. Retrieved July 4, 2014, from www.gatesfoundation.org/How-We-Work/Quick-Links/Grants-Database#q/k=stand%20for%20children

19. Bill and Melinda Gates Foundation. (2013, November). Stand for Children Leadership Center [Database search result]. Retrieved from www.gatesfoundation.org/How-We-Work/Quick-Links/Grants-Database/Grants/2013/11/OPP1098810

20. Bill and Melinda Gates Foundation. (2013, October). Stand for Children Leadership Center [Database search result]. Retrieved from www.gatesfoundation.org/How-We-Work/Quick-Links/Grants-Database/Grants/2013/10/OPP1087258

21. Bill and Melinda Gates Foundation. (2013, July). Stand for Children Leadership Center [Database search result]. Retrieved from www.gatesfoundation.org/How-We-Work/Quick-Links/Grants-Database/Grants/2013/07/OPP1087251

22. Stand for Children Louisiana. (2013, December). Louisiana's Common Core State Standards: Teacher Survey Report. Retrieved from stand.org/sites/default/files/Louisiana/CCSS%20EDUCATOR%20SURVEY%20REPORT_0.pdf

23. Jefferson Parish Public School System. (2013, August 22). Louisiana educator Common Core and Compass survey. Retrieved from jpschools.org/louisiana-educator-common-core-and-compass-survey/

24. Martin, Rayne. (2014, June 12). Tell Governor Jindal to leave Common Core alone [Web log post]. Retrieved from stand.org/louisiana/blog/2014/06/12/tell-governor-jindal-leave-common-core-alone

25. Magee, Kathleen Porter. (n.d.). What we stand for: Standards: Beyond high standards: Supporting the Common Core to improve student learning [White paper]. Retrieved July 4, 2014, from standleadershipcenter.org/what-we-stand-standards

26. Stand for Children Indiana. (n.d.). Common Core in Indiana. Retrieved July 4, 2014, from stand.org/indiana/common-core

27. Stand for Children Louisiana. (2013, December 4). [Common Core survey result press release]. Retrieved from deutsch29.files.wordpress.com/2013/12/sfc-press-release-12-04.docx

28. Schneider, Mercedes. (2014, March 22). 56 states tied to Common Core *in 2009*? [Web log post]. Retrieved from deutsch29.wordpress.com/2014/03/22/46-states-tied-to-common-core-in-2009/

29. See Note 23.

30. Common Core State Standards Initiative. (2014). About the standards. Retrieved from www.corestandards.org/about-the-standards/

31. See Note 30.

32. See Note 23.

33. Schneider, Mercedes. (2013, December 5). Stand for Children Louisiana: Teachers "like" Common Core [Web log post]. Retrieved from deutsch29.wordpress.com/2013/12/05/stand-for-children-louisiana-teachers-like-common-core/

34. *Sacramento Bee.* (2013, October 4). Teachers share their views. Retrieved October 14, 2014, from www.sacbee.com/2013/10/04/5793862/20000-teacher-share-their-views.html

35. Scholastic, & the Bill and Melinda Gates Foundation. (n.d.). Primary sources: America's teachers on teaching in an era of change: Common Core State Standards preview. Retrieved October 5, 2013, from www.scholastic.com/primarysources/2013preview/PrimarySourcesCCSS.pdf

36. Schneider, Mercedes. (2013, October 5). Bill Gates must be worried about Common Core survival [Web log post]. Retrieved from deutsch29.wordpress.

com/2013/10/05/bill-gates-must-be-worried-about-common-core-survival/

37. Bill and Melinda Gates Foundation. (2011, November). Scholastic, Inc. [Database search result]. Retrieved from www.gatesfoundation.org/How-We-Work/Quick-Links/Grants-Database/Grants/2011/11/OPP1033151

38. See Note 35.

39. Schneider, Mercedes. (2013, May 30). Hart, Weingarten, and Power Point deception [Web log post]. Retrieved from deutsch29.wordpress.com/2013/05/30/hart-weingarten-and-power-point-deception/

40. See Note 11.

41. See Note 35.

42. See Note 31.

43. See Note 35.

44. Tucker, Kaylen. (2013, December 13). NAESP releases two surveys of principals on Common Core State Standards Initiative [Press release]. Retrieved from deutsch29.files.wordpress.com/2013/12/naesp-ccss-survey-email-12-13-13.doc

45. Schneider, Mercedes. (2013, December 14). Guess who really wants Common Core now? Principals! [Web log post]. Retrieved from deutsch29.wordpress.com/2013/12/14/guess-who-really-wants-common-core-now-principals/

46. National Association of Elementary School Principals. (2013, December 13). NAESP releases two surveys of principals on Common Core State Standards Initiative [Press release]. Retrieved from deutsch29.files.wordpress.com/2013/12/naesp-ccss-survey-email-12-13-13.doc

47. National Association of Elementary School Principals. (2013, November). Leadership for the Common Core: More than one thousand school principals respond. Available at www.naesp.org/sites/default/files/LeadershipfortheCommonCore_0.pdf

48. National Association of Elementary School Principals. (n.d.). Leadership for the Common Core: Urban principals respond. Retrieved December 14, 2013, from www.naesp.org/leadership-common-core-urban-principals-respond

49.–54. See Note 47.

55. See Note 48.

56. See Note 47.

Chapter 8

1. Illinois State Board of Education. (2007, November 14). [Meeting minutes]. Retrieved from www.isbe.net/board/meetings/2007/nov07/2007-11.pdf

2. Council of Chief State School Officers. (2006, October). ESEA reauthorization policy statement. Retrieved from web.archive.org/web/20071011180840/www.ccsso.org/content/pdfs/ESEA_Policy_Stmnt.pdf

3. Student Achievement Partners. (n.d.). Achieve the core: Student Achievement Partners [Organization profile]. Retrieved June 18, 2014, from achievethecore.org/author/2/student-achievement-partners

4.–5. Achieve, Inc. (2008, July). *Out of many, one: Toward rigorous common core standards from the ground up* [Report]. Retrieved from www.achieve.org/OutofManyOne

6. State of Delaware. (2010, January 19). Race to the Top: Application for initial funding: Appendix [U.S. Department of Education archive]. Retrieved from www2.ed.gov/programs/racetothetop/phase1-applications/appendixes/delaware.pdf

7. Schneider, Mercedes. (2014, March 25). What Common Core looks like in desperation [Web log post]. Retrieved from deutsch29.wordpress.com/2014/03/25/what-common-core-looks-like-in-desperation/

8. Schneider, Mercedes. (2014, May 7). Weingarten wants Common Core; Lewis says we're done [Web log post]. Retrieved from deutsch29.wordpress.com/2014/05/07/weingarten-wants-common-core-lewis-says-were-done/

9.–10. Kober, Farra. (2014, May 9). Randi Weingarten: Common Core should be a guide, not a straitjacket. *MSNBC.com*. Retrieved from www.msnbc.com/all/you-asked-randi-weingarten-answered-common-core-standardized-testing

11. Schneider, Mercedes. (2013, October 13). The Common Core public license: Guess who wins? [Web log post]. Retrieved from deutsch29.wordpress.com/2013/10/13/the-common-core-public-license-guess-who-wins/

12. Schneider, Mercedes. (2014, April 2). The Common Core license: Open for NGA and CCSSO alteration [Web log post]. Retrieved from deutsch29.wordpress.com/2014/04/02/the-common-core-license-open-for-nga-and-ccsso-alteration/

13. *Google.com.* (n.d.). Copyright [Definition]. Retrieved April 2, 2014, from www.google.com/#psj=1&q=copyright+definition

14. *Google.com.* (n.d.). Public license [Definition]. Retrieved April 2, 2014, from www.google.com/#psj=1&q=public+license+definition

15. *Google.com.* (n.d.). Terms of use [Definition]. Retrieved April 2, 2014, from www.google.com/#psj=1&q=terms+of+use+definition

16. Google.com. (n.d.). Fair use [Definition]. Retrieved April 2, 2014, from www.google.com/#psj=1&q=fair+use+definition

17. National Council of Teachers of Mathematics. (2014). NCTM copyright policies. Retrieved from www.nctm.org/publications/content.aspx?id=522

18.–19. Copyright Clearance Center. (n.d.). [Copyright permission search engine]. Retrieved June 18, 2014, from www.copyright.com/

20. See Note 17.

21. National Council of Teachers of English. (n.d.). Standards. Retrieved June 18, 2014, from www.ncte.org/standards

22. National Council of Teachers of English. (n.d.). NCTE/IIRA Standards for the English language arts. Retrieved June 18, 2014, from www.ncte.org/standards/ncte-ira

23. National Council of Teachers of English. (n.d.). Resources for student-centered instruction in a time of Common Core Standards. Retrieved June 18, 2014, from www.ncte.org/standards/common-core

24. National Council of Teachers of English. (n.d.). NCTE press center. Retrieved June 18, 2014, from www.ncte.org/press

25. National Council of Teachers of English. (n.d.). Terms of use. Retrieved June 18, 2014, from www.ncte.org/terms

26.–28. Common Core State Standards Initiative. (2014). Public license. Retrieved from www.corestandards.org/public-license

29. Pearson. (n.d.). The Penguin Group contacts [Contact information]. Retrieved April 2, 2014, from www.pearson.com/contact-us/penguin-group.html

30.–31. See Note 26.

32. Common Core State Standards Initiative. (2014). Common Core State Standards Initiative [Web page]. Retrieved from www.corestandards.org/

33. See Note 26.

34. Common Core State Standards Initiative. (2010, November 24). Commercial license [Archived web page]. Retrieved from web.archive.org/web/20101124131009/www.corestandards.org/commercial-license

35. Common Core State Standards Initiative. (2011, September 13). Commercial license [Archived web page]. Retrieved from web.archive.org/web/20110913031243/www.corestandards.org/commercial-license

36. Common Core State Standards Initiative. (2012, April 15). Commercial license [Archived web page]. Retrieved from web.archive.org/web/20120415045341/www.corestandards.org/commercial-license

37. Common Core State Standards Initiative. (2014). About the Standards: Myths vs. facts. Retrieved from www.corestandards.org/about-the-standards/myths-vs-facts/

38. Schneider, Mercedes. (2014, April). My book: *A chronicle of echoes: Who's who in the implosion of American public education* [Web log page]. Retrieved from deutsch29.wordpress.com/my-book-a-chronicle-of-echoes-whos-who-in-the-implosion-of-american-public-education/

39. Bleiberg, Joshua, & West, Darrell. (2014, March 6). In defense of the Common Core Standards. *Brookings*. Retrieved from www.brookings.edu/research/papers/2014/03/06-common-core-education-standards-bleiberg-west

40. See Note 37.

Chapter 9

1. Layton, Lyndsey. (2014, June 7). How Bill Gates pulled off the swift Common Core revolution. *Washington Post*. Retrieved from www.washingtonpost.com/politics/how-bill-gates-pulled-off-the-swift-common-core-revolution/2014/06/07/a830e32e-ec34-11e3-9f5c-9075d5508f0a_story.html

2. Brockell, Gillian, & Layton, Lyndsey. (2014, June 5). Full interview: Bill Gates on the Common Core [Interview]. *Washington Post*. Retrieved from www.washingtonpost.com/posttv/national/full-interview-bill-gates-on-the-common-core/2014/06/07/e4c14cae-ecdc-11e3-b10e-5090cf3b5958_video.html

3. Bill and Melinda Gates Foundation. (2010, July). American Federation of Teachers Educational Foundation [Database search result]. Retrieved from www.gatesfoundation.org/How-We-Work/Quick-Links/Grants-Database/Grants/2010/07/OPP1015068

4. Bill and Melinda Gates Foundation. (2012, June). American Federation of Teachers Educational Foundation [Database search result]. Retrieved from www.gatesfoundation.org/How-We-Work/Quick-Links/Grants-Database/Grants/2012/06/OPP1060566

5. Bill and Melinda Gates Foundation. (2009, January). American Federation of Teachers Educational Foundation [Database search result]. Retrieved from www.gatesfoundation.org/How-We-Work/Quick-Links/Grants-Database/Grants/2009/01/OPP52599

6. American Federation of Teachers. (2008, July 14). Randi Weingarten elected AFT president [Archived press release]. Retrieved from web.archive.org/web/20080801094304/www.aft.org/presscenter/releases/2008/071408.htm web.archive.org/web/20080801094304/www.aft.org/presscenter/release/2008/071408.htm

7. Bill and Melinda Gates Foundation. (n.d.). AFT [Database search result].

Retrieved from June 24, 2014, from www.gatesfoundation.org/How-We-Work/
Quick-Links/Grants-Database#q/k=AFT

8. Bill and Melinda Gates Foundation. (2010, July 10). Bill Gates—American Federation of Teachers [Speech]. Retrieved from www.gatesfoundation.org/media-center/speeches/2010/07/american-federation-of-teachers

9.–10. Schmidt, George N. (2010, July 11). "Just because you're rich doesn't mean you're smart . . ." (Gerald Bracey): How Bill Gates received a totalitarians' welcome to the AFT national convention on July 10, 2010 and the complete text of the speech he delivered. Substance News. Retrieved from www.substancenews.net/articles.php?page=1529

11.–12. See Note 2.

13. Schneider, Mercedes. (2014, March 17). Gates dined on March 13, 2014, with 80 senators [Web log post]. Retrieved from deutsch29.wordpress.com/2014/03/17/gates-dined-on-march-13-2014-with-80-senators/

14. Bill and Melinda Gates Foundation. (2009, July 21). Bill Gates—National Conference of State Legislators [Speech]. Retrieved from www.gatesfoundation.org/media-center/speeches/2009/07/bill-gates-national-conference-of-state-legislatures-ncsl

15. North Denver News. (2014, March 17). Stunning revelation Bill Gates has spent $2.3 billion on Common Core. Retrieved from northdenvernews.com/stunning-revelation-bill-gates-has-spent-2-3-billion-on-common-core/

16. Bill and Melinda Gates Foundation. (2008, May). National Governors Association Center for Best Practices [Database search result]. Retrieved from www.gatesfoundation.org/How-We-Work/Quick-Links/Grants-Database/Grants/2008/05/OPP50433

17. Bill and Melinda Gates Foundation. (2009, November). National Governors Association Center for Best Practices [Database search result]. Retrieved from www.gatesfoundation.org/How-We-Work/Quick-Links/Grants-Database/Grants/2009/11/OPPSI084

18. Bill and Melinda Gates Foundation. (2011, February). National Governors Association Center for Best Practices [Database search result]. Retrieved from www.gatesfoundation.org/How-We-Work/Quick-Links/Grants-Database/Grants/2011/02/OPP1031294

19. Bill and Melinda Gates Foundation. (n.d.). NGA [Database search result]. Retrieved June 24, 2014, from www.gatesfoundation.org/How-We-Work/Quick-Links/Grants-Database#q/k=nga

20. National Governors Association. (1997, July). 1997 NGA annual meeting [Meeting summary]. Retrieved from www.nga.org/cms/home/about/nga-annual-winter-meetings/page-nga-annual-meetings/col2-content/main-content-list/1997-nga-annual-meeting.html

21. Crowley, Walt. (2000, December 26). Bill and Melinda Gates Foundation. Historylink.org. Retrieved from www.historylink.org/index.cfm?DisplayPage=output.cfm&File_Id=2907

22. Achieve, Inc. (2005, January 25). Bill Gates to join nation's governors, education and business leaders. Retrieved from www.achieve.org/bill-gates-join-nations-governors-education-and-business-leaders

23. Finne, Liv. (2011, March 2). Bill Gates provides guideposts for nation's governors on education: effective teachers, larger class sizes, charter public schools and no furlough days [Web log post]. Retrieved from www.washingtonpolicy.org/blog/post/

bill-gates-provides-guideposts-nations-governors-education-effective-teachers-larger-class

24. Bill and Melinda Gates Foundation. (2009, July). Council of Chief State School Officers [Database search result]. Retrieved from www.gatesfoundation.org/How-We-Work/Quick-Links/Grants-Database/Grants/2009/07/OPP50935

25. Bill and Melinda Gates Foundation. (2009, November). Council of Chief State School Officers [Database search result]. Retrieved from www.gatesfoundation.org/How-We-Work/Quick-Links/Grants-Database/Grants/2009/11/OPPad12

26. Bill and Melinda Gates Foundation. (2011, June). Council of Chief State School Officers [Database search result]. Retrieved from www.gatesfoundation.org/How-We-Work/Quick-Links/Grants-Database/Grants/2011/06/OPP1033998

27. Bill and Melinda Gates Foundation. (2013, July). Council of Chief State School Officers [Database search result]. Retrieved from www.gatesfoundation.org/How-We-Work/Quick-Links/Grants-Database/Grants/2013/07/OPP1089092

28. Bill and Melinda Gates Foundation. (n.d.). Council of Chief State School Officers [Database search result]. Retrieved June 24, 2014, from www.gatesfoundation.org/How-We-Work/Quick-Links/Grants-Database#q/k=council%20of%20chief%20state%20school%20officers

29. Bill and Melinda Gates Foundation. (2010, November 19). Bill Gates—Council of Chief State School Officers [Speech]. Retrieved from www.gatesfoundation.org/media-center/speeches/2010/11/bill-gates-council-of-chief-state-school-officers

30. Bill and Melinda Gates Foundation. (2008, February). Achieve, Inc. [Database search result]. Retrieved from www.gatesfoundation.org/How-We-Work/Quick-Links/Grants-Database/Grants/2008/02/OPP50031

31.–33. See Note 2.

34. Bill and Melinda Gates Foundation. (2003, July). Thomas B. Fordham Institute [Database search result]. Retrieved from www.gatesfoundation.org/How-We-Work/Quick-Links/Grants-Database/Grants/2003/07/OPP28659

35. Bill and Melinda Gates Foundation. (2009, October). Thomas B. Fordham Institute [Database search result]. Retrieved from www.gatesfoundation.org/How-We-Work/Quick-Links/Grants-Database/Grants/2009/10/OPP1005845

36. Bill and Melinda Gates Foundation. (2011, January). Thomas B. Fordham Institute [Database search result]. Retrieved from www.gatesfoundation.org/How-We-Work/Quick-Links/Grants-Database/Grants/2011/01/OPP1029612

37. Bill and Melinda Gates Foundation. (2013, April). Thomas B. Fordham Institute [Database search result]. Retrieved from www.gatesfoundation.org/How-We-Work/Quick-Links/Grants-Database/Grants/2013/04/OPP1081579

38. See Note 2.

39. Bill and Melinda Gates Foundation. (n.d). Grantseeker FAQ. Retrieved July 24, 2014, from www.gatesfoundation.org/How-We-Work/General-Information/Grantseeker-FAQ

40. Bill and Melinda Gates Foundation. (n.d.). Common Core implement [Database search result]. Retrieved June 24, 2014, from www.gatesfoundation.org/How-We-Work/Quick-Links/Grants-Database#q/k=common%20core%20implement

41. See Note 2.

42. Schneider, Mercedes K. (2014.) *A chronicle of echoes: Who's who in the implosion of public education*. Charlotte, NC: Information Age Publishing. p. 360

43. Ujifusa, Andrew. (2013, March 18). State chiefs spar with AFT and NEA

presidents over Common Core . *Education Week.* Retrieved from blogs.edweek.org/edweek/state_edwatch/2014/03/state_chiefs_spar_with_aft_and_nea_presidents_over_common_core.html

44. Schneider, Mercedes. (2014, May 7). Weingarten wants Common Core; Lewis says we're done [Web log post]. Retrieved from deutsch29.wordpress.com/2014/05/07/weingarten-wants-common-core-lewis-says-were-done/

45. Schneider, Mercedes. (2014, July 11). The problem with the AFT offer for teachers to "rewrite" the Common Core [Web log post]. Retrieved from deutsch29.wordpress.com/2014/07/11/the-problem-with-the-aft-offer-for-teachers-to-rewrite-the-common-core/

46. Ravitch, Diane. (2014, July 15). BATs blast Common Core standards and Arne Duncan [Web log post]. Retrieved from dianeravitch.net/2014/07/15/bats-blast-common-core-standards-and-arne-duncan/

47. Bidwell, Allie. (2013, September 12). Poll: Majority of teachers support Common Core. *US News and World Report.* Retrieved from www.usnews.com/news/articles/2013/09/12/poll-majority-of-teachers-support-common-core

48. See Note 43.

49. See Note 2.

50. Bill and Melinda Gates Foundation. (2012, June). American Enterprise Institute for Public Policy Research [Database search result]. Retrieved from www.gatesfoundation.org/How-We-Work/Quick-Links/Grants-Database/Grants/2012/06/OPP1062626

51. Schneider, Mercedes. (2014, April 27). Video: Bill Gates explains Common Core [Web log post]. Retrieved from deutsch29.wordpress.com/2014/04/27/video-bill-gates-explains-common-core/

52.–55. See Note 2.

56. Bill and Melinda Gates Foundation. (2005, September 23). Bill Gates—Lakeside School [Speech]. Retrieved from www.gatesfoundation.org/media-center/speeches/2005/09/bill-gates-lakeside-school

57. Ravitch, Diane. (2014, March 19). KrazyTA explains what Bill Gates wants for his own children [Web log post]. Retrieved from dianeravitch.net/2014/03/19/krazyta-explains-what-bill-gates-wants-for-his-own-children/

58. Westneat, Danny. (2011, March 8). Bill Gates, have I got a deal for you! *Seattle Times.* Retrieved from seattletimes.com/html/dannywestneat/2014437975_danny09.html

59. Diane Marie. (2014, April 26). Bill Gates crying in his vault [Web log post]. Available at truthabouteducation.wordpress.com/2014/04/26/bill-gates-crying-in-his-vault/

60. See Note 2.

61. Bill and Melinda Gates Foundation. (n.d.). Common Core [Database search result]. Retrieved June 22, 2014, from www.gatesfoundation.org/How-We-Work/Quick-Links/Grants-Database#q/k=common%20core

62. Bill and Melinda Gates Foundation. (2014, June). United Way Worldwide [Database search result]. Retrieved from www.gatesfoundation.org/How-We-Work/Quick-Links/Grants-Database/Grants/2014/06/OPP1107547

63. Bill and Melinda Gates Foundation. (2013, November). US Chamber of Commerce Foundation [Database search result]. Retrieved from www.gatesfoundation.org/How-We-Work/Quick-Links/Grants-Database/Grants/2013/11/OPP1081590

64. Bill and Melinda Gates Foundation. (2013, October). James B. Hunt, Jr., Institute for Educational Leadership and Policy Foundation, Inc. [Database search result]. Retrieved from www.gatesfoundation.org/How-We-Work/Quick-Links/Grants-Database/Grants/2013/10/OPP1082243

65. Bill and Melinda Gates Foundation. (2013, July). Harvard University [Database search result]. Retrieved from www.gatesfoundation.org/How-We-Work/Quick-Links/Grants-Database/Grants/2013/07/OPP1088797

66. Bill and Melinda Gates Foundation. (2013, June). National Association of State Boards of Education [Database search result]. Retrieved from www.gatesfoundation.org/How-We-Work/Quick-Links/Grants-Database/Grants/2013/06/OPP1082250

67. Bill and Melinda Gates Foundation. (2013, January). The Aspen Institute, Inc. Database search result]. Retrieved from www.gatesfoundation.org/How-We-Work/Quick-Links/Grants-Database/Grants/2013/01/OPP1079288

68. Bill and Melinda Gates Foundation. (2012, November). Fund for Public Schools, Inc. [Database search result]. Retrieved from www.gatesfoundation.org/How-We-Work/Quick-Links/Grants-Database/Grants/2012/11/OPP1077820

69. Bill and Melinda Gates Foundation. (2012, June). Student Achievement Partners [Database search result]. Retrieved from www.gatesfoundation.org/How-We-Work/Quick-Links/Grants-Database/Grants/2012/06/OPP1061551

70. Bill and Melinda Gates Foundation. (2011, November). Scholastic, Inc. [Database search result]. Retrieved from www.gatesfoundation.org/How-We-Work/Quick-Links/Grants-Database/Grants/2011/11/OPP1033151

71. Bill and Melinda Gates Foundation. (2011, August). Stanford University [Database search result]. Retrieved from www.gatesfoundation.org/How-We-Work/Quick-Links/Grants-Database/Grants/2011/08/OPP1033394

72. Bill and Melinda Gates Foundation. (2011, February). Association for Supervision of Curriculum and Development [Database search result]. Retrieved from www.gatesfoundation.org/How-We-Work/Quick-Links/Grants-Database/Grants/2011/02/OPP1030339

73. Bill and Melinda Gates Foundation. (2009, September). The Education Trust [Database search result]. Available at www.gatesfoundation.org/How-We-Work/Quick-Links/Grants-Database/Grants/2009/09/OPP1004820

Chapter 10

1. National Conference of State Legislatures. (n.d.). Policies on NCSL Standing Committee on Education as of the annual business meeting, which was held on August 15, 2013. Retrieved from www.ncsl.org/ncsl-in-dc/task-forces/policies-education.aspx

2. Ravitch, Diane. (1998, January- February). The controversy over National History Standards. *Bulletin of the Academy of Arts and Sciences* (51)3, 14–28. Retrieved from www.jstor.org/discover/10.2307/3824089?uid=3739688&uid=2134&uid=4582331577&uid=2&uid=70&uid=3&uid=4582331567&uid=3739256&uid=60&purchase-type=article&accessType=none&sid=21104202963857&showMyJstorPss=false&seq=4&showAccess=false

3. Achieve, Inc. (2008, July). *Out of many, one: Toward rigorous common core standards from the ground up* [Report]. Retrieved from www.achieve.org/files/OutofManyOne.pdf

4. Layton, Lyndsey. (2014, June 7). How Bill Gates pulled off the swift Common Core revolution. *Washington Post*. Retrieved from www.washingtonpost.com/politics/how-bill-gates-pulled-off-the-swift-common-core-revolution/2014/06/07/a830e32e-ec34-11e3-9f5c-9075d5508f0a_story.html

5. Schneider, Mercedes. (2014, June 22). Common Core memorandum of understanding not just for "development" [Web log post]. Retrieved from deutsch29.wordpress.com/2014/06/22/common-core-mou-not-just-for-development/

6. Schneider, Mercedes. (2014, April 5). Fordham's Mike Petrilli: Selling Common Core in states with better standards [Web log post]. Retrieved from deutsch29.wordpress.com/2014/04/05/fordhams-mike-petrilli-selling-common-core-in-states-with-better-standards/

7. State of Delaware. (2010, January 19). Race to the Top: Application for initial funding: Appendix [U.S. Department of Education archive]. Retrieved from www2.ed.gov/programs/racetothetop/phase1-applications/appendixes/delaware.pdf

8. Schneider, Mercedes. (2013, November 24). Common Core, aligned curriculum, and other NGA-Duncan-decided issues [Web log post]. Retrieved from deutsch29.wordpress.com/2013/11/24/common-core-aligned-curriculum-and-other-ngaduncan-decided-issues/

9. Bill and Melinda Gates Foundation. (2008, May). James B. Hunt, Jr., Institute for Educational Leadership and Policy Foundation, Inc. [Database search result]. Retrieved from www.gatesfoundation.org/How-We-Work/Quick-Links/Grants-Database/Grants/2008/05/OPP50361

10. National Governors Association. (2008, June 10). Governors explore strategies to make the United States a global leader in education [Press release]. Retrieved from www.nga.org/cms/home/news-room/news-releases/page_2008/col2-content/main-content-list/title_governors-explore-strategies-to-make-the-united-states-a-global-leader-in-education.html

11. One Hundred Eleventh Congress of the United States of America. (2009, January 6). American Recovery and Reinvestment Act of 2009 [Legislation]. Retrieved from www.gpo.gov/fdsys/pkg/BILLS-111hr1enr/pdf/BILLS-111hr1enr.pdf

12. Congressional Budget Office. (2012, February). Estimated impact of the American Recovery and Reinvestment Act on employment and economic output from October 2011 to December 2011 [Report]. Retrieved from www.cbo.gov/sites/default/files/cbofiles/attachments/02-22-ARRA.pdf

13.–15. See Note 11.

16. U.S. Department of Education. (2009, March 7). State Fiscal Stabilization Fund. Available at www2.ed.gov/policy/gen/leg/recovery/factsheet/stabilization-fund.html

17. American Recovery and Reinvestment Act of 2009. (2012, May 21). [Excerpts from Public Law 111-5 related to the State Fiscal Stabilization Fund administered by the U.S. Department of Education]. Retrieved from www2.ed.gov/policy/gen/leg/recovery/statutory/stabilization-fund.pdf

18. James B. Hunt, Jr., Institute for Educational Leadership and Policy, & National Governors Association Center for Best Practices. (2009). Perfecting the formula: Effective strategies = educational success: A report from the 2009 governors education symposium. Retrieved from www.nga.org/files/live/sites/NGA/files/pdf/0910GESREPORT.pdf

19. See Note 17.

20. See Note 18.

21. James B. Hunt, Jr., Institute for Educational Leadership and Policy. (n.d.). Common Core State Standards—general brief. Retrieved June 26, 2014, from www. edweek.org/media/fordham_event.pdf

22. See Note 18.

23. Schneider, Mercedes. (2014, March 22). 46 states tied to Common Core in 2009? [Web log post]. Retrieved from deutsch29.wordpress.com/2014/03/22/46-states-tied-to-common-core-in-2009/

24. See Note 17.

25. U.S. Department of Education. (2009, July 24). President Obama, U.S. Secretary of Education Duncan announces national competition to advance school reform [Press release]. Retrieved from www2.ed.gov/news/pressreleases/2009/07/07242009.html

26. See Note 16.

27. See Note 25.

28. U.S. Department of Education. (n.d.). Race to the Top: States' applications, scores and comments for phase 1. Retrieved June 26, 2014, from www2.ed.gov/programs/racetothetop/phase1-applications/index.html

29. U.S. Department of Education. (2010, March 29). Delaware and Tennessee win first Race to the Top grants [Press release]. Available at www2.ed.gov/news/pressreleases/2010/03/03292010.html

30. U.S. Department of Education. (n.d.). Race to the Top: States' applications for phase 2. Retrieved June 26, 2014, from www2.ed.gov/programs/racetothetop/phase2-applications/index.html

31. U.S. Department of Education. (n.d.). Race to the Top: States' applications for phase 3. Retrieved June 26, 2014, from www2.ed.gov/programs/racetothetop/phase3-applications/index.html

32.–33. See Note 17.

34. See Note 11.

35. Elementary and Secondary Education Act of 1965, Subpart 2, Section 9527 [Legislation]. Retrieved June 26, 2014, from www2.ed.gov/policy/elsec/leg/esea02/pg112.html#sec9527

36.–37. U.S. Department of Education. (2009, July 24). Race to the Top Application for Initial Funding, CFDA number 84.395A. Retrieved from www2.ed.gov/programs/racetothetop/application.doc

38. See Note 18.

39. See Note 36.

40. U.S. Department of Education Office of Elementary and Secondary Education Academic Improvement and Teacher Quality Programs. (2010, September 28). American Recovery and Reinvestment Act grant award letter for the Partnership for Assessment of Readiness for College and Careers (PARCC). Retrieved from www2.ed.gov/programs/racetothetop-assessment/parcc-award-letter.pdf

41. U.S. Department of Education Office of Elementary and Secondary Education Academic Improvement and Teacher Quality Programs. (2010, September 28). American Recovery and Reinvestment Act grant award letter for the Smarter Balanced Assessment Consortium (SBAC). Retrieved from www2.ed.gov/programs/racetothetop-assessment/sbac-award-letter.pdf

42. U.S. Department of Education. (n.d.). Race to the Top assessment program: Awards. Retrieved June 26, 2014, from www2.ed.gov/programs/racetothetop-assessment/awards.html

43. Berry, Susan. (2014, June 23). Tennessee abandons PARCC Common Core test consortium. Brietbart. Available at www.breitbart.com/Big-Government/2014/06/23/Tennessee-Abandons-PARCC-Common-Core-Test-Consortium

44. Solochek, Jeffrey S. (2013, November 21). Florida hands over fiscal responsibility for PARCC [Web log post]. *Tampa Bay Times.* Available at www.tampabay.com/blogs/gradebook/florida-hands-over-fiscal-responsibility-for-parcc/2153594

45. Partnership for Assessment of Readiness for College and Careers. (n.d.). Maryland takes on PARCC fiscal agent role; states gear up for 2014 field test. Retrieved June 26, 2014, from www.parcconline.org/maryland-takes-parcc-fiscal-agent-role

46. Partnership for Assessment of Readiness for College and Careers. (2013, March 12). PARCC becomes a nonprofit. Available at www.parcconline.org/parcc-becomes-non-profit

47. See Note 42.

48. Smarter Balanced Assessment Consortium. (n.d.). Governance. Retrieved June 26, 2014, from www.smarterbalanced.org/about/governance/

49. Smarter Balanced Assessment Consortium. (n.d.). Executive committee. Retrieved June 26, 2014, from www.smarterbalanced.org/about/executive-committee/

50. Smarter Balanced Assessment Consortium. (n.d.). Advisory committees. Retrieved June 26, 2014, from www.smarterbalanced.org/about/advisory-committees/

51. Smarter Balanced Assessment Consortium. (n.d.). Staff and advisors. Retrieved June 26, 2014 from www.smarterbalanced.org/about/smarter-balanced-staff/

52. U.S. Department of Education. (n.d.). Appendix B. scoring rubric [Race to the Top corrected scoring rubric]. Retrieved June 26, 2014 from www2.ed.gov/programs/racetothetop/scoringrubric.pdf

53. See Note 40.

54. See Note 41.

55.–57. U.S. Department of Education. (2011, January 7). Cooperative agreement between the U.S. Department of Education and the Partnership for Assessment of Readiness for College and Careers [Contract]. Retrieved from www2.ed.gov/programs/racetothetop-assessment/parcc-cooperative-agreement.pdf

58. U.S. Department of Education. (2011, January 7). Cooperative agreement between the U.S. Department of Education and the Smarter Balanced Assessment Consortium [Contract]. Retrieved from www2.ed.gov/programs/racetothetop-assessment/sbac-cooperative-agreement.pdf

59. Elliott, Scott. (2014, May 2). Feds put Indiana on notice: NCLB waiver in doubt. *Chalkbeat Indiana.* Retrieved from in.chalkbeat.org/2014/05/02/feds-put-indiana-on-notice-nclb-waiver-in-doubt/#.U6yLEJRdUYQ

60. Strauss, Valerie. (2013, November 16). Arne Duncan: "White suburban moms" upset that Common Core shows their kids aren't "brilliant" [Web log post]. Retrieved from www.washingtonpost.com/blogs/answer-sheet/wp/2013/11/16/arne-duncan-white-surburban-moms-upset-that-common-core-shows-their-kids-arent-brilliant/

61. Emma, Caitlin. (2014, August 28). Common Core repeal costs Oklahoma its NCLB waiver. *Politico Pro*. Retrieved from www.politico.com/story/2014/08/oklahoma-common-core-no-child-left-behind-waiver-110421.html

62. State of Oklahoma. (2014, June 5). Gov. Fallin signs HB 3399 to repeal and replace Common Core Standards [Press release]. Retrieved from www.ok.gov/triton/modules/newsroom/newsroom_article.php?id=223&article_id=14279

63.–64. Klein, Alyson. (2014, October 21). Oklahoma wants its NCLB waiver back, right now. *Education Week*. Retrieved from blogs.edweek.org/edweek/campaign-k-12/2014/10/oklahoma_wants_its_nclb_waiver.html

Chapter 11

1. Schneider, Mercedes. (2014, April 27). Video: Bill Gates explains Common Core [Web log post]. Retrieved from deutsch29.wordpress.com/2014/04/27/video-bill-gates-explains-common-core/

2. Brockell, Gillian, & Layton, Lyndsey. (2014, June 5). Full interview: Bill Gates on the Common Core [Interview]. *Washington Post*. Retrieved from www.washingtonpost.com/posttv/national/full-interview-bill-gates-on-the-common-core/2014/06/07/e4c14cae-ecdc-11e3-b10e-5090cf3b5958_video.html

3. Pearson. (n.d.). The Pearson timeline: Our history. Retrieved June 30, 2014, from timeline.pearson.com/

4. Grace's Guide. (2014, July 4). S. Pearson and Son [Company timeline]. Retrieved from www.gracesguide.co.uk/S._Pearson_and_Son

5. Wikipedia: The Free Encyclopedia. (2014, July 4). Nationalization [Search result]. Available at en.wikipedia.org/wiki/Nationalization

6. Investopedia. (2014). Acquisition [Definition]. Retrieved from www.investopedia.com/terms/a/acquisition.asp

7. See Note 4.

8.–9. See Note 3.

10. Reuters. (2014, June 29). Pearson PLC (PSO) [Stock exchange search engine result]. Retrieved from www.reuters.com/finance/stocks/companyProfile?symbol=PSO

11. Pearson Charitable Foundation. (2009). [IRS Form 990]. Retrieved December 15, 2013, from bulk.resource.org/irs.gov/eo/2010_12_EO/11-3690722_990_200912.pdf

12. Pearson Charitable Foundation. (2010). [IRS Form 990]. Retrieved December 15, 2013, from bulk.resource.org/irs.gov/eo/2011_12_EO/11-3690722_990_201012.pdf

13. Pearson Charitable Foundation. (2012). IRS Form 990. Retrieved December 15, 2013, from bulk.resource.org/irs.gov/eo/2013_03_EO/11-3690722_990_201112.pdf

14. Pearson Charitable Foundation. (2008). IRS Form 990. Retrieved December 15, 2013, from bulk.resource.org/irs.gov/eo/2009_12_EO/11-3690722_990_200812.pdf

15. Bill and Melinda Gates Foundation. (2011, February). Pearson Charitable Foundation [Database search result]. Retrieved from www.gatesfoundation.org/How-We-Work/Quick-Links/Grants-Database/Grants/2011/02/OPP1031713

16. Common Core State Standards Initiative. (2014). Public license. Retrieved June 29, 2014, from www.corestandards.org/public-license/

17. Pearson Foundation. (2014, November 18). Thank you [Public announcement]. Retrieved from www.pearsonfoundation.org/index.html?utm_source=EdsurgeLive&utm_campaign=fd5b456bb3-Innovate+197-HIREEDU&utm_medium=email&utm_term=0_0f1ec25b60-fd5b456bb3-291881961

18. Pearson. (2014, February 28). Pearson 2013 preliminary results (unaudited) [Financial summary press release]. Retrieved from www.pearson.com/content/dam/pearson-corporate/files/press-releases/2014/2013_RESULTS_FULL_RELEASE_AND_FINANCIALS_28-02-14.pdf

19. Schneider, Mercedes. (2014, May 2). Incompetent Pearson wins PARCC contract: Big surprise [Web log post]. Retrieved from deutsch29.wordpress.com/2014/05/02/incompetent-pearson-wins-parcc-contract-big-surprise/

20. Cavanagh, Sean. (2014, May 2). Pearson wins major contract from Common-Core testing consortium. *Education Week* [Web log post]. Retrieved from blogs.edweek.org/edweek/marketplacek12/2014/05/pearson_wins_major_contract_from_common-core_testing_consortium.html

21. See Note 19.

22. Partnership for Assessment of Readiness for College and Careers. (2013, March 12). PARCC announces launch of independent nonprofit, names leadership. Retrieved from www.parcconline.org/parcc-announces-launch-independent-nonprofit-names-leadership

23. Schneider, Mercedes. (2014, April 25). A tale of two NGA press releases and then some [Web log post]. Retrieved from deutsch29.wordpress.com/2014/04/25/a-tale-of-two-nga-press-releases-and-then-some/

24. Schneider, Mercedes. (2014, March 22). 46 states tied to Common Core in 2009? [Web log post]. Retrieved from deutsch29.wordpress.com/2014/03/22/46-states-tied-to-common-core-in-2009/

25. Cavanagh, Sean. (2014, May 6). American Institutes for Research fights Pearson Common-Core testing award. *Education Week* [Web log post]. Retrieved from blogs.edweek.org/edweek/marketplacek12/2014/05/american_institutes_for_research_challenges_pearson_common-core_testing_award_in_court.html

26. Chiaramonte, Perry. (2014, June 18). Bid-rigging lawsuit throws $240-million-a-year Common Core testing contract into limbo. *Fox News*. Retrieved from www.foxnews.com/us/2014/06/11/core-business-major-testing-company-pearson-lands-controversial-common-core/

27.–28. See Note 25.

29. See Note 26.

30. Cavanagh, Sean, (2013, June 3). Pearson, N.M. officials given deadline in Common-Core testing protest. *Education Week* [Web log post]. Retrieved from blogs.edweek.org/edweek/marketplacek12/2014/06/parties_in_common-core_testing_lawsuit_told_to_make_their_case.html

31. Ravitch, Diane. (2013, August 9). Who set the NY cut scores and what we still need to know [Web log post]. Retrieved from dianeravitch.net/2013/08/09/who-set-the-ny-cut-scores-and-what-we-still-need-to-know/

32. Seeking Alpha. (2014, February 28). Pearson management discusses 2013 results—earnings call transcript. Retrieved from seekingalpha.com/article/2058743-pearson-management-discusses-2013-results-earnings-call-transcript?page=1

33. Schneider, Mercedes. (2014, May 20). Pearson allows me to quote 400

board meeting words [Web log post]. Retrieved from deutsch29.wordpress. com/2014/05/20/pearson-allows-me-to-quote-400-board-meeting-words/

34.–36. See Note 32.

37. Fitzgerald, Bill. (2012, January 31). Pearson, PARCC, Smarter Balanced, and the money exchange [Web log post]. Retrieved from funnymonkey.com/blog/ pearson-parcc-smarter-balanced-and-money-exchange

38. National Governors Association. (2008, June 10). Governors explore strategies to make the United States a global leader in education [Press release]. Retrieved from www.nga.org/cms/home/news-room/news-releases/page_2008/col2-content/main-content-list/title_governors-explore-strategies-to-make-the-united-states-a-global-leader-in-education.html

39. Schneider, Mercedes. (2014, March 20). Bill Gates' sobering 2009 speech to legislators [Web log post]. Retrieved from deutsch29.wordpress.com/2014/03/20/ bill-gates-sobering-2009-speech-to-legislators/

40. Wikipedia, the Free Encyclopedia. (2014, June 29). General certificate of secondary education [Search result]. Retrieved from en.wikipedia.org/wiki/ General_Certificate_of_Secondary_Education

41. Wikipedia, the Free Encyclopedia. (2014, June 26). GCE advanced level (United Kingdom) [Search result]. Retrieved from en.wikipedia.org/wiki/GCE_ Advanced_Level_(United_Kingdom)

42. United Kingdom Department of Education. (2014, June 9). Reforming qualifications and the curriculum to better prepare pupils for life after school. Retrieved from www.gov.uk/government/policies/reforming-qualifications-and-the-curriculum-to-better-prepare-pupils-for-life-after-school

43. Eitel, Robert S., & Talbert, Kent D. (2012, February 16). The road to a national curriculum: Legal aspects of the Common Core standards, Race to the Top, and conditional waivers. *Federalist Society*. Retrieved from www.fed-soc.org/ publications/detail/the-road-to-a-national-curriculum-the-legal-aspects-of-the-common-core-standards-race-to-the-top-and-conditional-waivers

44. See Note 42.

45. Cornell University Law School Legal Information Institute. (n.d.). 20 US Code Section 1232a—prohibition against federal control of education [Public law]. Retrieved July 22, 2014, from www.law.cornell.edu/uscode/text/20/1232a

46.–48. See Note 32.

49. Molnar, Michelle. (2014, March 28). Review examines L.A. schools' decision on iPad, Pearson purchase. *Education Week* [Web log post]. Retrieved from blogs. edweek.org/edweek/marketplacek12/2014/03/review_examines_la_schools_ decision_on_ipad_pearson_purchase.html?r=1919073041&preview=1

50. See Note 32.

51. See Note 2.

Index

About the Author

Mercedes K. Schneider, PhD, is a career teacher. A native of southern Louisiana and a product of the St. Bernard Parish Public Schools, Schneider holds degrees in secondary education, English and German (BS, Louisiana State, 1991), guidance and counseling (MEd, West Georgia, 1998), and applied statistics and research methods (PhD, Northern Colorado, 2002). She is in her 20th year of full-time teaching and has taught from grade 7 to graduate school in several states (Louisiana, Georgia, Colorado, and Indiana). After 14 years away, Schneider returned home in 2007 in the aftermath of Hurricane Katrina and is in her 8th full-time year of teaching sophomore English in a southern Louisiana traditional public high school.

Common Core Dilemma: Who Owns Our Schools? is Schneider's second book. Her first, *A Chronicle of Echoes: Who's Who in the Implosion of American Public Education,* details individuals and organizations exploiting public education in the name of "reform."